Acclaim for Temple Grandin's

THINKING IN PICTURES

"How does a true marvel let you know it has arrived? . . . It's hard to imagine even an intellect as towering as Sacks's coming up with perceptions as rare and completely out of left field as Grandin herself does in this mind-blowing book."　　—*Newsday*

"Temple Grandin's window onto the subjective experience of autism is of value to all of us who hope to gain a deeper understanding of the human mind by exploring the ways in which it responds to the world's challenges."　　—*The Washington Times*

"Temple Grandin, the anthropologist from Mars, takes us on a journey through her inner life and, with exquisite scientific detail, offers us a near photograph of the workings of her visual mind."　　—John Ratey,
coauthor of *Driven to Distraction*

"Temple Grandin's legacy is the invaluable gift of compassion. This is a journey of courage, determination, and, above all, worth. Society is the better for Temple Grandin having left her mark on it."
—Alex Pacheco,
President, People for the Ethical Treatment of Animals

"*Thinking in Pictures* is a beautiful book. . . . Grandin has created a beautifully odd and fascinating picture of her life and mind, and her abiding love of animals."　　—*Elle*

TEMPLE GRANDIN

Thinking in Pictures

Temple Grandin has a Ph.D. in animal science from the University of Illinois and has designed one third of all the livestock-handling facilities in the United States, and many in other countries. She is currently an associate professor of animal sciences at Colorado State University and a frequent lecturer at autism meetings throughout the country. She lives in Fort Collins, Colorado.

BOOKS BY TEMPLE GRANDIN

Emergence: Labeled Autistic

Livestock Handling and Transport

Thinking in Pictures: And Other Reports from My Life with Autism

Genetics and the Behavior of Domestic Animals

Developing Talents

Animals in Translation

THINKING IN PICTURES

And Other Reports from My Life with Autism

TEMPLE GRANDIN

with a Foreword by

OLIVER SACKS

VINTAGE BOOKS
A Division of Random House, Inc.
New York

SECOND VINTAGE BOOKS EDITION, JANUARY 2006

Library of Congress Cataloging-in-Publication Data
Grandin, Temple.
Thinking in pictures : and other reports from my life with autism /
by Temple Grandin : with a foreword by Oliver Sacks.
p. cm.
Originally published : New York : Doubleday. c1995.
1. Grandin, Temple.   2. Autism—Patients—United States—Biography.
I. Title.
RC553.A88G74 1996
616.89′82′0092—dc20
[B]
96-10737
CIP

Vintage ISBN-10: 0-307-27565-5
Vintage ISBN-13: 978-0-307-27565-3

www.vintagebooks.com

Printed in the United States of America
20

I dedicate this book to my mother.
Her love, dedication, and insight
enabled me to succeed.

Acknowledgments

I would like to thank Diedra Enwright for typing the manuscript and Rosalie Winard for photography. I would also like to thank Betsy Lerner, my editor, for being patient and helping me organize my thoughts. Sequencing and organization are difficult for a visual thinker who has pictures for thoughts. I am also extremely grateful for the wonderful support from Dr. Oliver Sacks. Other people who have made this project possible were Pat Breinin, my agent, and Brandon Saltz, editorial assistant at Doubleday. I would like to conclude by thanking Mark Deesing, Mary Tanner, and Julie Struthers for library research.

Contents

A NOTE FROM THE AUTHOR

In the ten years since the initial publication of *Thinking in Pictures* our understanding of autism has changed a great deal. The Asperger's Syndrome diagnosis was rarely used in the United States, and now has become much more frequent. Our understanding of medications was not as advanced. There were fewer scientific references available. We have also learned a great deal about different kinds of autistic thinkers—not all autistic individuals are visual thinkers. In an effort to keep *Thinking in Pictures* as up-to-date and useful as possible I have taken into consideration the new studies, diagnoses, and treatments for autism and written updates following each chapter. The original text has not been changed. The updated sections are clearly marked. I have also added ninety new references and many new resources and useful Web sites.

Temple Grandin
August 4, 2005

FOREWORD

Oliver Sacks

IN 1986 a quite extraordinary, unprecedented and, in a way, unthinkable book was published, Temple Grandin's *Emergence: Labeled Autistic*. Unprecedented because there had never before been an "inside narrative" of autism; unthinkable because it had been medical dogma for forty years or more that there *was* no "inside," no inner life, in the autistic, or that if there was it would be forever denied access or expression; extraordinary because of its extreme (and strange) directness and clarity. Temple Grandin's voice came from a place which had never had a voice, never been granted real existence, before—and she spoke not only for herself, but for thousands of other, often highly gifted, autistic adults in our midst. She provided a glimpse, and indeed a revelation, that there might be people, no less human than ourselves, who constructed their worlds, lived their lives, in almost unimaginably different ways.

The word "autism" still conveys a fixed and dreadful meaning to most people—they visualize a child mute, rocking, screaming, inaccessible, cut off from human contact. And we almost always speak of autistic children, never of autistic adults, as if such children never grew up, or were somehow mysteriously spirited off the planet, out of society. Or else we think of an autistic "savant," a strange being with bizarre mannerisms and stereotypies, still cut off from normal life, but with uncanny powers of calculation, memory, drawing, whatever—like the savant portrayed in *Rain Man*. These pictures are not wholly false, but they fail to indicate that there are forms of autism which (while they may indeed go with ways of thinking and perceiving very different from the "normal") do not incapacitate in the same way, but may (especially if there is high intelligence, and understanding, and education) allow lives that are full of event and achievement, and a special sort of insight and courage too.

This was well realized by Hans Asperger, who described these "higher" forms of autism in 1944—but Asperger's paper, published in German, was virtually ignored for forty years. Then, in 1986, came Temple's startling book, *Emergence*. If her book, as a case history, was to have a sharp and salutary effect on medical and scientific thinking, allowing (indeed requiring) a broader and more generous concept of what it might mean to be "autistic," it was immensely appealing, too, as a human document.

Ten years have passed since Temple wrote her first book, ten years in which she has pursued her odd, solitary, stubborn, dedicated life—defining her own place as a professor of animal behavior and designer of livestock equipment, struggling for the understanding and humane treatment of animals, struggling for a deeper understanding of autism, struggling with the power of images and words, struggling not least to understand that odd species—*us*—and to define her own worth, her role, in a world that is not autistic. And now she has once more ventured into book-length writing (she has written scores of scientific papers and lectures in the interim) and given us a new, much more deeply pondered and integrated narrative-essay, *Thinking in Pictures*.

Here we can see, and relive, what it was like for Temple as a child—the overwhelming sensations of smell and sound and touch she could not blot out; how she would scream, or rock, endlessly, disconnected from others; or, in a sudden tantrum, fling feces around; or (with uncanny concentration, and a complete shutting out of the world) fix her attention for hours on a few sand grains, or the whorls of her fingers. We feel the chaos and terror of this fearful childhood, the looming sense that she might have to be institutionalized, confined, for her whole life. We seem to acquire, with her, the first, inchoate beginnings of speech, the sense of language as an almost miraculous power by which she might gain some mastery of herself, some contact with others, some intercourse with the world. We relive her schooldays with her—her total failure to understand or be understood by other children; her intense desire for, but fear of, contact; her bizarre daydreams—of a magic machine that could give her the contact, the "hugging" she craved, but in a way she could entirely control; and the impact of a remarkable science teacher who was able, behind all the bizarreness, the pathology, to recognize the unusual potential of this strange student, and to channel her obsessions into the opening of a scientific life.

We can also share, even if we cannot wholly understand, the extraordinary passion and understanding for cattle which consume Temple, and which have made her, by degrees, a world-renowned expert on cattle psychology and behavior, an inventor of devices and facilities for handling them, and a passionate advocate of their humane treatment. (Her original title for this book was *A Cow's Eye View.*) And we get a glimpse—this perhaps the least imaginable of all—of her total bewilderment about other people's minds, her inability to decipher their expressions and intentions, along with her determination to study them, study *us,* our alien behaviors, scientifically and systematically, as if (in her own words) she were "an anthropologist on Mars."

We sense all this despite (or perhaps partly because of) the touching simplicity and ingenuousness of Temple's writing, her curious lack of either modesty or immodesty, her incapacity for evasion or artifice of any kind.

It is fascinating to compare *Thinking in Pictures* with *Emergence.* The intervening ten years have been years of increasing professional recognition and fulfillment for Temple—she travels, consults, lectures continually, and her devices are now used for cattle management and corrals all over the world—and of increasing authority too in the field of autism (half her lectures and publications are dedicated to this). Writing did not come easily to her at first, not because she lacked verbal facility, but because she lacked an imagination of other minds, of the fact that her listeners were different from her, were not privy to the experiences, the associations, the background information in her own mind. There were strange discontinuities (people injected suddenly into the narrative without warning, for instance); casual reference to incidents of which the reader had no knowledge; and sudden, perplexing changes of topic. It is said by cognitive psychologists that autistic people lack "theory of mind"—any direct perception or idea of other minds, or other states of mind—and that this lies at the heart of their difficulties. What is remarkable is that Temple, now in her fifth decade, *has* developed some genuine appreciation of other people and other minds, their sensibilities and idiosyncrasies, in the ten years which have passed since writing *Emergence*. And it is this which now shows itself in *Thinking in Pictures,* and lends it a warmth and color rarely seen in her earlier book.

Indeed, when I first met Temple, in August of 1993, I found her so "normal" at first (or so adept in simulating normality) that I had difficulty realizing that she *was* autistic—but during the course of a weekend together this was to come through in innumerable ways. When we went for a stroll she confessed that she had never been able to "get" Romeo and Juliet ("I never knew what they were up to"), that she was stumped by complex human emotions of all sorts (of one man, a spiteful colleague, who tried to sabotage her work: "I had to learn to be suspicious, I had to learn it cognitively . . . I couldn't *see* the jealous look on his face").

She spoke repeatedly of the android in "Star Trek," Data, and how she identified with him as a "pure logical being"—but how, too, like him she was wistful about being human. But many sorts of humanness have become available for Temple in the past ten years. Not least among these is a capacity for humor and even subterfuge which one would have thought impossible in someone who is autistic. Thus, when she wanted to show me one of the plants she designed, she had me put on a hard hat and overalls ("You look just like a sanitary engineer now!"), and smuggled me gleefully past the security guards.

I was struck by her rapport with, her great understanding of, cattle—the happy, loving look she wore when she was with them—and her great awkwardness, by contrast, in many human situations. I was also struck, when we walked together, by her seeming inability to feel some of the simplest emotions. "The mountains are pretty," she said, "but they don't give me a special feeling, the feeling you seem to enjoy . . . You look at the brook, the flowers, I see what great pleasure you get out of it. I'm denied that."

And I was awed, as we drove to the airport before my departure, by a sudden revelation of moral and spiritual depths which I had thought no autistic person would have. Temple was driving, when suddenly she faltered and wept, and said, "I don't want my thoughts to die with me. I want to have done something . . . I want to know that my life has meaning . . . I'm talking about things at the very core of my existence."

Thus, in my brief (but very full) few days with Temple, I had a revelation of how, while in many ways so flat and constricted, her life was in other ways full of health, of depth, of deep human strivings.

Temple, now forty-seven, has never ceased to ponder and explore her own nature, which she feels is quintessentially concrete and visual (with the great strengths, and the weaknesses, which may go with this). She feels that "thinking in pictures" gives her a special rapport with cattle, and that her mode of thinking is, albeit at a much higher level, akin to their own mode of thinking—that she sees the world, in a sense, with a cow's eye. Thus though Temple often compares her own mind to a computer, she roots herself, and her own way of thought and feeling, in the creaturely and the organic. Her audacious chapters on sensation and autism, emotion and autism, relationships and autism, genius and autism, religion and autism, might seem strangely juxtaposed with her chapters on "connecting with animals," and "understanding animal thought"—but for Temple, clearly, there is a continuum of experience extending from the animal to the spiritual, from the bovine to the transcendent.

Thinking in pictures, she feels, represents a mode of perception, of feeling and thought and being, which we may call "primitive" if we wish, but not "pathological."

Temple does not romanticize autism, nor does she downplay how much her autism has cut her off from the social whirl, the pleasures, the rewards, the companionships, that for the rest of us may define much of life. But she has a strong, positive sense of her own being and worth, and how autism, paradoxically, may have contributed to this. At a recent lecture, she ended by saying, "If I could snap my fingers and be nonautistic, I would not—because then I wouldn't be me. Autism is part of who I am." If Temple is profoundly different from most of us, she is no less human for being so, but, rather, human in another way. *Thinking in Pictures* is finally a study of identity, the "who-ness" no less than the "what-ness" of a most gifted autistic person. It is a deeply moving and fascinating book because it provides a bridge between our world and hers, and allows us a glimpse into a quite other sort of mind.

Thinking in Pictures

I

Thinking in Pictures

Autism and Visual Thought

I THINK IN PICTURES. Words are like a second language to me. I translate both spoken and written words into full-color movies, complete with sound, which run like a VCR tape in my head. When somebody speaks to me, his words are instantly translated into pictures. Language-based thinkers often find this phenomenon difficult to understand, but in my job as an equipment designer for the livestock industry, visual thinking is a tremendous advantage.

Visual thinking has enabled me to build entire systems in my imagination. During my career I have designed all kinds of equipment, ranging from corrals for handling cattle on ranches to systems for handling cattle and hogs during veterinary procedures and slaughter. I have worked for many major livestock companies. In fact, one third of the cattle and hogs in the United States are handled in equipment I have designed. Some of the people I've worked for don't even know that their systems were designed by someone with autism. I value my ability to think visually, and I would never want to lose it.

One of the most profound mysteries of autism has been the remarkable ability of most autistic people to excel at visual spatial skills while performing so poorly at verbal skills. When I was a child and a teenager, I thought everybody thought in pictures. I had no idea that my thought processes were different. In fact, I did not realize the full extent of the differences until very recently. At meetings and at work I started asking other people detailed questions about how they accessed information from their memories. From their answers I learned that my visualization skills far exceeded those of most other people.

I credit my visualization abilities with helping me understand the animals I work with. Early in my career I used a camera to help give me the animals' perspective as they walked through a chute for their veterinary treatment. I would kneel down and take pictures through the chute from the cow's eye level. Using the photos, I was able to figure out which things scared the cattle, such as shadows and bright spots of sunlight. Back then I used black-and-white film, because twenty years ago scientists believed that cattle lacked color vision. Today, research has shown that cattle can see colors, but the photos provided the unique advantage of seeing the world through a cow's viewpoint. They helped me figure out why the animals refused to go in one chute but willingly walked through another.

Every design problem I've ever solved started with my ability to visualize and see the world in pictures. I started designing things as a child, when I was always experimenting with new kinds of kites and model airplanes. In elementary school I made a helicopter out of a broken balsa-wood airplane. When I wound up the propeller, the helicopter flew straight up about a hundred feet. I also made bird-shaped paper kites, which I flew behind my bike. The kites were cut out from a single sheet of heavy drawing paper and flown with thread. I experimented with different ways of bending the wings to increase flying performance. Bending the tips of the wings up made the kite fly higher. Thirty years later, this same design started appearing on commercial aircraft.

Now, in my work, before I attempt any construction, I test-run the equipment in my imagination. I visualize my designs being used in every possible situation, with different sizes and breeds of cattle and in different weather conditions. Doing this enables me to correct mistakes prior to construction. Today, everyone is excited about the new virtual reality computer systems in which the user wears special goggles and is fully immersed in video game action. To me, these systems are like crude cartoons. My imagination works like the computer graphics programs that created the lifelike dinosaurs in *Jurassic Park*. When I do an equipment simulation in my imagination or work on an engineering problem, it is like seeing it on a videotape in my mind. I can view it from any angle, placing myself above or below the equipment and rotating it at the same time. I don't need a fancy graphics program that can produce three-dimensional design simulations. I can do it better and faster in my head.

I create new images all the time by taking many little parts of images I have in the video library in my imagination and piecing them together. I have video memories of every item I've ever worked with—steel gates, fences, latches, concrete walls, and so forth. To create new designs, I retrieve bits and pieces from my memory and combine them into a new whole. My design ability keeps improving as I add more visual images to my library. I add videolike images from either actual experiences or translations of written information into pictures. I can visualize the operation of such things as squeeze chutes, truck loading ramps, and all different types of livestock equipment. The more I actually work with cattle and operate equipment, the stronger my visual memories become.

I first used my video library in one of my early livestock design projects, creating a dip vat and cattle-handling facility for John Wayne's Red River feed yard in Arizona. A dip vat is a long, narrow, seven-foot-deep swimming pool through which cattle move in single file. It is filled with pesticide to rid the animals of ticks, lice, and other external parasites. In 1978, existing dip vat designs were very poor. The animals often panicked because they were forced to slide into the vat down a steep, slick concrete decline. They would refuse to jump into the vat, and sometimes they would flip over backward and drown. The engineers who designed the slide never thought about why the cattle became so frightened.

The first thing I did when I arrived at the feedlot was to put myself inside the cattle's heads and look out through their eyes. Because their eyes are on the sides of their heads, cattle have wide-angle vision, so it was like walking through the facility with a wide-angle video camera. I had spent the past six years studying how cattle see their world and watching thousands move through different facilities all over Arizona, and it was immediately obvious to me why they were scared. Those cattle must have felt as if they were being forced to jump down an airplane escape slide into the ocean.

Cattle are frightened by high contrasts of light and dark as well as by people and objects that move suddenly. I've seen cattle that were handled in two identical facilities easily walk through one and balk in the other. The only difference between the two facilities was their orientation to the sun. The cattle refused to move through the chute where the sun cast harsh shadows across it. Until I made this observation, nobody in the feedlot industry had been able to explain why one veterinary facility worked better than the other. It was a matter of observing the small details that made a big difference. To me, the dip vat problem was even more obvious.

My first step in designing a better system was collecting all the published information on existing dip vats. Before doing anything else, I always check out what is considered state-of-the-art so I don't waste time reinventing the wheel. Then I turned to livestock publications, which usually have very limited information, and my library of video memories, all of which contained bad designs. From experience with other types of equipment, such as unloading ramps for trucks, I had learned that cattle willingly walk down a ramp that has cleats to provide secure, nonslip footing. Sliding causes them to panic and back up. The challenge was to design an entrance that would encourage the cattle to walk in voluntarily and plunge into the water, which was deep enough to submerge them completely, so that all the bugs, including those that collect in their ears, would be eliminated.

I started running three-dimensional visual simulations in my imagination. I experimented with different entrance designs and made the cattle walk through them in my imagination. Three images merged to form the final design: a memory of a dip vat in Yuma, Arizona, a portable vat I had seen in a magazine, and an entrance ramp I had seen on a restraint device at the Swift meat-packing plant in Tolleson, Arizona. The new dip vat entrance ramp was a modified version of the ramp I had seen there. My design contained three features that had never been used before: an entrance that would not scare the animals, an improved chemical filtration system, and the use of animal behavior principles to prevent the cattle from becoming overexcited when they left the vat.

The first thing I did was convert the ramp from steel to concrete. The final design had a concrete ramp on a twenty-five-degree downward angle. Deep grooves in the concrete provided secure footing. The ramp appeared to enter the water gradually, but in reality it abruptly dropped away below the water's surface. The animals could not see the drop-off because the dip chemicals colored the water. When they stepped out over the water, they quietly fell in, because their center of gravity had passed the point of no return.

Before the vat was built, I tested the entrance design many times in my imagination. Many of the cowboys at the feedlot were skeptical and did not believe my design would work. After it was constructed, they modified it behind my back, because they were sure it was wrong. A metal sheet was installed over the non-slip ramp, converting it back to an old-fashioned slide entrance. The first day they used it, two cattle drowned because they panicked and flipped over backward.

When I saw the metal sheet, I made the cowboys take it out. They were flabbergasted when they saw that the ramp now worked perfectly. Each calf stepped out over the steep drop-off and quietly plopped into the water. I fondly refer to this design as "cattle walking on water."

Over the years, I have observed that many ranchers and cattle feeders think that the only way to induce animals to enter handling facilities is to force them in. The owners and managers of feedlots sometimes have a hard time comprehending that if devices such as dip vats and restraint chutes are properly designed, cattle will voluntarily enter them. I can imagine the sensations the animals would feel. If I had a calf's body and hooves, I would be very scared to step on a slippery metal ramp.

There were still problems I had to resolve after the animals left the dip vat. The platform where they exit is usually divided into two pens so that cattle can dry on one side while the other side is being filled. No one understood why the animals coming out of the dip vat would sometimes become excited, but I figured it was because they wanted to follow their drier buddies, not unlike children divided from their classmates on a playground. I installed a solid fence between the two pens to prevent the animals on one side from seeing the animals on the other side. It was a very simple solution, and it amazed me that nobody had ever thought of it before.

The system I designed for filtering and cleaning the cattle hair and other gook out of the dip vat was based on a swimming pool filtration system. My imagination scanned two specific swimming pool filters that I had operated, one on my Aunt Brecheen's ranch in Arizona and one at our home. To prevent water from splashing out of the dip vat, I copied the concrete coping overhang used on swimming pools. That idea, like many of my best designs, came to me very clearly just before I drifted off to sleep at night.

Being autistic, I don't naturally assimilate information that most people take for granted. Instead, I store information in my head as if it were on a CD-ROM disc. When I recall something I have learned, I replay the video in my imagination. The videos in my memory are always specific; for example, I remember handling cattle at the veterinary chute at Producer's Feedlot or McElhaney Cattle Company. I remember exactly how the animals behaved in that specific situation and how the chutes and other equipment were built. The exact construction of steel fenceposts and pipe rails in each case is also part of my visual memory. I can run these images over and over and study them to solve design problems.

If I let my mind wander, the video jumps in a kind of free association from fence construction to a particular welding shop where I've seen posts being cut and Old John, the welder, making gates. If I continue thinking about Old John welding a gate, the video image changes to a series of short scenes of building gates on several projects I've worked on. Each video memory triggers another in this associative fashion, and my daydreams may wander far from the design problem. The next image may be of having a good time listening to John and the construction crew tell war stories, such as the time the backhoe dug into a nest of rattlesnakes and the machine was abandoned for two weeks because everybody was afraid to go near it.

This process of association is a good example of how my mind can wander off the subject. People with more severe autism have difficulty stopping endless associations. I am able to stop them and get my mind back on track. When I find my mind wandering too far away from a design problem I am trying to solve, I just tell myself to get back to the problem.

Interviews with autistic adults who have good speech and are able to articulate their thought processes indicate that most of them also think in visual images. More severely impaired people, who can speak but are unable to explain how they think, have highly associational thought patterns. Charles Hart, the author of *Without Reason,* a book about his autistic son and brother, sums up his son's thinking in one sentence: "Ted's thought processes aren't logical, they're associational." This explains Ted's statement "I'm not afraid of planes. That's why they fly so high." In his mind, planes fly high because he is not afraid of them; he combines two pieces of information, that planes fly high and that he is not afraid of heights.

Another indicator of visual thinking as the primary method of processing information is the remarkable ability many autistic people exhibit in solving jigsaw puzzles, finding their way around a city, or memorizing enormous amounts of information at a glance. My own thought patterns are similar to those described by A. R. Luria in *The Mind of a Mnemonist*. This book describes a man who worked as a newspaper reporter and could perform amazing feats of memory. Like me, the mnemonist had a visual image for everything he had heard or read. Luria writes, "For when he heard or read a word, it was at once converted into a visual image corresponding with the object the word signified for him." The great inventor Nikola Tesla was also a visual thinker. When he designed electric turbines for power generation, he built each turbine in his head. He operated it in his imagination and corrected faults. He said it did not matter whether the turbine was tested in his thoughts or in his shop; the results would be the same.

Early in my career I got into fights with other engineers at meat-packing plants. I couldn't imagine that they could be so stupid as not to see the mistakes on the drawing before the equipment was installed. Now I realize it was not stupidity but a lack of visualization skills. They literally could not see. I was fired from one company that manufactured meat-packing plant equipment because I fought with the engineers over a design which eventually caused the collapse of an overhead track that moved 1,200-pound beef carcasses from the end of a conveyor. As each carcass came off the conveyor, it dropped about three feet before it was abruptly halted by a chain attached to a trolley on the overhead track. The first time the machine was run, the track was pulled out of the ceiling. The employees fixed it by bolting it more securely and installing additional brackets. This only solved the problem temporarily, because the force of the carcasses jerking the chains was so great. Strengthening the overhead track was treating a symptom of the problem rather than its cause. I tried to warn them. It was like bending a paper clip back and forth too many times. After a while it breaks.

Different Ways of Thinking

The idea that people have different thinking patterns is not new. Francis Galton, in *Inquiries into Human Faculty and Development,* wrote that while some people see vivid mental pictures, for others "the idea is not felt to be mental pictures, but rather symbols of facts. In people with low pictorial imagery, they would remember their breakfast table but they could not see it."

It wasn't until I went to college that I realized some people are completely verbal and think only in words. I first suspected this when I read an article in a science magazine about the development of tool use in prehistoric humans. Some renowned scientist speculated that humans had to develop language before they could develop tools. I thought this was ridiculous, and this article gave me the first inkling that my thought processes were truly different from those of many other people. When I invent things, I do not use language. Some other people think in vividly detailed pictures, but most think in a combination of words and vague, generalized pictures.

For example, many people see a generalized generic church rather than specific churches and steeples when they read or hear the word *steeple*. Their thought patterns move from a general concept to specific examples. I used to become very frustrated when a verbal thinker could not understand something I was trying to express because he or she couldn't see the picture that was crystal clear to me. Further, my mind constantly revises general concepts as I add new information to my memory library. It's like getting a new version of software for the computer. My mind readily accepts the new "software," though I have observed that some people often do not readily accept new information.

Unlike those of most people, my thoughts move from video-like, specific images to generalization and concepts. For example, my concept of dogs is inextricably linked to every dog I've ever known. It's as if I have a card catalogue of dogs I have seen, complete with pictures, which continually grows as I add more examples to my video library. If I think about Great Danes, the first memory that pops into my head is Dansk, the Great Dane owned by the headmaster at my high school. The next Great Dane I visualize is Helga, who was Dansk's replacement. The next is my aunt's dog in Arizona, and my final image comes from an advertisement for Fitwell seat covers that featured that kind of dog. My memories usually appear in my imagination in strict chronological order, and the images I visualize are always specific. There is no generic, generalized Great Dane.

However, not all people with autism are highly visual thinkers, nor do they all process information this way. People throughout the world are on a continuum of visualization skills ranging from next to none, to seeing vague generalized pictures, to seeing semi-specific pictures, to seeing, as in my case, in very specific pictures.

I'm always forming new visual images when I invent new equipment or think of something novel and amusing. I can take images that I have seen, rearrange them, and create new pictures. For example, I can imagine what a dip vat would look like modeled on computer graphics by placing it on my memory of a friend's computer screen. Since his computer is not programmed to do the fancy 3-D rotary graphics, I take computer graphics I have seen on TV or in the movies and superimpose them in my memory. In my visual imagination the dip vat will appear in the kind of high-quality computer graphics shown on *Star Trek*. I can then take a specific dip vat, such as the one at Red River, and redraw it on the computer screen in my mind. I can even duplicate the cartoonlike, three-dimensional skeletal image on the computer screen or imagine the dip vat as a videotape of the real thing.

Similarly, I learned how to draw engineering designs by closely observing a very talented draftsman when we worked together at the same feed yard construction company. David was able to render the most fabulous drawings effortlessly. After I left the company, I was forced to do all my own drafting. By studying David's drawings for many hours and photographing them in my memory, I was actually able to emulate David's drawing style. I laid some of his drawings out so I could look at them while I drew my first design. Then I drew my new plan and copied his style. After making three or four drawings, I no longer had to have his drawings out on the table. My video memory was now fully programmed. Copying designs is one thing, but after I drew the Red River drawings, I could not believe I had done them. At the time, I thought they were a gift from God. Another factor that helped me to learn to draw well was something as simple as using the same tools that David used. I used the same brand of pencil, and the ruler and straight edge forced me to slow down and trace the visual images in my imagination.

My artistic abilities became evident when I was in first and second grade. I had a good eye for color and painted watercolors of the beach. One time in fourth grade I modeled a lovely horse from clay. I just did it spontaneously, though I was not able to duplicate it. In high school and college I never attempted engineering drawing, but I learned the value of slowing down while drawing during a college art class. Our assignment had been to spend two hours drawing a picture of one of our shoes. The teacher insisted that the entire two hours be spent drawing that one shoe. I was amazed at how well my drawing came out. While my initial attempts at drafting were terrible, when I visualized myself as David, the draftsman, I'd automatically slow down.

Processing Nonvisual Information

Autistics have problems learning things that cannot be thought about in pictures. The easiest words for an autistic child to learn are nouns, because they directly relate to pictures. Highly verbal autistic children like I was can sometimes learn how to read with phonics. Written words were too abstract for me to remember, but I could laboriously remember the approximately fifty phonetic sounds and a few rules. Lower-functioning children often learn better by association, with the aid of word labels attached to objects in their environment. Some very impaired autistic children learn more easily if words are spelled out with plastic letters they can feel.

Spatial words such as "over" and "under" had no meaning for me until I had a visual image to fix them in my memory. Even now, when I hear the word "under" by itself, I automatically picture myself getting under the cafeteria tables at school during an air-raid drill, a common occurrence on the East Coast during the early fifties. The first memory that any single word triggers is almost always a childhood memory. I can remember the teacher telling us to be quiet and walking single-file into the cafeteria, where six or eight children huddled under each table. If I continue on the same train of thought, more and more associative memories of elementary school emerge. I can remember the teacher scolding me after I hit Alfred for putting dirt on my shoe. All of these memories play like videotapes in the VCR in my imagination. If I allow my mind to keep associating, it will wander a million miles away from the word "under," to submarines under the Antarctic and the Beatles song "Yellow Submarine." If I let my mind pause on the picture of the yellow submarine, I then hear the song. As I start humming the song and get to the part about people coming on board, my association switches to the gangway of a ship I saw in Australia.

I also visualize verbs. The word *jumping* triggers a memory of jumping hurdles at the mock Olympics held at my elementary school. Adverbs often trigger inappropriate images—"quickly" reminds me of Nestle's Quik—unless they are paired with a verb, which modifies my visual image. For example, "he ran quickly" triggers an animated image of Dick from the first-grade reading book running fast, and "he walked slowly" slows the image down. As a child, I left out words such as "is," "the," and "it," because they had no meaning by themselves. Similarly, words like "of" and "an" made no sense. Eventually I learned how to use them properly, because my parents always spoke correct English and I mimicked their speech patterns. To this day certain verb conjugations, such as "to be," are absolutely meaningless to me.

When I read, I translate written words into color movies or I simply store a photo of the written page to be read later. When I retrieve the material, I see a photocopy of the page in my imagination. I can then read it like a TelePrompTer. It is likely that Raymond, the autistic savant depicted in the movie *Rain Man,* used a similar strategy to memorize telephone books, maps, and other information. He simply photocopied each page of the phone book into his memory. When he wanted to find a certain number, he just scanned pages of the phone book that were in his mind. To pull information out of my memory, I have to replay the video. Pulling facts up quickly is sometimes difficult, because I have to play bits of different videos until I find the right tape. This takes time.

When I am unable to convert text to pictures, it is usually because the text has no concrete meaning. Some philosophy books and articles about the cattle futures market are simply incomprehensible. It is much easier for me to understand written text that describes something that can be easily translated into pictures. The following sentence from a story in the February 21, 1994, issue of *Time* magazine, describing the Winter Olympics figure-skating championships, is a good example: "All the elements are in place—the spotlights, the swelling waltzes and jazz tunes, the sequined sprites taking to the air." In my imagination I see the skating rink and skaters. However, if I ponder too long on the word "elements," I will make the inappropriate association of a periodic table on the wall of my high school chemistry classroom. Pausing on the word "sprite" triggers an image of a Sprite can in my refrigerator instead of a pretty young skater.

Teachers who work with autistic children need to understand associative thought patterns. An autistic child will often use a word in an inappropriate manner. Sometimes these uses have a logical associative meaning and other times they don't. For example, an autistic child might say the word "dog" when he wants to go outside. The word "dog" is associated with going outside. In my own case, I can remember both logical and illogical use of inappropriate words. When I was six, I learned to say "prosecution." I had absolutely no idea what it meant, but it sounded nice when I said it, so I used it as an exclamation every time my kite hit the ground. I must have baffled more than a few people who heard me exclaim "Prosecution!" to my downward-spiraling kite.

Discussions with other autistic people reveal similar visual styles of thinking about tasks that most people do sequentially. An autistic man who composes music told me that he makes "sound pictures" using small pieces of other music to create new compositions. A computer programmer with autism told me that he sees the general pattern of the program tree. After he visualizes the skeleton for the program, he simply writes the code for each branch. I use similar methods when I review scientific literature and troubleshoot at meat plants. I take specific findings or observations and combine them to find new basic principles and general concepts.

My thinking pattern always starts with specifics and works toward generalization in an associational and nonsequential way. As if I were attempting to figure out what the picture on a jigsaw puzzle is when only one third of the puzzle is completed, I am able to fill in the missing pieces by scanning my video library. Chinese mathematicians who can make large calculations in their heads work the same way. At first they need an abacus, the Chinese calculator, which consists of rows of beads on wires in a frame. They make calculations by moving the rows of beads. When a mathematician becomes really skilled, he simply visualizes the abacus in his imagination and no longer needs a real one. The beads move on a visualized video abacus in his brain.

Abstract Thought

Growing up, I learned to convert abstract ideas into pictures as a way to understand them. I visualized concepts such as peace or honesty with symbolic images. I thought of peace as a dove, an Indian peace pipe, or TV or newsreel footage of the signing of a peace agreement. Honesty was represented by an image of placing one's hand on the Bible in court. A news report describing a person returning a wallet with all the money in it provided a picture of honest behavior.

The Lord's Prayer was incomprehensible until I broke it down into specific visual images. The power and the glory were represented by a semicircular rainbow and an electrical tower. These childhood visual images are still triggered every time I hear the Lord's Prayer. The words "thy will be done" had no meaning when I was a child, and today the meaning is still vague. Will is a hard concept to visualize. When I think about it, I imagine God throwing a lightning bolt. Another adult with autism wrote that he visualized "Thou art in heaven" as God with an easel above the clouds. "Trespassing" was pictured as black and orange NO TRESPASSING signs. The word "Amen" at the end of the prayer was a mystery: a man at the end made no sense.

As a teenager and young adult I had to use concrete symbols to understand abstract concepts such as getting along with people and moving on to the next steps of my life, both of which were always difficult. I knew I did not fit in with my high school peers, and I was unable to figure out what I was doing wrong. No matter how hard I tried, they made fun of me. They called me "workhorse," "tape recorder," and "bones" because I was skinny. At the time I was able to figure out why they called me "workhorse" and "bones," but "tape recorder" puzzled me. Now I realize that I must have sounded like a tape recorder when I repeated things verbatim over and over. But back then I just could not figure out why I was such a social dud. I sought refuge in doing things I was good at, such as working on reroofing the barn or practicing my riding prior to a horse show. Personal relationships made absolutely no sense to me until I developed visual symbols of doors and windows. It was then that I started to understand concepts such as learning the give-and-take of a relationship. I still wonder what would have happened to me if I had not been able to visualize my way in the world.

The really big challenge for me was making the transition from high school to college. People with autism have tremendous difficulty with change. In order to deal with a major change such as leaving high school, I needed a way to rehearse it, acting out each phase in my life by walking through an actual door, window, or gate. When I was graduating from high school, I would go and sit on the roof of my dormitory and look up at the stars and think about how I would cope with leaving. It was there I discovered a little door that led to a bigger roof while my dormitory was being remodeled. While I was still living in this old New England house, a much larger building was being constructed over it. One day the carpenters tore out a section of the old roof next to my room. When I walked out, I was now able to look up into the partially finished new building. High on one side was a small wooden door that led to the new roof. The building was changing, and it was now time for me to change too. I could relate to that. I had found the symbolic key.

When I was in college, I found another door to symbolize getting ready for graduation. It was a small metal trap door that went out onto the flat roof of the dormitory. I had to actually practice going through this door many times. When I finally graduated from Franklin Pierce, I walked through a third, very important door, on the library roof.

I no longer use actual physical doors or gates to symbolize each transition in my life. When I reread years of diary entries while writing this book, a clear pattern emerged. Each door or gate enabled me to move on to the next level. My life was a series of incremental steps. I am often asked what the single breakthrough was that enabled me to adapt to autism. There was no single breakthrough. It was a series of incremental improvements. My diary entries show very clearly that I was fully aware that when I mastered one door, it was only one step in a whole series.

April 22, 1970

Today everything is completed at Franklin Pierce College and it is now time to walk through the little door in the library. I ponder now about what I should leave as a message on the library roof for future people to find.

I have reached the top of one step and I am now at the bottom step of graduate school.

For the top of the building is the highest point on campus and I have gone as far as I can go now.

I have conquered the summit of FPC. Higher ones still remain unchallenged. Class 70

I went through the little door tonight and placed the plaque on the top of the library roof. I was not as nervous this time. I had been much more nervous in the past. Now I have already made it and the little door and the mountain had already been climbed. The conquering of this mountain is only the beginning for the next mountain.

The word "commencement" means beginning and the top of the library is the beginning of graduate school. It is human nature to strive, and this is why people will climb mountains. The reason why is that people strive to prove that they could do it.

After all, why should we send a man to the moon? The only real justification is that it is human nature to keep striving out. Man is never satisfied with one goal he keeps reaching. The real reason for going to the library roof was to prove that I could do it.

During my life I have been faced with five or six major doors or gates to go through. I graduated from Franklin Pierce, a small liberal arts college, in 1970, with a degree in psychology, and moved to Arizona to get a Ph.D. As I found myself getting less interested in psychology and more interested in cattle and animal science, I prepared myself for another big change in my life— switching from a psychology major to an animal science major. On May 8, 1971, I wrote:

> I feel as if I am being pulled more and more in the farm direction. I walked through the cattle chute gate but I am still holding on tightly to the gate post. The wind is blowing harder and harder and I feel that I will let go of the gate post and go back to the farm; at least for a while. Wind has played an important part in many of the doors. On the roof, the wind was blowing. Maybe this is a symbol that the next level that is reached is not ultimate and that I must keep moving on. At the party [a psychology department party] I felt completely out of place and it seems as if the wind is causing my hands to slip from the gate post so that I can ride free on the wind.

At that time I still struggled in the social arena, largely because I didn't have a concrete visual corollary for the abstraction known as "getting along with people." An image finally presented itself to me while I was washing the bay window in the cafeteria (students were required to do jobs in the dining room). I had no idea my job would take on symbolic significance when I started. The bay window consisted of three glass sliding doors enclosed by storm windows. To wash the inside of the bay window, I had to crawl through the sliding door. The door jammed while I was washing the inside panes, and I was imprisoned between the two windows. In order to get out without shattering the door, I had to ease it back very carefully. It struck me that relationships operate the same way. They also shatter easily and have to be approached carefully. I then made a further association about how the careful opening of doors was related to establishing relationships in the first place. While I was trapped between the windows, it was almost impossible to communicate through the glass. Being autistic is like being trapped like this. The windows symbolized my feelings of disconnection from other people and helped me cope with the isolation. Throughout my life, door and window symbols have enabled me to make progress and connections that are unheard of for some people with autism.

In more severe cases of autism, the symbols are harder to understand and often appear to be totally unrelated to the things they represent. D. Park and P. Youderian described the use of visual symbols and numbers by Jessy Park, then a twelve-year-old autistic girl, to describe abstract concepts such as good and bad. Good things, such as rock music, were represented by drawings of four doors and no clouds. Jessy rated most classical music as pretty good, drawing two doors and two clouds. The spoken word was rated as very bad, with a rating of zero doors and four clouds. She had formed a visual rating system using doors and clouds to describe these abstract qualities. Jessy also had an elaborate system of good and bad numbers, though researchers have not been able to decipher her system fully.

Many people are totally baffled by autistic symbols, but to an autistic person they may provide the only tangible reality or understanding of the world. For example, "French toast" may mean happy if the child was happy while eating it. When the child visualizes a piece of French toast, he becomes happy. A visual image or word becomes associated with an experience. Clara Park, Jessy's mother, described her daughter's fascination with objects such as electric blanket controls and heaters. She had no idea why the objects were so important to Jessy, though she did observe that Jessy was happiest, and her voice was no longer a monotone, when she was thinking about her special things. Jessy was able to talk, but she was unable to tell people why her special things were important. Perhaps she associated electric blanket controls and heaters with warmth and security. The word "cricket" made her happy, and "partly heard song" meant "I don't know." The autistic mind works via these visual associations. At some point in Jessy's life, a partly heard song was associated with not knowing.

Ted Hart, a man with severe autism, has almost no ability to generalize and no flexibility in his behavior. His father, Charles, described how on one occasion Ted put wet clothes in the dresser after the dryer broke. He just went on to the next step in a clothes-washing sequence that he had learned by rote. He has no common sense. I would speculate that such rigid behavior and lack of ability to generalize may be partly due to having little or no ability to change or modify visual memories. Even though my memories of things are stored as individual specific memories, I am able to modify my mental images. For example, I can imagine a church painted in different colors or put the steeple of one church onto the roof of another; but when I hear somebody say the word "steeple," the first church that I see in my imagination is almost always a childhood memory and not a church image that I have manipulated. This ability to modify images in my imagination helped me to learn how to generalize.

Today, I no longer need door symbols. Over the years I have built up enough real experiences and information from articles and books I have read to be able to make changes and take necessary steps as new situations present themselves. Plus, I have always been an avid reader, and I am driven to take in more and more information to add to my video library. A severely autistic computer programmer once said that reading was "taking in information." For me, it is like programming a computer.

Visual Thinking and Mental Imagery

Recent studies of patients with brain damage and of brain imaging indicate that visual and verbal thought may work via different brain systems. Recordings of blood flow in the brain indicate that when a person visualizes something such as walking through his neighborhood, blood flow increases dramatically in the visual cortex, in parts of the brain that are working hard. Studies of brain-damaged patients show that injury to the left posterior hemisphere can stop the generation of visual images from stored long-term memories, while language and verbal memory are not impaired. This indicates that visual imagery and verbal thought may depend on distinct neurological systems.

The visual system may also contain separate subsystems for mental imagery and image rotation. Image rotation skills appear to be located on the right side of the brain, whereas visual imagery is in the left rear of the brain. In autism, it is possible that the visual system has expanded to make up for verbal and sequencing deficits. The nervous system has a remarkable ability to compensate when it is damaged. Another part can take over for a damaged part.

Recent research by Dr. Pascual-Leone at the National Institutes of Health indicates that exercising a visual skill can make the brain's motor map expand. Research with musicians indicates that real practice on the piano and imagining playing the piano have the same effect on motor maps, as measured by brain scans. The motor maps expand during both real piano playing and mental imagery; random pushing of the keys has no effect. Athletes have also found that both mental practice and real practice can improve a motor skill. Research with patients with damage to the hippocampus has indicated that conscious memory of events and motor learning are separate neurological systems. A patient with hippocampal damage can learn a motor task and get better with practice, but each time he practices he will have no conscious memory of doing the task. The motor circuits become trained, but damage to the hippocampus prevents the formation of new conscious memories. Therefore, the motor circuits learn a new task, such as solving a simple mechanical puzzle, but the person does not remember seeing or doing the puzzle. With repeated practice, the person gets better and better at it, but each time the puzzle is presented, he says he has never seen it before.

I am fortunate in that I am able to build on my library of images and visualize solutions based on those pictures. However, most people with autism lead extremely limited lives, in part because they cannot handle any deviation from their routine. For me, every experience builds on the visual memories I carry from prior experience, and in this way my world continues to grow.

About two years ago I made a personal breakthrough when I was hired to remodel a meat plant that used very cruel restraint methods during kosher slaughter. Prior to slaughter, live cattle were hung upside down by a chain attached to one back leg. It was so horrible I could not stand to watch it. The frantic bellows of terrified cattle could be heard in both the office and the parking lot. Sometimes an animal's back leg was broken during hoisting. This dreadful practice totally violated the humane intent of kosher slaughter. My job was to rip out this cruel system and replace it with a chute that would hold the animal in a standing position while the rabbi performed kosher slaughter. Done properly, the animal should remain calm and would not be frightened.

The new restraining chute was a narrow metal stall which held one steer. It was equipped with a yoke to hold the animal's head, a rear pusher gate to nudge the steer forward into the yoke, and a belly restraint which was raised under the belly like an elevator. To operate the restrainer, the operator had to push six hydraulic control levers in the proper sequence to move the entrance and discharge gates as well as the head- and body-positioning devices. The basic design of this chute had been around for about thirty years, but I added pressure-regulating devices and changed some critical dimensions to make it more comfortable for the animal and to prevent excessive pressure from being applied.

Prior to actually operating the chute at the plant, I ran it in the machine shop before it was shipped. Even though no cattle were present, I was able to program my visual and tactile memory with images of operating the chute. After running the empty chute for five minutes, I had accurate mental pictures of how the gates and other parts of the apparatus moved. I also had tactile memories of how the levers on this particular chute felt when pushed. Hydraulic valves are like musical instruments; different brands of valves have a different feel, just as different types of wind instruments do. Operating the controls in the machine shop enabled me to practice later via mental imagery. I had to visualize the actual controls on the chute and, in my imagination, watch my hands pushing the levers. I could feel in my mind how much force was needed to move the gates at different speeds. I rehearsed the procedure many times in my mind with different types of cattle entering the chute.

On the first day of operation at the plant, I was able to walk up to the chute and run it almost perfectly. It worked best when I operated the hydraulic levers unconsciously, like using my legs for walking. If I thought about the levers, I got all mixed up and pushed them the wrong way. I had to force myself to relax and just allow the restrainer to become part of my body, while completely forgetting about the levers. As each animal entered, I concentrated on moving the apparatus slowly and gently so as not to scare him. I watched his reactions so that I applied only enough pressure to hold him snugly. Excessive pressure would cause discomfort. If his ears were laid back against his head or he struggled, I knew I had squeezed him too hard. Animals are very sensitive to hydraulic equipment. They feel the smallest movement of the control levers.

Through the machine I reached out and held the animal. When I held his head in the yoke, I imagined placing my hands on his forehead and under his chin and gently easing him into position. Body boundaries seemed to disappear, and I had no awareness of pushing the levers. The rear pusher gate and head yoke became an extension of my hands.

People with autism sometimes have body boundary problems. They are unable to judge by feel where their body ends and the chair they are sitting on or the object they are holding begins, much like what happens when a person loses a limb but still experiences the feeling of the limb being there. In this case, the parts of the apparatus that held the animal felt as if they were a continuation of my own body, similar to the phantom limb effect. If I just concentrated on holding the animal gently and keeping him calm, I was able to run the restraining chute very skillfully.

During this intense period of concentration I no longer heard noise from the plant machinery. I didn't feel the sweltering Alabama summer heat, and everything seemed quiet and serene. It was almost a religious experience. It was my job to hold the animal gently, and it was the rabbi's job to perform the final deed. I was able to look at each animal, to hold him gently and make him as comfortable as possible during the last moments of his life. I had participated in the ancient slaughter ritual the way it was supposed to be. A new door had been opened. It felt like walking on water.

Update: Brain Research and Different Ways of Thinking

Since I wrote *Thinking in Pictures*, brain imaging studies have provided more insights into how the brain of a person on the autism/Asperger spectrum processes information. Nancy Minshew at Carnegie Mellon University in Pittsburgh has found that normal brains tend to ignore the details while people on the autism spectrum tend to focus on the details instead of larger concepts. To view this phenomenon, she had normal, Asperger, and autistic people read sentences while they were in a scanner. The autistic brain was most active in the part of the brain that processes the individual words while the normal brain was most active in the part that analyzes the whole sentence. The Asperger brain was active in both areas.

Eric Courchesne at the University of California in San Diego states that autism may be a disorder of brain circuit disconnections. This would affect the ability to integrate detailed information from lower parts of the brain where sensory based memories are stored with higher level information processing in the frontal cortex. Lower level processing systems may be spared or possibly enhanced. He discovered in an autistic person that the only parts of the brain that are normal are the visual cortex and the areas in the rear of the brain that store memories. This finding helps explain my visual thinking. Scans of autistic brains have indicated that the white matter in the frontal cortex is overgrown and abnormal. Dr. Courchesne explains that white matter is the brain's "computer cables" connecting up different parts of the brain while the gray matter forms the information processing circuits. Instead of growing normally and connecting various parts of the brain together, the autistic frontal cortex has excessive overgrowth much like a thicket of tangled computer cables. In the normal brain, reading a word and speaking a word are processed in different parts of the brain. Connecting circuits between these two areas makes it possible to simultaneously process information from both of them. Both Courchesne and Minshew agree that a basic problem in both autistic and Asperger brains is a failure of the "computer cables" to fully connect together the many different localized brain systems. Local systems may have normal or enhanced internal connections but the long distance connections between the different local systems may be poor.

I am now going to use what I call visual symbol imagery to help you understand how the different parts of the normal brain communicate with each other. Think of the normal brain as a big corporate office building. All the different departments such as legal, accounting, advertising, sales, and the CEO's office are connected together by many communication systems such as e-mail, telephones, fax machines, and electronic messaging. The autistic/Asperger brain is like an office building where some of the interdepartmental communication systems are not hooked up. Minshew calls this underconnectivity in the brain. More systems would be hooked up in an Asperger brain than in the brain of a low-functioning individual. The great variability in austistic/Asperger symptoms probably depends on which "cables" get connected and which "cables" do not get connected. Poor communication between brain departments is likely the cause of uneven skills. People on the spectrum are often good at one thing and bad at something else. To use the computer cable analogy, the limited number of good cables may connect up one area and leave the other areas with poor connections.

Develop Talents in Specialized Brains

When I wrote *Thinking in Pictures* I thought most people on the autism spectrum were visual thinkers like me. After talking to hundreds of families and individuals with autism or Asperger's, I have observed that there are actually different types of specialized brains. All people on the spectrum think in details, but there are three basic categories of specialized brains. Some individuals may be combinations of these categories.

1. *Visual thinkers,* like me, think in photographically specific images. There are degrees of specificity of visual thinking. I can test run a machine in my head with full motion. Interviews with nonautistic visual thinkers indicated that they can only visualize still images. These images may range in specificity from images of specific places to more vague conceptual images. Learning algebra was impossible and a foreign language was difficult. Highly specific visual thinkers should skip algebra and study more visual forms of math such as trigonometry or geometry. Children who are visual thinkers will often be good at drawing, other arts, and building things with building toys such as Legos. Many children who are visual thinkers like maps, flags, and photographs. Visual thinkers are well suited to jobs in drafting, graphic design, training animals, auto mechanics, jewelry making, construction, and factory automation.

2. *Music and math thinkers* think in patterns. These people often excel at math, chess, and computer programming. Some of these individuals have explained to me that they see patterns and relationships between patterns and numbers instead of photographic images. As children they may play music by ear and be interested in music. Music and math minds often have

careers in computer programming, chemistry, statistics, engineering, music, and physics. Written language is not required for pattern thinking. The pre-literate Incas used complex bundles of knotted cords to keep track of taxes, labor, and trading among a thousand people.
3. *Verbal logic thinkers* think in word details. They often love history, foreign languages, weather statistics, and stock market reports. As children they often have a vast knowledge of sports scores. They are not visual thinkers and they are often poor at drawing. Children with speech delays are more likely to become visual or music and math thinkers. Many of these individuals had no speech delays, and they became word specialists. These individuals have found successful careers in language translation, journalism, accounting, speech therapy, special education, library work, or financial analysis.

Since brains on the autistic spectrum are specialized, there needs to be more educational emphasis on building up their strengths instead of just working on their deficits. Tutoring me in algebra was useless because there was nothing for me to visualize. If I have no picture, I have no thought. Unfortunately I never had an opportunity to try trigonometry or geometry. Teachers and parents need to develop the child's talents into skills that can eventually turn into satisfying jobs or hobbies.

Concept Formation

All individuals on the autism/Asperger spectrum have difficulties with forming concepts. Problems with conceptual thought occur in all of the specialized brain types. Conceptual thinking occurs in the frontal cortex. The frontal cortex is analogous to the CEO's office in a corporation. Researchers refer to frontal cortex deficits as problems with execution function. In normal brains, "computer cables" from all parts of the brain converge on the frontal cortex. The frontal cortex integrates information from thinking, emotional, and sensory parts of the brain. The degree of difficulty in forming concepts is probably related to the number and type of "computer cables" that are not hooked up. Since my CEO's office has poor "computer" connections, I had to use the "graphic designers" in my "advertising department" to form concepts by associating visual details into categories. Scientific research supports my idea. Detailed visual and musical memories reside in the lower primary visual and auditory cortex and more conceptual thinking is in association areas where inputs from different parts of the brain are merged.

Categories are the beginning of concept formation. Nancy Minshew found that people with autism can easily sort objects into categories such as red or blue, but they have difficulty thinking up new categories for groups of common objects. If I put a variety of common things on a table such as staplers, pencils, books, an envelope, a clock, hats, golf balls, and a tennis racquet, and asked an individual with autism to pick out objects containing paper, they could do it. However, they often have difficulty when asked to make up new categories. Teachers should work on teaching flexibility of thinking by playing a game where the autistic individual is asked to make up new categories for the objects like objects containing metal, or objects used in sports. Then the teacher should get the person to explain the reason for putting an object in a specific category.

When I was a child I originally categorized dogs from cats by size. That no longer worked when our neighbors got a small dachshund. I had to learn to categorize small dogs from cats by finding a visual feature that all the dogs had and none of the cats had. All dogs, no matter how small, have the same nose. This is sensory-based thinking, not language-based. The animals could also be categorized by sound, barking versus meowing. A lower-functioning person may categorize them by smell or touch because those senses provide more accurate information. Dividing information into distinct categories is a fundamental property of the nervous system. Studies with bees, rats, and monkeys all indicate that information is placed into categories with sharp boundaries. French scientists recorded signals from the frontal cortex of a monkey's brain while it was looking at computer-generated images of dogs that gradually turned into cats. There was a distinct change in the brain signal when the category switched to cat. In the frontal cortex, the animal image was either a dog or a cat. When categorizing cats from dogs by size no longer worked for me, I had to form a new category of nose type. Research by Itzahak Fried at UCLA has shown that individual neurons learn to respond to specific categories. Recordings taken from patients undergoing brain surgery showed that one neuron may respond only to pictures of food and another neuron will respond only to pictures of animals. This neuron will not respond to pictures of people or objects. In another patient, a neuron in the hippocampus responded to pictures of a movie actress both in and out of costume but it did not respond to pictures of other women. The hippocampus is like the brain's file finder for locating information in stored memory.

Becoming More Normal

More knowledge makes me act more normal. Many people have commented to me that I act much less autistic now than I did ten years ago. A person who attended one of my talks in 2005 wrote on my evaluation, "I saw Temple in 1996, it was fun to see the poise and presentation manner she has gained over the years." My mind works just like an Internet search engine that has been set to access only images. The more pictures I have stored in the Internet inside my brain the more templates I have of how to act in a new situation. More and more information can be placed in more and more categories. The categories can be placed in trees of master categories with many subcategories. For example, there are jokes that make people laugh and jokes that do not work.

There is then a subcategory of jokes that can only be told to close friends. When I was a teenager I was called "tape recorder" because I used scripted lines. As I gained experience, my conversation became less scripted because I could combine new information in new ways. To help understand the autistic brain I recommend that teachers and parents should play with an Internet search engine such as Google for images. It will give people who are more verbal thinkers an understanding into how visual associative thinking works. People with music and math minds have a search engine that finds associations between patterns and numbers.

The Asperger individual who is a verbal logic thinker uses verbal categories. For example, Dr. Minshew had an Asperger patient who had a bad side effect with a medication. Explaining the science of why he should try a different medication was useless. However, he became willing to try a new medication after he was simply told, the pink pills made you sick and I want you to try the blue pills. He agreed to try the blue pills.

The more I learn, the more I realize more and more that how I think and feel is different. My thinking is different from a normal person, but it is also very different from the verbal logic nonvisual person with Asperger's. They create word categories instead of picture categories. The one common denominator of all autistic and Asperger thinking is that details are associated into categories to form a concept. Details are assembled into concepts like putting a jigsaw puzzle together. The picture on the puzzle can be seen when only 20 percent of the puzzle is put together, forming a big picture.

2

THE GREAT CONTINUUM

Diagnosing Autism

THE FIRST SIGN that a baby may be autistic is that it stiffens up and resists being held and cuddled. It may be extremely sensitive to touch and respond by pulling away or screaming. More obvious symptoms of autism usually occur between twelve and twenty-four months of age. I was my mother's first child, and I was like a little wild animal. I struggled to get away when held, but if I was left alone in the big baby carriage I seldom fussed. Mother first realized that something was dreadfully wrong when I failed to start talking like the little girl next door, and it seemed that I might be deaf. Between nonstop tantrums and a penchant for smearing feces, I was a terrible two-year-old.

At that time, I showed the symptoms of classic autism: no speech, poor eye contact, tantrums, appearance of deafness, no interest in people, and constant staring off into space. I was taken to a neurologist, and when a hearing test revealed that I was not deaf, I was given the label "brain-damaged." Most doctors over forty years ago had never heard of autism. A few years later, when more doctors learned about it, that label was applied.

I can remember the frustration of not being able to talk at age three. This caused me to throw many a tantrum. I could understand what people said to me, but I could not get my words out. It was like a big stutter, and starting words was difficult. My first few words were very difficult to produce and generally had only one syllable, such as "bah" for ball. I can remember logically thinking to myself that I would have to scream because I had no other way to communicate. Tantrums also occurred when I became tired or stressed by too much noise, such as horns going off at a birthday party. My behavior was like a tripping circuit breaker. One minute I was fine, and the next minute I was on the floor kicking and screaming like a crazed wildcat.

I can remember the day I bit my teacher's leg. It was late in the afternoon and I was getting tired. I just lost it. But it was only after I came out of it, when I saw her bleeding leg, that I realized I had bitten her. Tantrums occurred suddenly, like epileptic seizures. Mother figured out that like seizures, they had to run their course. Getting angry once a tantrum started just made it worse. She explained to my elementary school teachers that the best way to handle me if I had a tantrum was not to get angry or excited. She learned that tantrums could be prevented by getting me out of noisy places when I got tired. Privileges such as watching *Howdy Doody* on TV were withdrawn when I had a bad day at school. She even figured out that I'd sometimes throw a tantrum to avoid going to class.

When left alone, I would often space out and become hypnotized. I could sit for hours on the beach watching sand dribbling through my fingers. I'd study each individual grain of sand as it flowed between my fingers. Each grain was different, and I was like a scientist studying the grains under a microscope. As I scrutinized their shapes and contours, I went into a trance which cut me off from the sights and sounds around me.

Rocking and spinning were other ways to shut out the world when I became overloaded with too much noise. Rocking made me feel calm. It was like taking an addictive drug. The more I did it, the more I wanted to do it. My mother and my teachers would stop me so I would get back in touch with the rest of the world. I also loved to spin, and I seldom got dizzy. When I stopped spinning, I enjoyed the sensation of watching the room spin.

Today, autism is regarded as an early childhood disorder by definition, and it is three times more common in boys than girls. For the diagnosis to be made, autistic symptoms must appear before the age of three. The most common symptoms in young children are no speech or abnormal speech, lack of eye contact, frequent temper tantrums, oversensitivity to touch, the appearance of deafness, a preference for being alone, rocking or other rhythmic stereotypic behavior, aloofness, and lack of social contact with parents and siblings. Another sign is inappropriate play with toys. The child may spend long periods of time spinning the wheel of a toy car instead of driving it around on the floor.

Diagnosing autism is complicated by the fact that the behavioral criteria are constantly being changed. These criteria are listed in the *Diagnostic and Statistical Manual* published by the American Psychiatric Association. Using those in the third edition of the book, 91 percent of young children displaying autistic symptoms would be labeled autistic. However, using the newest edition of the book, the label would apply to only 59 percent of the cases, because the criteria have been narrowed.

Many parents with an autistic child will go to many different specialists looking for a precise diagnosis. Unfortunately, diagnosing autism is not like diagnosing measles or a specific chromosomal defect such as Down syndrome. Even though autism is a neurological disorder, it is still diagnosed by observing a child's behavior. There is no blood test or brain scan that can give an absolute diagnosis, though brain scans may partially replace observation in the future.

The new diagnostic categories are autism, pervasive developmental disorder (PDD), Asperger's syndrome, and disintegrative disorder, and there is much controversy among professionals about them. Some consider these categories to be true separate entities, and others believe that they lie on an autistic continuum and there is no definite distinction between them.

A three-year-old child would be labeled autistic if he or she lacked both social relatedness and speech or had abnormal speech. This diagnosis is also called classic Kanner's syndrome, after Leo Kanner, the physician who first described this form of autism, in 1943. These individuals usually learn to talk, but they remain very severely handicapped because of extremely rigid thinking, poor ability to generalize, and no common sense. Some of the Kanner people have savant skills, such as calendar calculation. The savant group comprises about 10 percent of the children and adults who are diagnosed.

A child with classic Kanner's syndrome has little or no flexibility of thinking or behavior. Charles Hart describes this rigidity in his autistic brother, Sumner, who had to be constantly coached by his mother. He had to be told each step of getting undressed and going to bed. Hart goes on to describe the behavior of his autistic son, Ted, during a birthday party when ice cream cones were served. The other children immediately began to lick them, but Ted just stared at his and appeared to be afraid of it. He didn't know what to do, because in the past he had eaten ice cream with a spoon.

Another serious problem for people with Kanner's syndrome is lack of common sense. They can easily learn how to get on a bus to go to school, but have no idea what to do if something interrupts the routine. Any disruption of routine causes a panic attack, anxiety, or a flight response, unless the person is taught what to do when something goes wrong. Rigid thinking makes it difficult to teach people with Kanner-type autism the subtleties of socially appropriate behavior. For example, at an autism meeting, a young man with Kanner's syndrome walked up to every person and asked, "Where are your earrings?" Kanner autistics need to be told in a clear simple way what is appropriate and inappropriate social behavior.

Uta Frith, a researcher at the MRC Cognitive Development Unit in London, has found that some people with Kanner's syndrome are unable to imagine what another person is thinking. She developed a "theory of mind" test to determine the extent of the problem. For example, Joe, Dick, and a person with autism are sitting at a table. Joe places a candy bar in a box and shuts the lid. The telephone rings, and Dick leaves the room to answer the phone. While Dick is gone, Joe eats the candy bar and puts a pen in the box. The autistic person who is watching is asked, "What does Dick think is in the box?" Many people with autism will give the wrong answer and say "a pen." They are not able to figure out that Dick, who is now outside the room, thinks that the box still contains a candy bar.

People with Asperger's syndrome, who tend to be far less handicapped than people with Kanner-type autism, can usually pass this test and generally perform better on tests of flexible problem-solving than Kanner's syndrome autistics. In fact, many Asperger individuals never get formally diagnosed, and they often hold jobs and live independently. Children with Asperger's syndrome have more normal speech development and much better cognitive skills than those with classic Kanner's. Another label for Asperger's syndrome is "high-functioning autism." One noticeable difference between Kanner's and Asperger's syndromes is that Asperger children are often clumsy. The diagnosis of Asperger's is often confused with PDD, a label that is applied to children with mild symptoms which are not quite serious enough to call for one of the other labels.

Children diagnosed as having disintegrative disorder start to develop normal speech and social behavior and then regress and lose their speech after age two. Many of them never regain their speech, and they have difficulty learning simple household chores. These individuals are also referred to as having low-functioning autism, and they require supervised living arrangements for their entire lives. Some children with disintegrative disorder improve and become high-functioning, but overall, children in this category are likely to remain low-functioning. There is a large group of children labeled autistic who start to develop normally and then regress and lose their speech before age two. These early regressives sometimes have a better prognosis than late regressives. Those who never learn to talk usually have severe neurological impairments that show up on routine tests. They are also more likely to have epilepsy than Kanner or Asperger children. Individuals who are low-functioning often have very poor ability to understand spoken words. Kanner, Asperger, and PDD children and adults usually have a much better ability to understand speech.

Children in all of the diagnostic categories benefit from placement in a good educational program. Prognosis is improved if intensive education is started before age three. I finally learned to speak at three and a half, after a year of intensive speech therapy. Children who regress at eighteen to twenty-four months of age respond to intensive educational programs when speech loss first occurs, but as they become older they may require calmer, quieter teaching methods to prevent sensory overload. If an educational program is successful, many autistic symptoms become less severe.

The only accurate way to diagnose autism in an adult is to interview the person about his or her early childhood and obtain descriptions of his or her behavior from parents or teachers. Other disorders with autistic symptoms, such as acquired aphasia (loss of speech), disintegrative disorder, and Landau-Kleffner syndrome, occur at an older age. A child may have normal or near-normal speech and then lose it between the ages of two and seven. In some cases disintegrative disorder and Landau-Kleffner syndrome may have similar underlying brain abnormalities. Landau-Kleffner syndrome is a type of epilepsy that often causes a child to lose speech. Small seizures scramble hearing and make it difficult or impossible for the child to understand spoken words. A proper diagnosis requires very sophisticated tests, because the seizures are difficult to detect. They will not show up on a simple brain-wave (EEG) test. These disorders can often be successfully treated with anticonvulsants (epilepsy drugs) or corticosteroids such as prednisone. Anticonvulsant medications may also be helpful to autistic children who have abnormal EEGs or sensory scrambling. Other neurological disorders that have symptoms of autism are Fragile X syndrome, Rhett's syndrome, and tuberous sclerosis. Educational and treatment programs that help autistic children are usually helpful for children with these disorders also.

There is still confusion in diagnosing between autism and schizophrenia. Some professionals claim that children with autism develop schizophrenic characteristics in adulthood. Like autism's, schizophrenia's current diagnostic criteria are purely behavioral, though both are neurological disorders. In the future, brain scans will be sophisticated enough to provide an accurate diagnosis. Thus far, brain research has shown that these conditions have different patterns of abnormalities. By definition, autism starts in early childhood, while the first symptoms of schizophrenia usually occur in adolescence or early adulthood. Schizophrenia has two major components, the positive symptoms, which include full-blown hallucinations and delusions accompanied by incoherent thinking, and the negative symptoms, such as flat, dull affect and monotone speech. These negative symptoms often resemble the lack of affect seen in adults with autism.

In the *British Journal of Psychiatry,* Dr. P. Liddle and Dr. T. Barnes wrote that schizophrenia may really be two or three separate conditions. The positive symptoms are entirely different from symptoms of autism, but the negative ones may partially overlap with autistic symptoms. Confusion of the two conditions is the reason that some doctors attempt to treat autism with neuroleptic drugs such as Haldol and Mellaril. But neuroleptics should not be the first-choice medications for autism, because other, safer drugs are often more effective. Neuroleptic drugs have very severe side effects and can damage the nervous system.

Over ten years ago, Dr. Peter Tanguay and Rose Mary Edwards, at UCLA, hypothesized that distortion of auditory input during a critical phase in early childhood development may be one cause of handicaps in language and thinking. The exact timing of the sensory processing problems may determine whether a child has Kanner's syndrome or is a nonverbal, low-functioning autistic. I hypothesize that oversensitivity to touch and auditory scrambling prior to age two may cause the rigidity of thinking and lack of emotional development found in Kanner-type autism. These children partially recover the ability to understand speech between the ages of two and a half and three. Disintegrative disorder children, who develop normally up to two years of age, may be more emotionally normal because emotional centers in the brain have had an opportunity to develop before the onset of sensory processing problems. It may be that a simple difference in timing determines which type of autism develops. Early sensory processing problems may prevent development of the emotional centers of the brain in Kanner-type autistics, while the acquisition of language is more disturbed when sensory processing difficulties occur slightly later.

Research has very clearly shown that autism is a neurological disorder that reveals distinct abnormalities in the brain. Brain autopsy research by Dr. Margaret Bauman has shown that those with both autism and disintegrative disorder have immature development of the cerebellum and the limbic system. Indications of a delay in brain maturation can also be seen in autistic children's brain waves. Dr. David Canter and his associates at the University of Maryland found that low-functioning children between the ages of four and twelve have EEG readings that resemble the brain-wave pattern of a two-year-old. The question is what causes these abnormalities. Studies by many researchers are showing that there may be a cluster of genes that can put a person at risk for many disorders, including autism, depression, anxiety, dyslexia, attention deficit disorder, and other problems.

There is no single autism gene, though most cases of autism have a strong genetic basis. If a person is autistic, his or her chances of having an autistic child are greatly increased. There is also a tendency for the siblings of autistic children to have a higher incidence of learning problems than other children. Studies by Susan Folstein and Mark Rutter in London showed that in 42 percent of the families surveyed, either a sibling or a parent of an autistic child had delayed speech or learning problems.

Genetics, however, does not completely control brain development. Studies of identical twins by Folstein and Rutter show that sometimes one twin is severely autistic and the other has only a few autistic traits. MRI (magnetic resonance imaging) brain scans of identical twin schizophrenics have shown that the more severely afflicted twin has greater brain abnormalities. The brain is so complex that genetics cannot tell every little developing neuron exactly where it should be connected. There is a 10 percent variation in brain anatomical structure that is not controlled by genetics. Brain scans of normal identical twins by Michael Gazzaniga, at the Dartmouth Medical School, showed an easily observable variation in brain structure, but twins' brains are more similar than the brains of unrelated people. Likewise, the personalities of identical twins are similar. Studies at the University of Minnesota by Thomas Bouchard and his colleagues of twins reared in different families show that basic traits such as mathematical ability, athletic ability, and temperament are highly inheritable. A summary of these studies concluded that roughly half of what a person becomes is determined by genetics and the other half is determined by environment and upbringing.

Other theories suggest that if a fetus is exposed to certain toxins and viruses, these may interact with genes to cause the abnormal brain development typical of autism. If either parent is exposed to chemical toxins that slightly damage his or her genetic material, that could increase the likelihood of autism or some other developmental disorder. Some parents suspect that an allergic reaction to early childhood vaccinations triggers autistic regression. If this is true it is likely that the vaccine interacts with genetic factors. Another possibility is immune system abnormalities which interfere with brain development. However, there is still too much that is not known, and neither parent should be held responsible for an autistic child. Scientific studies and interviews with families indicate that both the father's and the mother's side contribute genetically to autism.

The Autistic Continuum

Countless researchers have attempted to figure out what factors determine the difference between high- and low-functioning autism. High-functioning children with Kanner's or Asperger's syndrome usually develop good speech and often do well academically. Low-functioning children are often unable to speak or can say only a few words. They also have trouble learning simple skills such as buttoning a shirt. At age three, both types have similar behaviors, but as they grow older the difference becomes more and more apparent.

When my speech therapist held my chin and directed me to look at her, it jerked me out of my private world, but for others forcing eye contact can cause the opposite reaction—brain overload and shutdown. For instance, Donna Williams, the author of *Nobody Nowhere,* explained that she could use only one sensory channel at a time. If a teacher had grabbed her chin and forced eye contact, she would have turned off her ears. Her descriptions of sensory jumbling provide an important bridge to understanding the difference between high-functioning and low-functioning autism, which I would describe as a sensory processing continuum. At one end of the continuum is a person with Asperger's or Kanner's autism who has mild sensory oversensitivity problems, and at the other end of the spectrum is the low-functioning person who receives jumbled, inaccurate information, both visually and aurally.

I was able to learn to speak because I could understand speech, but low-functioning autistics may never learn to speak because their brains cannot discriminate among speech sounds. Many of these people are mentally retarded, but a few individuals may have a near-normal brain trapped inside a sensory system that does not work. Those who escape the prison of low-functioning autism probably do so because just enough undistorted information gets through. They do not totally lose contact with the world around them.

Twenty years ago, Carl Delacato, a therapist who worked with autistic children, speculated that low-functioning individuals may have "white noise" in their sensory channels. In his book *The Ultimate Stranger,* he described three kinds of sensory processing problems: hyper, hypo, and white noise. Hyper means oversensitive, hypo means undersensitive, and white noise means internal interference.

In questioning many people with autism, I soon found that there was a continuum of sensory abnormalities that would provide insight into the world of nonverbal people with autism. I imagine that the extent of sensory jumbling they experience would be equivalent to taking Donna's sensory problems and multiplying them tenfold. I am lucky in that I responded well when my mother, teachers, and governess kept encouraging social interaction and play. I was seldom allowed to retreat into the soothing world of rocking or spinning objects. When I daydreamed, my teachers yanked me back to reality.

Almost half of all very young children with autism respond well to gently intrusive programs in which they are constantly encouraged to look at the teacher and interact. Brightly colored wall decorations made learning fun for me, but they may be too distracting for a child with sensory jumbling. The popular Lovaas program, developed at UCLA, is being used successfully there to mainstream nearly half of young autistic children into a normal kindergarten or first grade. The Lovaas method pairs words with objects, and the children are rewarded with praise and food when they correctly match a word with an object. While this program is wonderful for some kids, it is certain to be confusing and possibly painful for children with severe sensory jumbling and mixing problems.

These children require a different approach. Touch is often their most reliable sense, and they learn best if teachers use a tactile system. One mother taught her nonverbal daughter to draw a circle by holding her hand and guiding it to make a circle. Plastic letters that can be felt are often useful for teaching words. The more protected these children are from distracting sights and sounds, the more likely it is that their dysfunctional nervous system will be able to perceive speech accurately. To help them hear better, teachers must protect them from visual stimuli that will cause sensory overload. They may hear best in a quiet, dimly illuminated room that is free of fluorescent lights and bright wall decorations. Sometimes hearing is enhanced if the teacher whispers or sings softly. Teachers need to speak slowly to accommodate a nervous system that processes information slowly. And sudden movements that will cause sensory confusion should also be avoided.

Children who are echolalic—who repeat what they hear—may be at a midpoint on the sensory processing continuum. Enough recognizable speech gets through for them to be able to repeat the words. Dr. Doris Allen, at the Albert Einstein Hospital in New York, emphasizes that echolalia should not be discouraged, so as not to inhibit speech. The child repeats what has been said to verify that he heard it correctly. Research by Laura Berk, at Illinois State University, has shown that normal children talk to themselves to help them control their behavior and learn new skills. Since autism is caused by immature brain development, it is likely that echolalia and self-talking, which occur in older autistic children, are the result of immature speech patterns.

Unlike normal children, who naturally connect language to the things in their lives at a remarkable rate, autistic children have to learn that objects have names. They have to learn that words communicate. All autistic children have problems with long strings of verbal information. Even very high-functioning people have difficulty following verbal instructions and find it easier to follow written instructions, since they are unable to remember the sequence of the information. My college math teacher once commented that I took excessive notes. He told me that I should pay attention and understand the concept. The problem was that it was impossible for me to remember the sequence of the problems without the notes. I learned to read with phonics and sounding out words, because I was able to understand speech by age three. Children with more severe auditory processing problems often learn to read before they can speak. They learn best if a written word is paired with an object, because many of them have very poor comprehension of spoken words.

As an adult my method for learning a foreign language may be similar to how a more severely impaired autistic child learns to understand language. I cannot pick words out of a conversation in a foreign language until I have seen them written first.

Two basic patterns of autistic symptoms can help identify which children will respond well to intensive, gently intrusive teaching methods, and which will not. The first kind of child may appear deaf at age two, but by age three he or she can understand speech. I was this kind. When adults spoke directly to me, I could understand them, but when they talked among themselves, it sounded like gibberish. The second kind of child appears to develop normally until one and a half or two and then loses speech. As the syndrome progresses, the ability to understand speech deteriorates and autistic symptoms worsen. A child that has been affectionate withdraws into autism as his sensory system becomes more and more scrambled. Eventually he may lose awareness of his surroundings, because his brain is not able to process and understand sights and sounds around him. There are also children who are mixtures of the two kinds of autism.

Children of the first kind will respond well to intensive, structured educational programs that pull them out of the autistic world, because their sensory systems provide a more or less accurate representation of things around them. There may be problems with sound or touch sensitivity, but they still have some realistic awareness of their surroundings. The second kind of child may not respond, because sensory jumbling makes the world incomprehensible. Gently intrusive teaching methods will work on some children who lose their speech before age two if teaching is started before their senses become totally scrambled. Catherine Maurice describes her successful use of the Lovaas program with her two children, who lost speech at fifteen and eighteen months of age, in her book, *Let Me Hear Your Voice*. Teaching was started within six months of the onset of symptoms. The regression into autism was not complete, and her children still had some awareness. If she had waited until they were four or five, it is very likely that the Lovaas method would have caused confusion and sensory overload.

My experience and that of others has shown that an effective teaching method coupled with reasonable amounts of effort should work. Desperate parents often get hooked into looking for magic cures that require ten hours a day of intensive treatment. To be effective, educational programs do have to be done every day, but they usually do not require heroic amounts of effort. My mother spent thirty minutes five days a week for several months teaching me to read. Mrs. Maurice had a teacher spend twenty hours a week on the Lovaas method with her children. In addition to participating in formal educational programs, young autistic children need a structured day, both in the school and at home. Several studies have shown that twenty to twenty-five hours a week of intensive treatment which required the child to constantly interact with his teacher was most effective. A neurologist gave my mother some very good advice: to follow her own instincts. If a child is improving in an educational program, then it should be continued, but if there is no progress, something else should be tried. Mother had a knack for recognizing which people could help me and which ones could not. She sought out the best teachers and schools for me, in an era when most autistic children were placed in institutions. She was determined to keep me out of an institution.

A controversial technique called facilitated communication is now being used with nonverbal people with autism. Using the technique, the teacher supports the person's hand while he or she taps out messages on a typewriter keyboard. Some severely handicapped people have problems with stopping and starting hand movements, and they also have involuntary movements that make typing difficult. Supporting the person's wrist helps to initiate motion of the hand toward the keyboard and pulls his fingers off the keyboard after he pushes a key to prevent perseveration and multiple pushing of a single key. Merely touching the person's shoulder can help him initiate hand movements.

Several years ago, facilitated communication was hailed as a major breakthrough, and wild claims were made that the most severely handicapped autistic people had completely normal intelligence and emotions. Fifty scientific studies have now shown that in the vast majority of cases, the teacher was moving the person's hand, as if it were a planchet on a Ouija board. The teacher was communicating, instead of the person with autism. A summary of forty-three studies in the *Autism Research Review* showed that 5 percent of nonverbal, severely handicapped people can communicate with simple one-word responses. In the few cases where facilitated communication has been successful, someone has spent many hours teaching the person to read first.

It is likely that the truth about facilitated communication is somewhere between wishful hand-pushing and real communication. Carol Berger, of New Breakthroughs in Eugene, Oregon, found that low-functioning autistics could achieve 33 percent to 75 percent accuracy in typing one-word answers. Some of the poor results in controlled studies may have been due to sensory overload caused by the presence of strange people. Reports from parents indicate that a few adults and children initially need wrist support and then gradually learn to type independently. But the person must know how to read, and facilitator influence cannot be completely ruled out until wrist or arm support is removed.

Parents who are desperate to reach their autistic children often look for miracles. It's hard not to get caught up in new promises of hope, because there have been so few real breakthroughs in the understanding of autism.

The Autistic Continuum

It appears that at one end of the spectrum, autism is primarily a cognitive disorder, and at the other end, it is primarily a sensory processing disorder. At the severely impaired sensory processing end, many children may be diagnosed as having disintegrative disorder. At a midpoint along the spectrum, autistic symptoms appear to be caused by equal amounts of cognitive and sensory problems. There can be mild and severe cases at all points along the continuum. Both the severity and the ratio of these two components are variable, and each case of autism is different. When a person with autism improves because of either educational or medical intervention, the severity of a cognitive or sensory problem may diminish, but the ratio between the two seems to stay the same. What remains inexplicable, however, are rigid thinking patterns and lack of emotional affect in many high-functioning people. One of the perplexing things about autism is that it is almost impossible to predict which toddler will become high-functioning. The severity of the symptoms at age two or three is often not correlated with the prognosis.

The world of the nonverbal person with autism is chaotic and confusing. A low-functioning adult who is still not toilet-trained may be living in a completely disordered sensory world. It is likely that he has no idea of his body boundaries and that sights, sounds, and touches are all mixed together. It must be like seeing the world through a kaleidoscope and trying to listen to a radio station that is jammed with static at the same time. Add to that a broken volume control, which causes the volume to jump erratically from a loud boom to inaudible. Such a person's problems are further compounded by a nervous system that is often in a greater state of fear and panic than the nervous system of a Kanner-type autistic. Imagine a state of hyperarousal where you were being pursued by a dangerous attacker in a world of total chaos. Not surprisingly, new environments make low-functioning autistics fearful.

Puberty often makes the problem worse. Birger Sellin describes in his book *I Don't Want to Be Inside Me Anymore* how his well-behaved son developed unpredictable screaming fits and tantrums at puberty. The hormones of adolescence further sensitized and inflamed an overaroused nervous system. Dr. John Ratey, at Harvard University, uses the concept of noise in the nervous system to describe such hyperarousal and confusion. Medications such as beta-blockers and clonidine are often helpful because they can calm an overaroused sympathetic nervous system.

Autistics with severe sensory problems sometimes engage in self-injurious behavior such as biting themselves or hitting their heads. Their sensory sensations are so disordered that they may not realize they are hurting themselves. Though a recent study by Reed Elliot published in the *Journal of Autism and Developmental Disabilities* showed that very vigorous aerobic exercise reduced aggression and self-injury in half of mentally retarded autistic adults, educational and behavioral training will help almost all people with autism to function better. Early intervention in a good program can enable about 50 percent of autistic children to be enrolled in a normal first grade. Though most autistics will not function at my level, their ability to live a productive life will be improved. Medication can help reduce the hyperarousal of many low-functioning older children and help them control their behavior. Many nonverbal autistics are capable of doing simple jobs such as washing windows or routine manual work. Few nonverbal autistic adults are able to read and are capable of doing normal schoolwork.

Many parents and teachers have asked me where I fit on the autistic continuum. I still have problems with rapid responses to unexpected social situations. In my business dealings I can handle new situations, but every once in a while I panic when things go wrong. I've learned to deal with the fear of traveling, so that I have a backup plan if, for example, my plane is late. I have no problems if I mentally rehearse every scenario, but I still panic if I'm not prepared for a new situation, especially when I travel to a foreign country where I am unable to communicate. Since I can't rely on my library of social cues, I feel very helpless when I can't speak the language. Often I withdraw.

If I were two years old today, I would be diagnosed with classic Kanner's syndrome, because I had delayed abnormal speech development. However, as an adult I would probably be diagnosed as having Asperger's syndrome, because I can pass a simple theory-of-mind test and I have greater cognitive flexibility than a classic Kanner autistic. All of my thinking is still in visual images, though it appears that thinking may become less visual as one moves along the continuum away from classic Kanner's syndrome. My sensory oversensitivities are worse than the mild difficulties some Kanner autistics have, but I do not have sensory mixing and jumbling problems. Like most autistics, I don't experience the feelings attached to personal relationships. My visual world is a literal one, though I have made progress by finding visual symbols to carry me beyond the fixed and rigid worlds of other people with classic Kanner autism.

In an article written by Oliver Sacks in *The New Yorker,* I was quoted as saying, "If I could snap my fingers and be nonautistic, I would not. Autism is part of what I am." In contrast, Donna Williams says, "Autism is not me. Autism is just an information processing problem that controls who I am." Who is right? I think we both are, because we are on different parts of the autism spectrum. I would not want to lose my ability to think visually. I have found my place along the great continuum.

Update: Diagnosis and Education

Both parents and teachers make the mistake of thinking a diagnosis of autism, PDD (Pervasive Developmental Disorder), ADHD (Attention Deficit Hyperactivity Disorder), or Asperger's is precise. It is not precise the way a diagnosis for measles or meningitis is precise. It is a behavioral profile and different doctors and psychologists often come up with a different diagnosis because they interpret the child's behavior differently. At the time of writing this update, there is no definitive brain imaging or laboratory test for the diagnosis of autism.

Since *Thinking in Pictures* was written, the mild Asperger diagnosis is being used more and more. At the many autism conferences that I attend, I am observing more and more very smart children with a diagnosis of Asperger's. Some of these children should be in a gifted and talented class instead of being sent to special education. There are other Asperger's individuals who may need special education in their area of weakness and be in an advanced class in their area of strength. I am worried that students who would be capable of a challenging career in science, engineering, or computers may be shunted into a special education rut. In fairness to special education teachers, it is difficult to work with a spectrum that can range from nonverbal to genius.

Diane Kennedy, author of *ADHD Autism Connection,* was one of the first people to write about the confusion of Asperger's with attention deficit problems. I talk to more and more parents of children with a diagnosis that switches back and forth between Asperger's and ADHD. Many parents have told me that stimulant ADHD medications such as Ritalin (metehylphenidate) and Adderall (a combination of four different types of amphetamines) have greatly helped their children. It is likely that some individuals on the high-functioning end of the autism spectrum share traits with ADHD. Children or adults who have more classical types of autism or are nonverbal often become agitated and worse on stimulants. A trial of only one or two pills is all that is needed to determine if stimulants will be helpful or terrible.

Brain Research and Early Diagnosis

During the last ten years, there has been an increased understanding of autistic brain abnormalities. A normal child's brain grows at a steady rate. Detailed brain scans of autistic children in Dr. Eric Courchesne's lab indicated that in the first year of life there is premature overgrowth of the brain followed by an arrest of growth. Children with greater amounts of abnormal overgrowth usually have more severe autism. Research has also shown that the serotonin systems in the autistic child's brain are highly abnormal. This may explain why doses for SSRI antidepressants often need to be kept very low to prevent agitation. The degree and pattern of abnormal overgrowth will be highly variable from child to child. David Amarel at the University of California found that the variability of overgrowth was greatest in low-functioning autism. He also discovered that the immune system is often abnormal and may affect the brain.

The excess of brain overgrowth causes the infant's head to become abnormally large between the ages of one and two. Later in childhood, the head size returns to normal due to later undergrowth of the brain. Measuring a young infant's head circumference (hat size) with a tape measure could be used as a simple screening tool for detecting babies who might be at risk for autism.

Other early screening tools that are being developed test for joint attention. Joint attention occurs when normal babies orient and follow an adult's gaze. When the adult is playing a little game, asking the baby to look at the pretty birdie, the baby will look where the adult is looking. The infant at risk for developmental problems will not follow an adult's gaze. Patricia Kohl at the University of Washington is working on another screening tool. This tool will detect children at risk for developmental problems who do not orient toward normal speech sounds. This is due to being unable to hear consonant sounds. Normal babies prefer to listen to "motherese"—expressive slowed down speech where the mother enunciates the words. Autistic babies prefer computerized warbling nonspeech sounds. The test would be conducted by observing the infant to determine which sounds he orients toward.

Early Education

Both scientific studies and practical experience have fully confirmed that young children with autism need at least twenty hours a week of intensive one to one teaching by an adult. All experts agree that the *worst* thing to do with an autistic two- to five-year-old is to let him watch TV all day. There is much debate about the best early education programs. I have observed that the best teachers tend to use the same methods regardless of the theoretical basis of the program. A review of teaching methods by Sally Rogers at the University of California at Davis indicated that discrete trial or ABA (Applied Behavioral Analysis) teaching methods were the most effective to get language started. This structured highly repetitive method helps jump-start language in young two- to five-year-olds. The discrete trial programs used today are usually more natural and less rigid than the older Lovaas method. To teach socialization and play skills methods such as Greenspan's floor-time and Dr. Lynn Kern Koegel's program are more effective. Dr. Koegel's book *Overcoming Autism* is full of practical teaching methods. In the floor-time method, the teacher engages the child in many interactive games and encourages social play.

Autism and PDD are highly variable and the methods that work for each child should be used. Dr. Koegel found that some little children respond well to a highly structured Lovaas-style program and other types of autistic children, who are more socially engaged, may make more progress with a less structured program. Do not get too single-minded on one method. Use things that work and eliminate things that do not work. Sometimes a combination of methods is best. For older high-functioning children, highly repetitious programs are boring and they need lessons that will stimulate their minds. In elementary school children a child's fixation can be used to motivate learning. If a child loves trains, then read a book about a train or do a math problem involving trains.

If shooting-type video games had been available when I was little, I would have become a total addict and I may not have developed more career-related interests such as building things or flying kites and airplanes. The video games with lots of rapid movement are the most addictive. For me, rapid movement video games would have just been another way to "stim" and "zone out." I would rather encourage the older child to become really interested in doing science on a computer or learning programming. Free software is available that will turn a kid's computer into part of a super computer that crunches numbers on a real scientific project. The May 6, 2005, issue of *Science* is devoted to these fascinating projects. Looking at the NASA Web site and following a space probe during its journey is a wonderful way to use computers. The problem with video games is that both parents and teachers tell me that some students get so addicted that they have no other interests. I get hypnotized by screen savers with changing patterns that move rapidly. I cannot stop looking at them and for me to get any work done I have to shut them off. Video games or screen savers that move slowly do not have this effect.

Totally banning shooting-type games is probably a bad idea, but the time playing them should be severely limited. This is especially important for a child like me. They provide an activity that the autistic child can discuss with other kids at school and this may help the child socially. However, I want to direct the autistic child's interests into more constructive activities.

Genetics and Autism

Research during the last ten years confirms that autism, PDD, and Asperger's all have a strong genetic basis. Craig Newschaffer, Johns Hopkins School of Medicine, estimates that 60 to 90 percent of autism cases are genetic. Dr. Isabel Rapin and her colleagues at Albert Einstein College of Medicine reviewed papers published between 1961 and 2003. They concluded that interactions between multiple genes explain the highly variable nature of autism. Genome scans of families with many cases of autism indicate that at least ten genes are involved. They also found that the probability of having a second autistic child is 2 to 8 percent. Researchers have also confirmed previous studies that show that relatives of people with autism will often have many milder autistic-like symptoms. I have observed that the probability of having a child with low-functioning autism increases when *both* parents and their families have many autistic traits.

Many computer programmers exhibit autistic traits. Steve Silberman asked in an article entitled "The Geek Syndrome" in *Wired* magazine—are math and tech genes to blame? The computer and technical industries depend on people with attention to detail. The real social people are not interested in computers. Herbert Schreir of the Children's Hospital in Oakland, California, believes that intermarriage of "techies" explains why people have noticed high pockets of autism around Stanford and MIT Universities.

In 2004 and 2005, my webmaster for www.grandin.com (my livestock website) started giving me a list every month of the cities with the most hits on my webpage. Month after month, Redmond, Washington, where Microsoft is located and San Mateo, California, near Stanford University are in my top five cities. There is a total of one hundred cities on the list. The number one page downloaded is the first chapter of *Thinking in Pictures*. Even though my site is a livestock site, the autism book chapter gets the heaviest traffic. Is this because people in these areas are especially interested in the ways brains work, or does autism affect them more directly?

There are differences of opinion in the autism field about the relationship between autism and Asperger's. Are they really separate syndromes? Family and genetic studies done in the United Kingdom indicate that autism and Asperger's are part of the same spectrum. Research by Fred Volkmar at Yale showed that Asperger individuals with no speech delay are often poor at a visual thinking task such as the block design test on the WISC and high-functioning autistic individuals are more likely to be good at this test. In the block design test, the task is to assemble colored blocks to match patterns shown in a book. This difference could be explained by the differences in where the "computer cables" hook up. The underlying brain abnormality of underconnectivity problems would still be similar.

There is concern among people with Asperger's that genetic testing could eliminate them. This would be a terrible price to pay. Many gifted and talented people could be wiped out. A little bit of autism genetics may provide an advantage though too much creates a low-functioning, nonverbal individual. The development of genetic tests for autism will be extremely controversial.

Autism Epidemic

Many researchers agree that the increase in Asperger's syndrome is mostly increased detection. People who used to be labeled as science geeks or computer nerds are now diagnosed with Asperger's. Research in Sweden by Christopher Gillberg showed that some severe cases that used to be labeled mentally retarded are now labeled autistic. Another cause of the increase may be changes made to the DSMIV (Diagnostic and Statistical Manual) published by the American Psychiatric Association in 1994 to expand the diagnostic criteria to include Asperger's and Pervasive Developmental Disorders (PDD). The Centers for Disease Control (CDC) estimate that there are three to four autism cases per one thousand children. A CDC study in Atlanta, Georgia, indicated that 40 percent of all children on the spectrum are only diagnosed at school and 41 percent of special education students are on the autism spectrum. A fully verbal child with mild Asperger's will often not have any problems until he/she enrolls in school. Unfortunately there are severe cases of autism who do not receive services until they go to school. From my own observations there is one type of autism that I think has increased. The regressive type where the child loses language at age eighteen to twenty-four months. David Geier and Mark Geir, two autism consultants, state that exposure to mercury causes regression-type autism. Mercury has now been removed from many vaccines, but fish and power plant emissions are other sources of mercury.

Other scientists question the effect of mercury in the incidence of autism.

There is increasing concern about environmental effects on the fetus during pregnancy. If these factors affect the incidence of autism, they probably could interact with susceptible genetics. An outside insult like toxic exposure could turn a brilliant Asperger baby into a nonverbal one. This is purely speculation. New research supports the idea that genetics susceptibility interacts with environmental insults. Scientists have developed a genetic line of mice that are highly susceptible to mercury toxicity. When the mice are given injections that mimic a vaccination schedule the normal mice have no ill effects and the susceptible mice develop autistic-like symptoms such as tail chewing and repetitive behaviors. Possibly there are some children who would have a similar susceptibility to mercury. Mady Horning at the Columbia University School of Public Health has a three-strikes model. The factors that all interact with each other to cause a developmental disability are:

1. Genetic susceptibility
2. Exposure to a toxic agent
3. The timing during development that exposure to a toxic agent occurs. A toxic agent may have no effect at one stage of development and bad effects at another stage.

Twin studies show further evidence of an interaction between environment and genetics. Mady Horning states that the concordance rate for autism in genetically identical twins is 90 percent. This means that 90 percent of the time both twins are autistic. In genetically different nonidentical twins the concordance rate is 35 percent and the autism rate in siblings is 4 percent. Further information on the mercury controversy can be found at the Autism Research Institute in San Diego, California, or in a new book by David Kirby entitled *Evidence of Harm*.

3

THE SQUEEZE MACHINE

Sensory Problems in Autism

FROM AS FAR BACK as I can remember, I always hated to be hugged. I wanted to experience the good feeling of being hugged, but it was just too overwhelming. It was like a great, all-engulfing tidal wave of stimulation, and I reacted like a wild animal. Being touched triggered flight; it flipped my circuit breaker. I was overloaded and would have to escape, often by jerking away suddenly.

Many autistic children crave pressure stimulation even though they cannot tolerate being touched. It is much easier for a person with autism to tolerate touch if he or she initiates it. When touched unexpectedly, we usually withdraw, because our nervous system does not have time to process the sensation. One autistic woman told me that she enjoys touch, but she needs to initiate it in order to have time to feel it. Parents used to report that their autistic children loved to crawl under mattresses and wrap up in blankets or wedge themselves in tight places, long before anyone made sense of this strange behavior.

I was one of these pressure seekers. When I was six, I would wrap myself up in blankets and get under sofa cushions, because the pressure was relaxing. I used to daydream for hours in elementary school about constructing a device that would apply pressure to my body. I visualized a box with an inflatable liner that

I could lie in. It would be like being totally encased in inflatable splints.

After visiting my aunt's ranch in Arizona, I got the idea of building such a device, patterned after the cattle squeeze chute I first saw there. When I watched cattle being put in the squeeze chute for their vaccinations, I noticed that some of them relaxed when they were pressed between the side panels. I guess I had made my first connection between those cows and myself, because a few days later, after I had a big panic attack, I just got inside the squeeze chute at the ranch. Since puberty I had experienced constant fear and anxiety coupled with severe panic attacks, which occurred at intervals of anywhere from a few weeks to several months. My life was based on avoiding situations that might trigger an attack.

I asked Aunt Ann to press the squeeze sides against me and to close the head restraint bars around my neck. I hoped it would calm my anxiety. At first there were a few moments of sheer panic as I stiffened up and tried to pull away from the pressure, but I couldn't get away because my head was locked in. Five seconds later I felt a wave of relaxation, and about thirty minutes later I asked Aunt Ann to release me. For about an hour afterward I felt very calm and serene. My constant anxiety had diminished. This was the first time I ever felt really comfortable in my own skin. Ann went along with my odd request to get in the cattle chute. She recognized that my mind worked in visual symbols, and she figured that the squeeze chute was an important part of my journey in the visual symbol world. I don't think she realized at the time that it was the pressure from the chute that relaxed me.

I copied the design and built the first human squeeze machine out of plywood panels when I returned to school. Entering the machine on hands and knees, I applied pressure to both sides of my body. The headmaster of my school and the school psychologist thought my machine was very weird and wanted to take it away. Professionals in those days had no understanding of autistic sensory problems; they still believed that autism was caused by psychological factors. Since they wanted to get rid of my machine, they alerted my mother, who became very concerned. Like the professionals, she had no idea that my attraction to pressure was biological.

Over the years I improved on the design of my machine. The most advanced version has two soft foam-padded panels that apply pressure along each side of my body and a padded opening that closes around my neck. I control the amount of pressure by pushing an air valve lever that pulls the two panels tight against my body. I can precisely control how much pressure my body receives. Slowly increasing and decreasing it is the most relaxing. Using the squeeze machine on a daily basis calms my anxiety and helps me to unwind.

When I was young I wanted very intense pressure, almost to the point of pain. This machine provided great relief. The earliest version of the squeeze machine, with its hard wood sides, applied greater amounts of pressure than later versions with soft padded sides. As I learned to tolerate the pressure, I modified the machine to make it softer and gentler. Now that medication has reduced the hyperarousal of my nervous system, I prefer much less pressure.

Since many people were trying to convince me to give up the machine, I had many ambivalent feelings about using it. I was torn between two opposing forces: I wanted to please my mother and the school authorities by giving the machine up, but my biology craved its calming effect. To make matters worse, I had no idea at that time that my sensory experiences were different from those of other people. Since then I've learned that other people with autism also crave pressure and have devised methods to apply it to their bodies. Tom McKean wrote in his book *Soon Will Come the Light* that he feels a low-intensity pain throughout his body which is relieved by pressure. He finds that very tight pressure works best. The amount of pressure a person desires may be related to his or her nervous arousal level.

Tom's overall sensory processing problems are more severe than mine. It is possible that for people with such problems, pressure to the point of pain functions as an attempt to reduce sensory discomfort. Tom wears very tight wristwatch straps on both wrists. He makes the bands as tight as he can without cutting off blood circulation. He also made a pressure suit consisting of a wet suit with an inflatable life jacket under it. He can adjust the pressure by blowing air into the valve on the jacket. Other adults with autism have also sought relief through the application of pressure. One man wore very tight belts and shoes, and a woman reported that pressure applied to certain parts of her body helped her senses to work better.

Even though the sense of touch is often compromised by excessive sensitivity, it can sometimes provide the most reliable information about the environment for people with autism. Therese Joliffe, an autistic woman from England, preferred using touch to learn about her environment because it was easier to understand things through her fingers. Her vision and hearing were distorted and provided unreliable information, but touching something gave her a relatively accurate representation of the world. She learned to do things like setting a table by feel. She did not learn to put her shoes on the correct feet until somebody held her hands and had her run her fingers down her legs and along the sides of her feet and along her shoes. Doing this enabled her to learn what the right and left shoe looked like. She had to feel them before she could see them. Her method of learning was similar to that of a blind man whose vision was restored when he was an adult. In his essay "To See and Not to See," Dr. Oliver Sacks described how this man had to touch things in order to see them with his eyes. For objects like houses, which were too big to be touched all over, he touched a model, which enabled him to see the real thing.

Touching can also be used to teach words. Therese Joliffe reported that she learned reading by feeling letters. Margaret

Eastham describes in her book *Silent Words* how she taught her nonverbal son to read by having him feel sandpaper letters. Many totally nonverbal children with autism touch and smell things. Some constantly tap everything. They may be doing this to figure out where the boundaries are in their environment, like a blind person tapping with a cane. Their eyes and ears function, but they are not able to process incoming visual and auditory information.

I was always able to determine where my body ended and where the outside world began, but some people with autism have severe body boundary problems. If they cannot see their legs, then they do not know where they are. Jim Sinclair, a young man with autism, reports not being able to find his body. Donna Williams describes a fractured perception of her body in which she could perceive only one part at a time. Similar fracturing occurred when she looked at things around her. She could only look at one small part of an object at a time. Donna tapped rhythmically and some-times slapped herself to determine where her body boundaries were. When her senses became overloaded with painful stimuli, she bit herself, not realizing that she was biting her own body.

Overly sensitive skin can also be a big problem. Washing my hair and dressing to go to church were two things I hated as a child. A lot of kids hate Sunday clothes and taking baths. But shampooing actually hurt my scalp. It was as if the fingers rubbing my head had sewing thimbles on them. Scratchy petticoats were like sandpaper scraping away at raw nerve endings. In fact, I couldn't tolerate changes in clothing altogether. When I got accustomed to pants, I could not bear the feeling of bare legs when I wore a skirt. After I became accustomed to wearing shorts in the summer, I couldn't tolerate long pants. Most people adapt in several minutes, but it still takes me at least two weeks to adapt. New underwear is a scratchy horror. I wear my bras until they are falling apart, and new ones require no fewer than ten washings to make them comfortable. Even today I prefer to wear them inside out, because the stitching often feels like pins pricking my skin. Parents can avoid many problems with sensory-induced tantrums simply by dressing kids in soft clothes that cover most of their body.

Auditory Problems

When I was little, loud noises were also a problem, often feeling like a dentist's drill hitting a nerve. They actually caused pain. I was scared to death of balloons popping, because the sound was like an explosion in my ear. Minor noises that most people can tune out drove me to distraction. When I was in college, my roommate's hair dryer sounded like a jet plane taking off. Some of the sounds that are most disturbing to autistic children are the high-pitched, shrill noises made by electrical drills, blenders, saws, and vacuum cleaners. Echoes in school gymnasiums and bathrooms are difficult for people with autism to tolerate. The kinds of sounds that are disturbing vary from person to person. A sound that caused me pain may be pleasurable to another child. One autistic child may love the vacuum cleaner, and another will fear it. Some are attracted to the sound of flowing, splashing water and will spend hours flushing the toilet, while others may wet their pants in panic because the flushing sounds like the roar of Niagara Falls.

Children with autism often appear to be deaf. They respond to some sounds and not to others. Jane Taylor McDonnell reported in her book *News from the Border* that her autistic son was suspected of being deaf to particular pitches and frequencies. When certain musical instruments were played, he responded, while other instruments produced no effect. I still have problems with losing my train of thought when distracting noises occur. If a pager goes off while I am giving a lecture, it fully captures my attention and I completely forget what I was talking about. Intermittent high-pitched noises are the most distracting. It takes me several seconds to shift my attention back. Several research studies have shown that rapid shifting of attention between two different stimuli is very difficult for people with autism. Eric Courchesne and his colleagues at the San Diego School of Medicine found that people with autism could not rapidly shift their attention between a visual and an auditory task. Further research by Ann Wainwright Sharp and Susan Bryson, in Canada, suggests that there is a fundamental impairment in the brain's ability to process incoming information rapidly.

When two people are talking at once, it is difficult for me to screen out one voice and listen to the other. My ears are like microphones picking up all sounds with equal intensity. Most people's ears are like highly directional microphones, which only pick up sounds from the person they are pointed at. In a noisy place I can't understand speech, because I cannot screen out the background noise. When I was a child, large noisy gatherings of relatives were overwhelming, and I would just lose control and throw temper tantrums. Birthday parties were torture when all the noisemakers went off. My mother recognized that I had difficulty with noisy gatherings of people, but she did not know why. Fortunately, I attended an elementary school that had quiet classrooms where all the students worked on the same task. I would have drowned in a cacophony of confusion if I had been in an open classroom with thirty students doing ten different projects.

Recently I was given a highly sophisticated hearing test that was developed by Joan Burleigh, in the Electrical Engineering Department at Colorado State University. The combination of her expertise in speech pathology and the electronics skills of the engineers there created a test that is able to determine the degree of autism-related hearing problems people have. People with autism usually seem to have normal hearing when tested with the standard test, which measures the ability to hear faint pure tones. My hearing tested normal on that test. The problem arises in processing complex sounds such as spoken words.

I did very badly on two segments of Joan Burleigh's test, both of which measure the ability to hear two conversations going on at once. In the first test, a man spoke a sentence in one ear and a

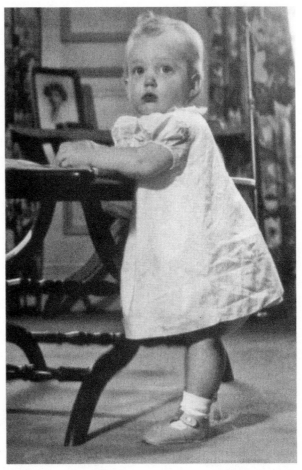

Here I am as a toddler. At that time, my retreat from touch was the only obvious sign of autism.

At two and a half, I had no speech and no interest in people. I appeared to be deaf, and often threw tantrums out of frustration at not being able to talk. Like many autistic children, I looked normal.

In high school, my life revolved around 4-H and showing horses. A deep connection with animals has been a constant in my life.

One of my mentors, Aunt Brecheen, helped me channel my fixations. This picture was taken in front of her ranch house in Arizona, where I first observed the cattle chute and made the connection between its calming pressure and my own hyperaroused nervous system.

Here is an example of the kind of cattle chute used for holding animals during veterinary procedures. Two panels apply pressure to the animal's body, and its head is restrained by a stanchion closed around its neck.

I constructed my first makeshift version of the squeeze machine out of used plywood. Here I am in the current version of the machine, which I also constructed. By manipulating the lever, I can precisely control the amount of pressure applied to my body. (*Photograph copyright © by Rosalie Winard*)

This is a commercially available squeeze machine manufactured by the Therafin Corporation, based on my design and used in the treatment of people with autism. (*Photograph copyright © by Rosalie Winard*)

One of my first designs for a curved lane leads into the dip vat at John Wayne's Red River feed yard. I figured out that cattle would move more easily through a curved lane because it makes use of their natural circling behavior.

I later applied the curved-lane design to systems for meatpacking plants. When I designed this chute, I was able to visualize the whole system in my imagination.

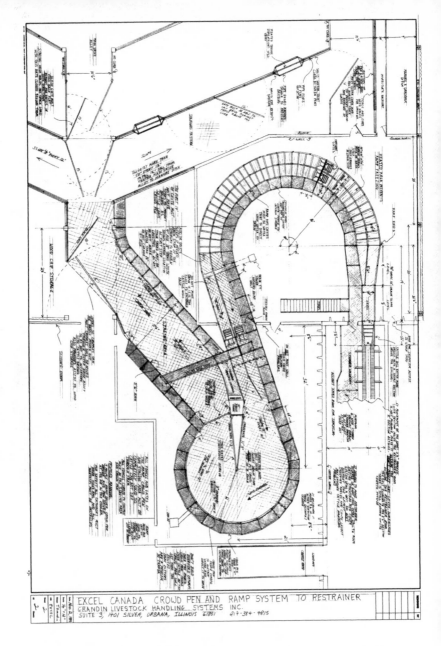

Here is one of my blueprints for a curved-chute system. As I draw, I visualize how each part will operate from every angle in my imagination. Many autistics share these intense visualization skills.

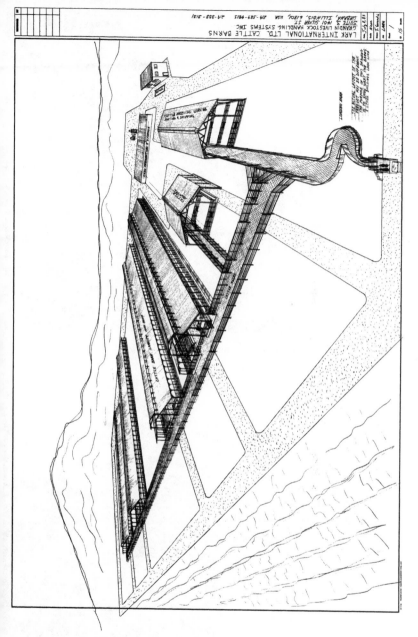

Even though I had little experience with drawing in perspective, I was able to come up with this blueprint in one try. Drawing skills often appear in young autistic children, perhaps as a compensation for their lack of verbal skills.

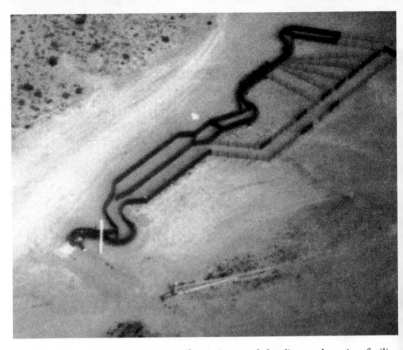

I call this my ground sculpture. In fact it is a truck loading and sorting facility in Nevada.

I love nothing more than surveying a plant I've designed where the animals are calm and quiet. One third of the cattle in the United States are moved through handling facilities that I have designed. (*Photograph copyright © by Rosalie Winard*)

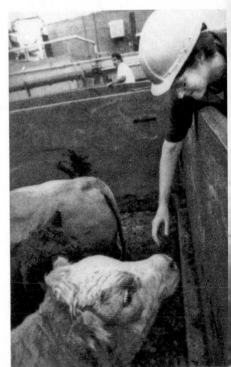

This is an aerial view of my most intricate design, a buffalo-handling facility at the Wichita Mountains Wildlife Refuge. It took 26 drawings to complete this facility, which is operated by the U.S. Fish and Wildlife Service.

I have designed humane restraint systems for both sheep and cattle. As a result of my autism, I have heightened sensory perceptions that help me work out how an animal will feel moving through the system.

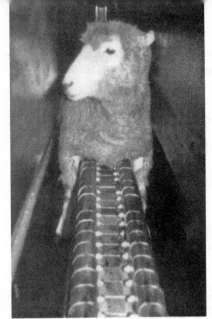

In my work on cattle behavior at Colorado State University, I sometimes like to get a cow's eye view of the situation. (*Photograph copyright © by Rosalie Winard*)

I met Dr. Oliver Sacks when he first wrote about me in *An Anthropologist on Mars*. His groundbreaking descriptions of people with various neurological disabilities have improved our understanding of the often enigmatic workings of the human mind. (*Photograph copyright © by Rosalie Winard*)

In 1994 I testified at a congressional hearing on the humane handling of crippled animals. (*Photograph copyright © by Rosalie Winard*)

I regularly lecture all over the United States on livestock handling and autism. Here I am addressing the annual meeting of the Autism Society of America. (*Photograph copyright © Rosalie Winard*)

woman spoke another sentence in the other ear. I was instructed to ignore one sentence and repeat the other. This task was hard and I got only 50 percent of the sentence correct. A normal person gets almost 100 percent correct. On the next test, two different voices said different sentences simultaneously in the same ear. I was instructed to ignore one voice and tell what the other one said. My left ear was very bad compared to my right ear. Performance in my left ear was only 25 percent of normal, whereas my right ear was 66 percent of normal. These tests showed very clearly that my ability to process and attend to one voice against the background of another voice is severely impaired. On some of the sentences I could distinguish only one or two words, usually from the middle of the sentence.

A third test given by Joan Burleigh, called the binaural fusion test, showed that I have a distinct deficiency in timing sound input between my two ears. In this test a word is electronically split so that the high-frequency sounds go to one ear and the low-frequency sounds go to the other. When the low-frequency part of the word went to my right ear, I was able to hear 50 percent of the words correctly. When the low frequency was sent to my left ear, I became functionally deaf and only got 5 percent of the words correct. "Woodchuck" became "workshop," "doormat" became "floor lamp," "padlock" became "catnap," "therefore" became "air force," and "lifeboat" became "lightbulb." While taking the test I knew that "catnap" and "floor lamp" were wrong, but I thought that "workshop" and "lightbulb" were correct. I often figure out words by the context. If I am at work on an equipment design project, I know that an engineer probably will be talking about a workshop instead of a woodchuck.

Dr. Burleigh has tested other people with autism, and they show the same pattern of hearing deficiencies. She has been able to improve the hearing abilities of some people with auditory processing problems by placing a plug that filters certain frequencies in the most impaired ear. She explained to me that the kinds of problems I have in processing speech indicate defects in my brain stem and possibly the corpus callosum, the bundle of neurons that allows the two halves of the brain to communicate. The brain stem is one of the relay stations that send input from the ears to the thinking parts of the brain.

The techniques used during some of these tests have been available for more than twenty years, but nobody used them on people with autism, mostly owing to a lot of old-fashioned thinking. Working with the electrical engineers helped Dr. Burleigh to look at sensory processing in a new light. Professionals in the field of educating autistic children have largely ignored sensory problems and favored behavioral theory. Edward Ornitz and Peter Tanguay at UCLA documented abnormalities in the brain stem of autistic children more than ten years ago. Dr. Ornitz wrote a major review of the scientific literature on sensory processing problems in autism in the *Journal of the American Academy of Child Psychiatry* in 1985. He stated that people with autism either overreact or underreact to different stimuli, and suggested that some of their deficits could be caused by distorted sensory input. But his important paper was overlooked by educators, who had completely embraced behavior modification methods at the time and ignored the impact of sensory problems.

My auditory problems are very mild compared with those of individuals who are more severely afflicted with autism. Some people have lost all or almost all ability to understand speech. Others have such acute hearing that everyday noises are completely intolerable. One person said that rain sounded like gunfire; others claim they hear blood whooshing through their veins or every sound in an entire school building. Their world is a confusing mass of noise. One woman said she could not tolerate the sound of a baby crying even when she was wearing a combination of earplugs and industrial sound-protector earmuffs. These symptoms are similar to those of people who have had brain stem injuries in an accident, some of whom cannot abide the smallest amount of noise or bright light. Certain types of head injuries create symptoms that partially mimic autistic auditory problems. A girl who was hit on the head during a riot told me that she had auditory problems similar to mine and could no longer ignore distracting background noise. I sometimes have small auditory tuneouts when my ears shut off and I start to daydream. If I work hard to pay attention, I can prevent these lapses, but when I get tired I have a greater tendency to tune out. Now I have control over this, but a person with greater auditory processing difficulties may not be able to gain such control.

Darren White, a young man with autism, wrote that his hearing faded in and out. Sometimes it was loud and sometimes it was soft. He described the sensation in the journal *Medical Hypothesis:* "Another trick my ears played was to change the volume of sounds around me. Sometimes when other kids spoke to me I would scarcely hear, then sometimes they sounded like bullets." Other hearing problems can include a buzzing sound in the ears. I sometimes hear my heartbeat in my ears, or I hear a kind of electronic noise like the sound that accompanies a TV test pattern.

Some autistic children do not pay attention to spoken language. Jane Taylor McDonnell wrote that her two-year-old son could not respond to simple spoken commands. He had to figure out what people wanted by looking at their gestures and the things in the room. Autistic children with echolalia help themselves understand what has been said by repeating it; Donna Williams stated that if she didn't repeat the words, she only understood 5 to 10 percent of what was said. Children with echolalia appear to have severe speech perception problems. In *Somebody Somewhere,* Donna writes, "As a child I had been echolalic and had difficulty learning the purpose and significance of language." She had problems with perceiving both the words and the intonation or tone of speech as a seamless whole. When she was young, she thought that the intonation of a voice *was* the words. If she listened to the intonation, she could not hear the words.

Therese Joliffe also used echolalia to help her learn language. In the December 1992 issue of *Communication,* published by the National Autistic Society in England, she explained how she usually loses the first few words when someone speaks to her, because it takes her a while to realize that somebody has spoken. It was a long time before she figured out the purpose of speech. When she was young, speech had no more significance than other sounds. To learn that speech had meaning, she had to see words written on paper. After seeing the words, she began to recognize them in speech.

Jim Sinclair also had to learn that spoken words had meaning. He described the difficulties he experienced in *High-Functioning Individuals with Autism,* explaining that "speech therapy was just a lot of meaningless drills in repeating meaningless sounds for incomprehensible reasons. I had no idea that this could be a way to exchange meaning with other minds."

It is likely that some of the people who are nonverbal fail to develop language because not enough speech gets through their dysfunctional auditory system. Both Joan Burleigh's auditory test and recent research by Japanese scientists at the University of Tokushima School of Medicine indicate that abnormal brain stem functioning is the cause of at least some of the problems with understanding speech. Dr. Hashimoto and his colleagues found that nonverbal people with autism have smaller brain stems than normal, and D. G. McClelland and his colleagues at Queen's University in Belfast, Ireland, found that so-called low-functioning individuals who are unable to speak show abnormalities in brain stem function when measured by a test that determines the brain stem's ability to transmit nerve impulses.

Therapists have learned from experience that sometimes non-verbal children can be taught to sing before they can speak. In some people the brain circuits used for singing may be more normal than the circuits used for speech. Possibly the song rhythm helps to stabilize auditory processing and block out intruding sounds. This may explain why some autistic children use commercial jingles as an attempt to communicate. The pairing of a visual cue and a sung slogan makes a rhythmic and visual impression. Therese Joliffe's parents told her that when she was a child, she would speak when certain music was played. I used to hum to myself to block out bothersome noise.

Visual Problems

Some people have very severe visual processing problems, and sight may be their most unreliable sense. Some nonverbal people with autism act as though they are blind when they are in a strange place, and others have problems with visual tuneouts and whiteouts, where vision completely shuts down. During a whiteout they see snow, as if they were tuned to a vacant television channel. Several autistic people with normal vision have told me that they have depth perception problems and have difficulty going down stairs. The eyes and the retina usually function normally, and the person can pass an eye examination. The problem arises in processing visual information in the brain.

As a child I was attracted to bright colors and moving objects that were visually stimulating, such as kites and flying model airplanes. I loved striped shirts and Day-Glo paint, and I loved to watch supermarket sliding doors go back and forth. When I watched the edge of the door move across my visual field, I'd get a little pleasurable chill up my back. Minor sensory processing deficits heightened my attraction to certain stimulation, whereas a greater sensory processing defect might cause another child to fear and avoid that same stimulus. Some of the problems autistics have with making eye contact may be nothing more than an intolerance for the movement of the other person's eyes. One autistic person reported that looking at other people's eyes was difficult because the eyes did not stay still. Face recognition also presents certain problems for many people with autism.

I often get into embarrassing situations because I do not remember faces unless I have seen the people many times or they have a very distinct facial feature, such as a big beard, thick glasses, or a strange hairstyle. Barbara Jones, a woman with autism, told me that to remember a face, she has to see the person fifteen times. Barbara works in a laboratory identifying cancer cells under a microscope. Her ability to recognize patterns has made her one of the best technicians in the lab. Her visual abilities enable her to spot abnormal cells instantly, because they just jump out at her. But there is some evidence that facial recognition involves different neural systems from those used for imagery of objects such as buildings. Antonio Damasio, at the University of Iowa College of Medicine, reports that patients with damage to the ventral occipital and temporal association cortices may fail to identify a person's face, but they can identify his voice. These patients can also identify a person accurately by using other visual information, such as a gait or posture, even though they fail to recognize his face. Fortunately, people who have difficulty recognizing a particular face have no difficulty discriminating between a person's face and a dog's face.

Fluorescent lighting causes severe problems for many autistic people, because they can see a sixty-cycle flicker. Household electricity turns on and off sixty times each second, and some autistic people see this. Problems with flickering can range from excessive eyestrain to seeing a room pulsate on and off. Fluorescent lighting in the classroom was a big problem for Donna Williams. Reflections bounced off everything, and the room looked like an animated cartoon. Fluorescent lighting in a kitchen with yellow walls blinded her. There were also situations in which things disappeared and lost their meaning. Donna described moving quickly through a hall: "Perceptually the hall did not exist. I saw shapes and colors as it whooshed by." When her visual system became completely overloaded with stimuli, all meaning in visual sensation was lost.

Distorted visual images may possibly explain why some children with autism favor peripheral vision. They may receive more reliable information when they look out of the corners of their eyes. One autistic person reported that he saw better from the side and that he didn't see things if he looked straight at them.

Smell and Taste

Many autistic children like to smell things, and smell may provide more reliable information about their surroundings than either vision or hearing. A survey of sensory problems in thirty adults and children was conducted by Neil Walker and Margaret Whelan from the Geneva Center in Toronto. Eighty to eighty-seven percent of the people reported oversensitivity to touch or sound. Eighty-six percent had problems with vision. However, only 30 percent reported taste or smell oversensitivities.

Many children with autism are finicky and will eat only certain foods. Their eating problems usually have a sensory basis. They are unable to tolerate the texture, smell, taste, or sound of the food in their mouth. I hated anything that was slimy, like Jell-O or undercooked egg whites. Many autistic children hate crunchy foods because they sound too loud when chewed. Sean Barron writes in *There's a Boy in Here* that he was supersensitive to food texture. He would only eat bland foods—Cream of Wheat was one of his favorites, because it was "perfectly bland." For some people, foods with strong odors or tastes can overpower an overly sensitive nervous system. Neil Walker reported that one person refused to walk on a lawn because he could not bear the smell of grass. Several autistic people have told me that they remember people by smell, and one reported that he liked safe smells such as the smell of pots and pans, which he associated with his home.

Sensory Mixing

In people with severe sensory processing deficits, vision, hearing, and other senses mix together, especially when they are tired or upset. Laura Cesaroni and Malcolm Garber, at the Ontario Institute for Studies in Education in Canada, interviewed a twenty-seven-year-old male graduate student with autism. He described difficulty hearing and seeing at the same time as his sensory channels got mixed up. Sound came through as color, while touching his face produced a soundlike sensation. Donna Williams describes herself as mono channel; in other words, she cannot see and hear at the same time. When she is listening to somebody speak, visual input loses its meaning. She is unable to perceive a cat jumping on her lap while she is listening to a friend talk. She often handles telephone conversations more easily than face-to-face meetings, because distracting visual input is eliminated. Other people with autism have also reported that the phone is a preferred method of socializing.

People with severe sensory problems have a horrible time trying to figure out what reality is. Therese Joliffe succinctly summarizes the chaos caused by autistic sensory problems:

> Reality to an autistic person is a confusing interacting mass of events, people, places, sounds and sights. There seem to be no clear boundaries, order or meaning to anything. A large part of my life is spent just trying to work out the pattern behind everything. Set routines, times, particular routes and rituals all help to get order into an unbearably chaotic life.

Jim Sinclair has also reported sensory mixing problems. Vision is his weakest sense, and sometimes when the phone rings he has to stop and remember what it is. Jim explains his problem in the language of computer technology: "I have an interface problem, not a core processing problem."

Donna Williams found the world incomprehensible, and she had to fight constantly to get meaning from her senses. When she gave up trying to get meaning, she would let her attention wander into fractured patterns, which were entertaining, hypnotic, and secure. In *Somebody Somewhere* she writes, "This was the beautiful side of autism. This was the sanctuary of the prison." People with severe sensory processing problems can also go into total shutdown when they become overstimulated.

Many therapists and doctors confuse autistic perceptual problems with the hallucinations and delusions of schizophrenics, but true schizophrenic delusions and hallucinations follow a different pattern. Autistic fantasies can be confused with hallucinations, but the autistic person knows they are fantasies, whereas the schizophrenic believes they are reality. People with autism do not report such classic delusions associated with schizophrenia as believing that the FBI has planted a radio transmission in their head or thinking they're King Henry the VIII. The problem for most autistic people is that they do not realize that their sensory processing is different. I thought other people were better and stronger than I when I couldn't tolerate scratchy clothes or loud noise. My sensory sensitivities became much less bothersome after I started taking the antidepressant Tofranil. My senses are still easily overstimulated, but the medication calms down my reactions to stimuli.

In the book *Sound of a Miracle,* Georgie Stehli describes how her life changed when a procedure called Berard auditory training greatly reduced her incredible sound sensitivity. It was a relief for her no longer to be terrified of sounds such as that made by surf on a beach. The auditory training consists of listening to music that is electronically distorted at random intervals for two thirty-minute periods for ten days. The machine also contains filters to block the frequencies where hearing is supersensitive. For about half the people who try it, it has helped reduce sound sensitivity, and for some people it has reduced buzzing and other noises in the ears. It is not a cure for autism, but it can have beneficial effects.

Donna Williams has been greatly helped by Irlen tinted glasses, which filter out irritating color frequencies and enable her defective visual system to handle sharp contrast. The glasses stopped fractured visual perception. She is now able to see an entire garden instead of bits and pieces of flowers. Tom McKean has less severe visual processing problems, but he finds that wearing rust-colored glasses with a purplish tint has stopped areas of high contrast from vibrating. Another woman with mild visual problems has also been greatly helped by rose-colored glasses; her depth perception improved, and now she can drive at night. Regular brown sunglasses are helpful for some people.

It is likely that there is a continuum of visual and auditory processing problems for most people with autism, which goes from fractured, disjointed images at one end to a slight abnormality at the other. A slight visual processing abnormality may cause a child to be attracted to bright objects with contrasting colors, but a greater abnormality will cause the child to avoid them. Colored glasses and Berard auditory training are not going to help everybody. These sensory methods can be of value, but neither one is a cure.

It came as a kind of revelation, as well as a blessed relief, when I learned that my sensory problems weren't the result of my weakness or lack of character. When I was a teenager, I was aware that I did not fit in socially, but I was not aware that my method of visual thinking and my overly sensitive senses were the cause of my difficulties in relating to and interacting with other people. Many autistic people know that there is something about them that is different, but they don't know what it is. I only learned the full extent of my differences after reading many books and carefully questioning many people about their thinking and sensory processes. I hope that as more educators and doctors understand these differences, more children with autism will be helped from their terrible isolation at younger ages.

Sensory Integration

Jean Ayres, an occupational therapist in California, has developed a treatment called sensory integration which has been very helpful for most autistic children. It aids both fully verbal children and those with little or no meaningful speech. It is especially useful for reducing touch sensitivity and calming the nervous system. Two of the main components of this treatment are application of deep pressure and slow vestibular stimulation done on a swing that moves ten to twelve times per minute. Swinging must always be fun and done as a game, and the therapist should actively encourage speech and social interaction while the child is swinging. It must never be forced. Gentle swinging helps to stabilize abnormal sensory processing.

It is easy to apply comforting deep pressure over large areas of the body to little children by placing them under large pillows or rolling them up in heavy gym mats. These procedures are most effective if they are done twice a day for fifteen minutes. They need to be done every day, but they do not have to be done for hours and hours. Depending on the children's anxiety level, some will need access to deep pressure or swinging throughout the day, using it to calm themselves down when they become overstimulated. Another useful aid for calming hyperactive children is a padded weighted vest. To help autistic children sleep at night, a snug mummy-type sleeping bag provides comfort and pressure.

When I built my squeeze machine and Tom McKean made his pressure suit, we did not realize that we were inventing a therapy method that has now helped many children. Many of the behaviors of people with autism seem strange, but they are reactions to distorted or overly intense sensory input. Observation of the behaviors can provide clues to the underlying sensory problems. A child who flicks his fingers in front of his eyes may have a visual processing problem, and a child who puts his hands over his ears probably has hypersensitive hearing.

Touch sensitivity in autistic children can also be reduced by massaging the body and stroking with soft surgical scrub brushes. It is important to use relatively firm pressure, which is calming and comforting. A light tickle must be avoided, because it triggers fear in the child's immature nervous system. A good therapist is gently insistent, gradually desensitizing the nervous system to touch. Touching is never forced, but the therapist has to be somewhat insistent; otherwise no progress will be made.

It is likely that sensory integration programs will have the greatest effect on very young children, while the brain is still developing. Touching and stroking babies when they first stiffen and pull away may be helpful as well. But even though these exercises work best on young children, they are also helpful for adults. Tom McKean reports that firmly brushing his skin with soft brushes temporarily made his body pain go away. Donna Williams told me that she hated brushing her body, but it helped integrate her senses and enabled her to see and hear at the same time. Somehow, the brushing helped her to integrate information from different senses. When pressure or rubbing stimulation is first applied, a child may resist, but gradually the nervous system will become less sensitive and the person will enjoy touching that he initially rejected.

As I developed my squeeze machine, I designed it to enhance the feeling of being embraced. Now, if I suddenly resist, I cannot pull my head out of the softly padded neck opening. In order to open the latch, I have to relax and lean forward. I am never locked in the machine, but I am prevented from suddenly pulling away from the soothing pressure. At all times I am in control of the amount of pressure applied to my body. The new design has enabled me to give in completely to the gentle feeling of being held.

Margaret Creedon from the Easter Seals Therapeutic Day School in Chicago has been successfully using the squeeze machine on young children. Over a period of months, each child gradually learns to tolerate the pressure until he or she can enjoy it for five minutes or more. Most children prefer to lie prone in the machine. They are never forced to use it, and they themselves always control the amount of pressure. Researchers found that children who were using the squeeze machine for more than five minutes a day were calmer and had a greater ability to inhibit a motor response than children who did not use the machine. They also performed better on a test of mechanical problem-solving. Helping autistic children fulfill that most basic human need, the comfort of touch, is like taming an animal. At first they pull away, but then they learn that touching feels good.

Update: Sensory Processing Problems

During the last ten years, I have had additional tests of auditory processing and was shocked at how badly I failed one of them. In one test I was asked to discriminate the difference in pitch between two short sounds that were separated by a half-second gap. I was not able to do the task because I heard the sounds as one continuous sound. Nathalie Boddaert and her colleagues in France used a PET scanner to determine that people with autism have abnormalities in the part of the brain that processes complex sounds. One reason why some children with autism fail to learn to speak is due to a poor ability to hear *auditory detail*. Even though a child is able to pass the simple pure tone hearing test, he/she may not be hearing the consonants in the words. My speech teacher helped me to hear words by enunciating the consonants of words such as *cup*. She said *ccc u pp. Auditory detail* and *auditory threshold* (ability to perceive faint sounds) are two different processes. Some nonverbal individuals may be hearing only vowel sounds.

Another problem that individuals with both autism and dyslexia have is slow shifting of attention. It takes much longer to shift back and forth between two different things that attract their attention. For example, if a mobile phone rings it distracts a normal person for a fraction of a second, but it takes much longer for the person with autism to shift away from the distraction. Distractions in the classroom may prevent a person with autism from hearing the first few words of a sentence.

Echolalia

Children who have difficulty hearing auditory detail will often repeat back TV commercials and videos. This is called echolalia.

Parents and teachers should be happy if a child can recite a perfect commercial because the brain is programmed for speech. The reason why TV commercials are learned first is due to the fact that every time the words are said with exactly the same tone and pronunciation.

Adults who were echolalic as children reported that when they recited a commercial, they had no idea that the words had meaning. They thought that the tone of voice was the communication. They had to be taught that the words had meaning. One method that may be effective is to make hundreds of flash cards with nouns on them. The picture of an object such as a cup and the word *cup* must be on the same side of the card. Each card is held up and the child can hear the teacher say the word and look at the picture and the printed word all at the same time. If the child says a word such as *juice,* give him the juice. If he says *spoon* and you know he really was trying to ask for juice, do not correct him and give him a spoon. He/she has to learn the association between a word and certain objects.

Auditory Training

There is much controversy about the use of auditory training to reduce sound sensitivity and improve the ability to hear auditory detail. There are many variations of these programs, but in all of the programs, the person listens to electronically modified music. The music sounds like an old-fashioned record player that is speeding up and slowing down.

Some studies have shown that auditory training is effective and others have not. This is probably due to the huge variation in the wiring problems in different autistic brains. Fortunately a large review of the literature by Dr. Sinha at the Royal Children's Institute in Australia showed that auditory training is safe. However, the music must not be played too loudly. Reports from parents and individuals with autism indicate that auditory training may be helpful for some individuals. Another method that may be useful for reducing sound sensitivity is recording the fire alarm or other sounds that hurt the child's ears. The child is then allowed to play the sound back at a greatly reduced volume. It is essential that the child controls the volume and turns on the sound. Sounds a child initiates are better tolerated. Gradually the volume could be raised.

Visual Problems

Many individuals on the spectrum have difficulty tolerating fluorescent lights. To them the room will flicker like a disco. Placing a lamp with an old-fashioned incandescent lightbulb next to the individual's desk will reduce the flicker effect. Individuals with autism, dyslexia, and other learning problems often prefer to use a flat panel computer screen because it flickers less than a TV-type monitor. The best flat panels are either laptops or a really thin desk unit. Avoid desktop flat panels that have fluorescent lights inside them.

Children with visual processing problems will often look out the corners of their eyes. They do this so they can see more clearly. They are often afraid of escalators because they have difficulty judging how to step on and off of them. If visual processing problems are suspected, the child should see a developmental optometrist. This is a special eye doctor who can do therapy and exercises to help the processing problems that are inside the brain. In many of these children, the eye itself is normal but faulty wiring in the brain is causing the problem.

British researchers have done extensive studies in the use of colored overlays and colored glasses to improve reading in individuals who have visual processing problems. They have found that they are often helpful. It is important for the person to pick the exact colors they prefer. A U.S. study indicated that colored lenses had no significant effect. The poor result was probably due to everybody being given the same color.

I had a dyslexic student who had severe visual processing problems. When she tried to read, the print appeared to wriggle on the page. Colored glasses and printing her work on tan paper to reduce contrast improved both her reading and the organization of her writing. In my livestock equipment design class 1 to 2 percent of normal college students have visual processing problems. These students absolutely cannot draw. They are unable to figure out how to draw a half circle freehand and locate the center in the correct place. When I question them they say they see waves. I always tell them about colored glasses and some of them have reported back to me that colored glasses were helpful. Some students went to a sunglass store and tried reading a book with many different pale colored glasses until they found a color that made the print stop jiggling. Prescription reading glasses can be custom tinted with the preferred color. Irlen centers can help people find the precise shade that works the best. Refer to the directory in the back of the book.

Brain System Fragmentation

When I met Tito Mukhopadhyay he looked like a typical nonverbal low-functioning teenager with autism. When he came into the room he grabbed a magazine and smelled it. His mother taught him to type on a keyboard by constant prompting to make him pay attention. His typing is truly independent and he was not touched by a person while he was typing a sentence. He had to be prompted after he typed each short sentence to keep him on task and to prevent him from running across the room. To make sure that he was not using prerehearsed phrases, I asked Tito to tell me about a picture he had never seen before. The picture was from an advertisement and it showed an astronaut on a horse. Tito immediately typed "Apollo 11 on a horse." This convinced me that Tito was not being cued by his mother. Tito's description of how he thinks and feels indicates that the different subsystems in his brain are not working together. He has written about a thinking self and an acting self. When I questioned him about visual perception he typed that he saw fragments of color, shapes, and motions. He is not able to hear and see at the same time.

In the normal visual system, the brain has circuits for color, shape, and motion. These circuits must work together to create stable images. Tito's description of how he sees things may be an indicator that these systems are working independently. His descriptions may also indicate that he has localized brain systems that are working but the connections among the different brain areas are highly abnormal. I asked Tito what it was like before he could type. He typed out one word: *emptiness.* Tito's writings have more emotion that the writings of many fully verbal people on the autism/Asperger spectrum. I have observed that sometimes emotions are more normal in individuals who have either fragmented sensory processing or poor verbal skills. Tito's achievements indicate that some individuals who appear to be low-functioning have good brains hidden inside. It is likely that many nonverbal individuals will not have Tito's abilities. It depends on which brain circuits get connected.

Deep Pressure

Therapists have found that providing deep pressure by rolling a child in mats or putting him under pillows can calm the nervous system. Discrete trial training (Applied Behavioral Analysis) and speech therapy are sometimes more effective if done while the child is experiencing deep pressure. The calming effect may help the miswired nervous system to perceive speech better. Many of these children's brains are like poor mobile phone signals. The speech may fade in and out.

Pressure applied by a padded, weighted vest can help a hyperactive child sit still. For best results, the vest should be worn for twenty minutes and then taken off for twenty minutes. Sleeping can often be helped by using a weighted blanket to apply soothing pressure. Steve Edelson and his colleague at the Autism Research Institute in San Diego found that the squeeze machine had a calming effect.

An amazing experiment done with Great Danes who bit out of fear showed that deep pressure is calming. Nancy Williams and Peter Borchelt placed aggressive Great Danes in a box filled with grain to apply pressure all over their bodies. The dog's head protruded through a padded opening. While the dogs were in the box, other dogs and strangers were brought up to them. The calming pressure reduced aggressive snarling or attempts to bite. The dog's behavior was improved for several months after treatment. The pressure reduced the dog's anxiety. This experiment shows the calming effects of pressure. When pressure is used on individuals with autism, it should be done as a fun activity and never forced onto the child or adult.

Why is Progress on Sensory Problems Slow?

I am frustrated by the fact that some teachers and therapists still do not recognize the importance of sensory over sensibility. It must be difficult for them to imagine a totally different way of perceiving the world where sounds and lights are super intense. A question people ask is if a child is so sensitive to sounds why don't his own screams bother him? The reason is because sound sensitivity occurs only at specific sound pitches that vary from child to child. Fortunately there are more books available now on sensory over sensitivity problems. Research by S. J. Rogers and others at the Department of Psychiatry, University of California at Davis clearly shows that autistic children have abnormal sensory reactivity. They were also more likely to have abnormal responses to taste and smell compared to children with other developmental abnormalities. Individuals who scream and tantrum every time they go into a large supermarket have the most severe problems with sensory oversensitivity. They probably feel like they are inside the speaker and the light show at a rock concert. Problems with sensory overload get worse when a person is tired. These individuals will need a quiet environment that is free of fluorescent lights and distractions in order to learn.

There is a need for research on the differences in brain function in children and adults with autism. If the area of the brain that is miswired could be identified, then therapy could be targeted at it. It is likely that abnormalities in brain wiring will vary greatly between individuals. One individual may have a visual processing problem and another one may not.

4

LEARNING EMPATHY

Emotion and Autism

TO HAVE FEELINGS of gentleness, one must experience gentle bodily comfort. As my nervous system learned to tolerate the soothing pressure from my squeeze machine, I discovered that the comforting feeling made me a kinder and gentler person. It was difficult for me to understand the idea of kindness until I had been soothed myself. It wasn't until after I had used the modified squeeze machine that I learned how to pet our cat gently. He used to run away from me because I held him too tightly. Many autistic children hold pets too tightly, and they have a disproportionate sense of how to approach other people or be approached. After I experienced the soothing feeling of being held, I was able to transfer that good feeling to the cat. As I became gentler, the cat began to stay with me, and this helped me understand the ideas of reciprocity and gentleness.

From the time I started using my squeeze machine, I understood that the feeling it gave me was one that I needed to cultivate toward other people. It was clear that the pleasurable feelings were those associated with love for other people. I built a machine that would apply the soothing, comforting contact that I craved as well as the physical affection I couldn't tolerate when I was young. I would have been as hard and as unfeeling as a rock if I had not built my squeeze machine and followed through with its use. The relaxing feeling of being held washes negative thoughts away. I believe that the brain needs to receive comforting sensory input. Gentle touching teaches kindness.

I always thought about cattle intellectually until I started touching them. I was able to remain the neutral scientist until I placed my hands on them at the Swift plant and feedlots in 1974. When I pressed my hand against the side of a steer, I could feel whether he was nervous, angry, or relaxed. The cattle flinched unless I firmly put my hand on them, but then touching had a calming effect. Sometimes touching the cattle relaxed them, but it always brought me closer to the reality of their being.

People have a need to touch animals in order to connect with them. I still vividly remember an experience I had while handling cattle at the Arlington feedlot in Arizona. We were working them through a squeeze chute to give them vaccinations. I was operating the chute and giving the animals their vaccinations. When I gave an injection, I always placed my hand on the animal's back, which had a calming effect on me. This calmness seemed to be reciprocal, because when I was calm, the cattle remained calm. I think they sensed this, and each animal walked quietly into the chute. I mentally asked him to relax so he would not get hit by the head restraint. Everything remained calm until the side of the squeeze chute broke and knocked over a bucket. This got me and all the cattle completely rattled for the rest of the afternoon. The spell had been broken.

The application of physical pressure has similar effects on people and animals. Pressure reduces touch sensitivity. For instance, gentle pressure on the sides of a piglet will cause it to fall asleep, and trainers have found that massaging horses relaxes them. The reactions of an autistic child and a scared, flighty horse are similar. Both will lash out and kick anything that touches them. Wild horses can be desensitized and relaxed by pressure. Recently I watched a demonstration of a pressure device for breaking them. The horse used in the demonstration had been sold by a rancher because he was unrideable, and he kicked and reared when people approached. The effect of the pressure device on his nervous system was similar to that of my squeeze machine. Pressure helped this frightened horse to overcome his intense fear of being touched.

The machine was built by Robert Richardson of Prescott, Arizona, and it used sand to immobilize the horse gently as it applied pressure. The wild horse was placed in a narrow stall similar to a horse trailer, with two gentle horses in adjacent stalls to keep it company because wild horses will panic when they are alone. The horse's head protruded through a padded opening in the front of the stall, and a rear pusher gate prevented him from backing up and pulling his head inside. Sand from an overhead hopper flowed down the stall walls and slowly filled up the stall so that the horse hardly felt it until he was buried up to his back. Slow application of pressure is the most calming. It wasn't until the sand came up to his belly that he jerked slightly, but then he appeared to relax. He seldom put his ears back, which is a sign of fear or aggression, and he never tried to bite anybody. He was alert and curious about his surroundings, and he acted like a normal horse in a stall, even though his body was now completely buried. He was free to move his head, and eventually he allowed people to touch his face and rub his ears and mouth. Touching that had been intolerable was now being tolerated.

After fifteen minutes, the sand was removed from the stall by draining through a grating in the floor. The horse now tolerated being touched on the rest of his body. The effect of the pressure lasted for thirty minutes to one hour. During that time the horse learned to trust people a little more and to experience touch as a positive sensation.

The effects of gentle touching work at a basic biological level. Barry Keverne and his colleague at the University of Cambridge in England found that grooming in monkeys stimulated increased levels of endorphins, which are the brain's own opiates. Japanese researchers have found that pressure on the skin produces a relaxed muscle tone and makes animals drowsy. Pigs will roll over and solicit scratching on their bellies when rubbed. The drive for contact comfort is great. Harry Harlow's famous monkey experiments showed that baby monkeys that had been separated from their mother needed a soft surface to cling to. If a baby monkey was deprived of contact with either a real mother or a mother substitute such as the soft fluffy paint roller Harlow gave them, then its capacity for future affection was weakened. Baby animals need to feel contact and comfort and to have normal sensory experiences to develop normally. Harlow also found that gentle rocking helped prevent abnormal, autistic-like behavior in baby monkeys who were separated from their mothers. Every parent knows that rocking calms a cranky baby, and both children and adults enjoy rocking. That's why rocking horses and rocking chairs continue to sell well.

The old theory of autism, popular until the 1970s, placed blame on the "refrigerator mother," whose supposed rejection of the child caused the autism. The psychologist Bruno Bettelheim's theories, popularized in his book *The Empty Fortress,* held that psychological difficulties caused autism. We now know that autism is caused by neurological abnormalities that shut the child off from normal touching and hugging. It is the baby's abnormal nervous system that rejects the mother and causes it to pull away when touched. There is the further possibility that secondary damage to the brain, caused by a defective nervous system, adds to the child's further retreat from normal comforting touch.

Studies of the brain show that sensory problems have a neurological basis. Abnormalities of the cerebellum and the limbic system may cause sensory problems and abnormal emotional responses. Margaret Bauman and her colleagues at Massachusetts General Hospital autopsied the brains of people with autism and found that both the cerebellum and the limbic system had immature neuron development. Eric Courchesne also found abnormalities in the cerebellum on MRI brain scans. Research on rats and cats has shown that the center part of the cerebellum, the vermis, acts as a volume control for the senses. As early as 1947, Dr. William Chambers wrote an article in the *American Journal of Anatomy* reporting that stimulating a cat's vermis with an electrode caused the cat to become supersensitive to sound and touch. A series of abnormalities in lower brain centers probably causes sensory oversensitivity, jumbling, and mixing.

Tests done in many different laboratories around the world clearly indicate that people with autism have abnormal results on brain stem function tests, and that nonverbal people with severe impairments have the most abnormal results. Neurological problems occur during fetal development and are not caused by psychological factors. However, it's possible that if a baby does not receive comforting touch, the feeling and kindness circuits in the brain shrivel up.

Autism and Animal Behavior

Zoo animals kept in barren concrete cages become bored and often develop abnormal behavior such as rocking, pacing, and weaving. Young animals placed alone in such environments become permanently damaged and exhibit strange, autistic-like behavior, becoming overly excitable and engaging in stereotypical behaviors such as self-mutilation, hyperactivity, and disturbed social relations. The effects of sensory deprivation are very bad for their nervous systems. Total rehabilitation of these animals is extremely difficult.

Animal and human studies show that restriction of sensory experiences causes the central nervous system to become hypersensitive to sound and touch. The effects of early sensory restriction are often long-lasting. Puppies reared in empty concrete kennels become very excited when they hear a noise. Their brain waves still show signs of excessive excitability six months after they are removed from the kennel and housed on a farm. The brain waves of autistic children show similar signs of excessive arousal. Further experiments with rats have illustrated the damaging effects of restricting normal sensory experiences. Trimming the whiskers on baby rats causes the parts of the brain that receive sensations from the whiskers to become oversensitive, because there are no incoming touch sensations. This abnormality is relatively permanent; the brain areas are still abnormal after the whiskers grow back. It may be that the autistic child's abnormal sensory functioning causes his or her brain to develop secondary abnormalities because of distorted sensory input or a lack of such input. And these distortions may affect what are considered normal emotions.

The environment a young animal is raised in will affect the structural development of its brain. Research by Bill Greenough, at the University of Illinois, indicated that rearing rats in cages with toys and ladders to play with increased the number of dendrites, or nerve endings, in the visual and auditory parts of their brains. I conducted research as part of my Ph.D. dissertation that indicated that pigs engaging in abnormal rooting, owing to being raised in a barren plastic pen, grew extra dendrites in the part of the brain that received sensations from the snout. Construction of this abnormal "dendrite highway" may explain why it is so difficult to rehabilitate zoo animals that have engaged in years of stereotypical pacing. This is why it is so important to start therapy and education when an autistic child is young, so that developing nerve endings can connect in the right places.

Autistic Emotions

Some people believe that people with autism do not have emotions. I definitely do have them, but they are more like the emotions of a child than of an adult. My childhood temper tantrums were not really expressions of emotion so much as circuit overloads. When I calmed down, the emotion was all over. When I get angry, it is like an afternoon thunderstorm; the anger is intense, but once I get over it, the emotion quickly dissipates. I become very angry when I see people abusing cattle, but if they change their behavior and stop abusing the animals, the emotion quickly passes.

Both as a child and as an adult, I have felt a happy glee. The happiness I feel when a client likes one of my projects is the same kind of glee I felt as a child when I jumped off the diving board. When one of my scientific papers is accepted for publication, I feel the same happiness I experienced one summer when I ran home to show my mother the message I had found in a wine bottle on the beach. I feel a deep satisfaction when I make use of my intellect to design a challenging project. It is the kind of satisfied feeling one gets after finishing a difficult crossword puzzle or playing a challenging game of chess or bridge; it's not an emotional experience so much as an intellectual satisfaction.

At puberty, fear became my main emotion. When the hormones hit, my life revolved around trying to avoid a fear-inducing panic attack. Teasing from other kids was very painful, and I responded with anger. I eventually learned to control my temper, but the teasing persisted, and I would sometimes cry. Just the threat of teasing made me fearful; I was afraid to walk across the parking lot because I was afraid somebody would call me a name. Any change in my school schedule caused intense anxiety and fear of a panic attack. I worked overtime on my door symbols because I believed that I could make the fear go away if I could figure out the secrets of my psyche.

The writings of Tom McKean and Therese Joliffe indicate that fear is also a dominant emotion in their autism. Therese stated that trying to keep everything the same helped her avoid some of the terrible fear. Tony W., another man with autism, wrote in the *Journal of Autism and Developmental Disorders* that he lived in a world of daydreaming and fear and that he was afraid of everything. In my case the terrible fear did not begin until puberty, but for some autistic people it starts in early childhood. Sean Barron reported that he felt pure terror during the first five or six years of his life. The highly structured environment of the classroom reduced some of his fear, but he was often afraid and anxious in the hallways.

The intense fear and anxiety I used to experience has been almost eliminated by the antidepressant medication I've been on for the last thirteen years. The elimination of most of my fears and panic attacks has also attenuated many of my emotions. The strongest feeling I have today is one of intense calm and serenity as I handle cattle and feel them relax under my care. The feeling of peacefulness and bliss does not dissipate quickly like my other emotions. It is like floating on clouds. I get a similar but milder feeling from the squeeze machine. I get great satisfaction out of doing clever things with my mind, but I don't know what it is like to feel rapturous joy. I know I am missing something when other people swoon over a beautiful sunset. Intellectually I know it is beautiful, but I don't feel it. The closest thing I have to joy is the excited pleasure I feel when I have solved a design problem. When I get this feeling, I just want to kick up my heels. I'm like a calf gamboling about on a spring day.

My emotions are simpler than those of most people. I don't know what complex emotion in a human relationship is. I only understand simple emotions, such as fear, anger, happiness, and sadness. I cry during sad movies, and sometimes I cry when I see something that really moves me. But complex emotional relationships are beyond my comprehension. I don't understand how a person can love someone one minute and then want to kill him in a jealous rage the next. I don't understand being happy and sad at the same time. Donna Williams succinctly summarizes autistic emotions in *Nobody Nowhere:* "I believe that autism results when some sort of mechanism that controls emotions does not function properly, leaving an otherwise relatively normal body and mind unable to express themselves with the depth that they would otherwise be capable of." As far as I can figure out, complex emotion occurs when a person feels two opposite emotions at once. Samuel Clemens, the author of *Tom Sawyer,* wrote that "the secret source of humor is not joy but sorrow," and Virginia Woolf wrote, "The beauty of the world has two edges, one of laughter, one of anguish, cutting the heart asunder." I can understand these ideas, but I don't experience emotion this way.

I am like the lady referred to as S. M. in a recent paper by Antonio Damasio in *Nature*. She has a damaged amygdala. This part of the brain is immature in autism. S. M. has difficulty judging the intentions of others, and she makes poor social judgments. She is unable to recognize subtle changes in facial expression, which is common in people with autism. In developing many varied, complex ways to operate the squeeze machine on myself, I keep discovering that slight changes in the way I manipulate the control lever affect how it feels. When I slowly increase the pressure, I make very small variations in the rate and timing of the increase. It is like a language of pressure, and I keep finding new variations with slightly different sensations. For me, this is the tactile equivalent of a complex emotion and this has helped me to understand complexity of feelings.

I have learned how to understand simple emotional relationships that occur with clients. These relationships are usually straightforward; however, emotional nuances are still incomprehensible to me, and I value concrete evidence of accomplishment and appreciation. It pleases me to look at my collection of hats that clients have given me, because they are physical evidence that the clients liked my work. I am motivated by tangible accomplishment, and I want to make a positive contribution to society.

I still have difficulty understanding and having a relationship with people whose primary motivation in life is governed by complex emotions, as my actions are guided by intellect. This has caused friction between me and some family members when I have failed to read subtle emotional cues. For instance, it was difficult for my younger sister to have a weird sister. She felt she always had to tiptoe around me. I had no idea that she felt this way until years later, when she told me about her childhood feelings toward me. Motivated by love, my mother worked with me and kept me out of institutions. Yet sometimes she feels that I don't love her.

She is a person for whom emotional relationships are more important than intellect and logic. It pains her that I kicked like a wild animal when I was a baby and that I had to use the squeeze machine to get the feeling of love and kindness. The irony is that if I had given up the machine, I would have been a cold, hard rock. Without the machine, I would have had no kind feelings toward her. I had to feel physical comfort in order to feel love. Unfortunately, it is difficult for my mother and other highly emotional people to understand that people with autism think differently. For her, it is like dealing with somebody from another planet. I relate better to scientists and engineers, who are less motivated by emotion.

At a conference a man with autism told me that he feels only three emotions, fear, sadness, and anger. He has no joy. He also has problems with the intensity of his emotions, which both fluctuate and get mixed up, similar to sensory jumbling. My emotions don't get mixed up, but they are reduced and simplified in some areas. The emotional jumbling described by this man may be like the sudden emotional changes that normally occur in two-year-old children. They can be laughing one minute and having a tantrum the next. The tendency to shift emotional states rapidly often occurs in autistic children at a later age, whereas older autistic children may have the emotional patterns of a younger child.

During the last couple of years, I have become more aware of a kind of electricity that goes on between people which is much subtler than overt anger, happiness, or fear. I have observed that when several people are together and having a good time, their speech and laughter follow a rhythm. They will all laugh together and then talk quietly until the next laughing cycle. I have always had a hard time fitting in with this rhythm, and I usually interrupt conversations without realizing my mistake. The problem is that I can't follow the rhythm. Twenty years ago, Dr. Condon, a Boston physician, observed that babies with autism and other developmental disorders failed to move in synchrony with adult speech. Normal infants will tune into adult speech and get in synch with it.

The work I do is emotionally difficult for many people, and I am often asked how I can care about animals and be involved in slaughtering them. Perhaps because I am less emotional than other people, it is easier for me to face the idea of death. I live each day as if I will die tomorrow. This motivates me to accomplish many worthwhile things, because I have learned not to fear death and have accepted my own mortality. This has enabled me to look at slaughtering objectively and perceive it the way the cattle do. However, I am not just an objective, unfeeling observer; I have a sensory empathy for the cattle. When they remain calm I feel calm, and when something goes wrong that causes pain, I also feel their pain. I tune in to what the actual sensations are like to the cattle rather than having the idea of death rile up my emotions. My goal is to reduce suffering and improve the way farm animals are treated.

People with autism are capable of forming very strong emotional bonds. Hans Asperger, the German doctor after whom the syndrome is named, states that the commonly held assumption of poverty of emotion in autism is inaccurate. However, my strong emotional bonds are tied up with places more than people. Sometimes I think my emotional life may appear more similar to those of animals than humans, because my feelings are simpler and more overt, and like cattle, I have emotional memories that are place-specific. For instance, I am not aware of a subconscious full of memories that are too painful to think about, and my emotional memory is very weak. It is highly doubtful that cattle become emotionally aroused when they think about a cowboy who whipped them, but they will have a measurable fear response, such as increased heart rate or stress hormone release, when they see that particular cowboy or return to the place where they were whipped. They often associate danger with a specific place. People with autism also have place- or object-specific memories. Going back to the place where something good happened or looking at an object associated with good feelings helps us reexperience the pleasure. Just thinking about it is not enough.

I have emotional reactions to places where I've stayed for a number of days or weeks while working on designing a livestock system. One of my clients told me that I fussed over a project for two weeks like a mother with a new baby. Places where I invest a lot of time become emotionally special. When I return to one of these spots, I am often overwhelmed with fear as I approach. I panic, thinking that I will be denied entry to my special place. Even though I know it's irrational, I always survey each place I work in to make sure I can get back in. Large meat-packing plants have security guards, but in almost every plant I have figured out how to evade security, just in case it becomes one of my special places and I need to get back in. Driving by, I will see every hole in the fence and every unlocked gate and imprint them in my memory forever. My fear of blocked passages feels very primal, as though I were an animal that has been trapped.

For me, finding these holes and gaps is similar to the way a wary animal surveys new territory to make sure it has safe escape routes and passages, or crosses an open plain that may be full of predators. Will the people try to stop me? Some of the surveying is automatic and unconscious. I'll find the unlocked gate even when I am not looking for it. I can't help but see it. And when I spot an opening, I get a rush of happy excitement. Finding all the holes in the fence also reduces fear. I know I am emotionally safe if I can get through the fence. My fear of blocked passages is one of the few emotions that is so great that it's not fully suppressed by my antidepressant medication.

I had similar fearful reactions when I approached my symbolic doors. I was partly afraid that the door would be locked, like the blocked burrow of a tunneling animal. It was as if an antipredator system deep in my brain was activated. Basic instincts that we share with animals may be triggered by certain stimuli. This idea has been suggested by respected scientists such as Carl Sagan in his book *The Dragons of Eden* and Melvin Konner in *The Tangled Wing*. Judith Rapoport suggests in *The Boy Who Couldn't Stop Washing* that obsessive-compulsive disorders, where people wash their hands for hours or repeatedly check whether the stove is off, may be the result of an activation of old animal instincts for safety and grooming.

The fear of blocked passages persisted in both my visual symbolic world of doors and in the real world long after I stopped using door symbols. In my early days I would find the doors that opened up to the roofs of the highest buildings on the school campus. From a high vantage point I could survey the danger that lurked in the next stage of my life. Emotionally I was like an animal surveying the plains for lions, but symbolically the high place signified striving to find the meaning of life. My intellect was trying to make sense of the world, but it was being driven by an engine of animal fears.

Nearly thirty years ago, when I was navigating my visual symbolic world of doors, I recognized that fear was my great motivator. At that time I didn't realize that other people experience other major emotions. Since fear was my major emotion, it spilled over into all events that had any emotional significance. The following diary entry shows very clearly how I attempted to deal with fear in my symbolic world.

October 4, 1968

I opened the little door and went through tonight. To lift up the door and see the wide expanse of the moonlight roof before me. I have put all my fears anxieties about other people on the door. Using the trap door is risky because if it were sealed shut I would have no emotional outlet. Intellectually the door is just a symbol but on the emotional level the physical act of opening the door brings on the fears. The act of going through is my overcoming my fears and anxiety towards other people.

The intellectual side of me always knew that making changes in my life would be a challenge, and I deliberately chose symbolic doors to help me get through after the first door almost magically appeared. Sometimes I had massive activation of my sympathetic nervous system—the system that enables an animal or person to flee from danger—when I went through a door. It was like facing a lion. My heart would race and I would sweat profusely. These reactions are now controlled with antidepressant drugs. In conjunction with vast amounts of stored information in my memory, the drugs have enabled me to leave the visual symbolic world behind and venture out into the so-called real world.

Yet, it has only been during the last two or three years that I have discovered that I do not experience the full range of emotions. My first inkling that my emotions were different came in high school, when my roommate swooned over the science teacher. Whatever it was she was feeling, I knew I didn't feel that way toward anyone. But it was years before I realized that other people are guided by their emotions during most social interactions. For me, the proper behavior during all social interactions had to be learned by intellect. I became more skilled at social interactions as I became more experienced. Throughout my life I have been helped by understanding teachers and mentors. People with autism desperately need guides to instruct and educate them so they will survive in the social jungle.

Update: Empathy and Emotions

There are some situations where "normal" people have a horrific lack of empathy. Some of this lack of empathy is beyond my comprehension. Time after time I read in the paper about a company that is in financial trouble and they need to ask the workers to take a cut in pay. The workers agree to a pay cut, but the chairman of the board gives himself a bonus. This often makes the workers really angry. The workers would be more willing to undergo hardship if their leader had some hardship. This is a situation where ego and emotion blinds empathy. Why does this blindness occur? Power and ego circuits that I do not have cause this blindness. These managers seem to be incapable of learning from this same mistake made by other companies. Possibly these managers do not have empathy because they do not directly see how the workers react. In most cases, he or she does not face them. New research is revealing how empathy works. Brain circuits called mirror areas are activated when a person sees another person hurt. These circuits enable a person to experience the other person's pain. Brain imaging studies by Finnish scientists have shown that the mirror circuits in people with Asperger's syndrome have less activation compared to normal people.

People have empathy when they directly experience suffering. In my work with restaurant companies, I have taken many top executives on their first tours to farms and slaughter plants. Prior to the site visits, animal welfare was just an abstract thing. After they saw suffering firsthand, they made big changes and forced their suppliers to comply with animal welfare guidelines. Executives who had been apathetic jumped into action. One of them was totally disgusted after he saw a half-dead dairy cow going into their product. My job was to implement an auditing system for measuring animal welfare standards in slaughter plants. There was only one executive who reacted differently. On the flight home he clapped on a headset and told silly airline pilot jokes. He wanted to avoid discussing his visit to a slaughter plant because his reaction had conflicted with his beliefs. His company is one of the few companies that has failed to implement strong welfare guidelines.

This brings up another human emotion that I do not understand: denial. Some parents with children who are still not talking until age four cannot admit to themselves that something is wrong. I do not understand this kind of emotional lock on logic. Children with autism have to be taught what it is like to be in another person's shoes in a very concrete way. When I threw dirt on another person, my mother explained that I should not throw dirt because I would not like it if they threw dirt on me.

I think there are different types of empathy. For me to have empathy I have to visually put myself in the other person's place. I can really emphasize with a laid-off worker because I can visualize his family sitting at the dining room table trying to figure out how the bills will get paid. If the worker fails to pay the mortgage he will lose his house. I really relate to physical hardship. I have observed that normal people have bad visual empathy. They are often not able to perceive how another person would see something. Many people leave out essential details when they give driving directions because they are not able to imagine what the other driver would be seeing. People have told me that they do not get lost with my directions. Normal people have emotional empathy but some of them lack empathy for sensory over sensitivity in autistic people. Some of the best therapists who work with individuals with sensory problems can empathize with these difficulties because they themselves have struggled with sound, touch, or visual oversensitivity. The people who have the best sensory empathy have experienced the pain or total sense of chaos caused by faulty sensory processing.

Sometimes Consequences are Needed

The subject of consequences is controversial. Some people think that nothing aversive should ever be done. I was always testing the limits. I knew that a tantrum in school had a penalty of no TV for one day. Discipline between home and school was consistent. Mother and the teachers were a team. I would have been out of control if there had been no consequences for bad behavior. Even though I was raised in a strict household, my abilities in art were always encouraged and never taken away as a punishment. I want to emphasize that I am totally against the use of aversives such as electric shocks. The repeated use of many aversives is wrong and abusive.

Positive methods should always be used for teaching and educating, but there are some situations where a single aversive event is needed to teach the child how another person feels. Three different teachers have told me that they had students who would constantly spit on them. They had tried all of the nonaversive methods such as ignoring it or explaining why they did not like it. Then one day after the teachers had been spat on one hundred times they got fed up and spat back. The child responded by saying, "Ick, I don't like that." The teacher said, "Now you know how I feel when you spit on me." In all three cases, the spitting stopped. Now the child really understood how it felt to the other person when he spat.

Emotional Brain Versus Thinking Brain Type

Simon Baron-Cohen of University of Cambridge in England introduced the idea of people as one of two emotional brain types. He states that people are either empathizers or systematizers. Empathizers are people who relate to other people through their emotions. Systematizers are people who are more interested in things than people. Normal people tend to be empathizers while people on the autism/Asperger's spectrum tend to be systematizers. I scored high on Baron-Cohen's test for being a systematizer.

In the update of Chapter 1 I describe the three thinking types: visual, music and math, and verbal logic. Both emotional types of brain may have the different thinking types, but people in the autism/Asperger spectrum may have the most extreme variations of the thinking types. I hypothesize that some emotional circuits may fail to hook up and local networks in the "art" or "math" department may have extra connections. Brains will be highly variable depending on which "computer cables" get connected.

5

THE WAYS OF THE WORLD

Developing Autistic Talent

AT AGE two and a half I was enrolled in a nursery school for speech-handicapped children. It was staffed by an older, experienced speech therapist and another teacher. Each child received one-to-one work with the therapist while the teacher worked with the other five children. The teachers there knew how much to intrude gently into my world to snap me out of my daydreams and make me pay attention. Too much intrusion would cause tantrums, but without intervention there would be no progress. Autistic children will remain in their own little worlds if left to their own devices.

I would tune out, shut off my ears, and daydream. My daydreams were like Technicolor movies in my head. I would also become completely absorbed in spinning a penny or studying the wood-grain pattern on my desktop. During these times the rest of the world disappeared, but then my speech teacher would gently grab my chin to pull me back into the real world.

When I was three my mother hired a governess to take care of my younger sister and me. This woman kept us constantly occupied with games and outdoor activities and was an important part of my education and treatment. She actively participated in everything we did to encourage me to stay connected. We would make snowmen, play ball, jump rope, and go skating and sledding. When I got a little older, she painted pictures with us, which helped develop my interest in art. It is important for an autistic child to have structured activities both at home and at school. Meals were always at the same time, and we were taught good table manners. Our governess taught me at an early age to be polite, and safety rules were drilled into my head. I was taught to look both ways before I crossed the street. All kids have to learn that the street is dangerous, but autistic children need to learn everything by rote. One or two warnings won't do.

I was enrolled in a normal kindergarten at a small elementary school. Each class had only twelve to fourteen pupils and an experienced teacher who knew how to put firm but fair limits on children to control behavior. The day before I entered kindergarten, Mother attended the class and explained to the other children that they needed to help me. This prevented teasing and created a better learning environment. I am indebted to the good teachers at that school, who ran an old-fashioned, highly structured classroom, with lots of opportunity for interesting hands-on activities.

I vividly remember learning about the solar system by drawing it on the bulletin board and taking field trips to the science museum. Going to the science museum and doing experiments in my third- and fourth-grade classrooms made science real to me. The concept of barometric pressure was easy to understand after we made barometers out of milk bottles, rubber sheeting, and drinking straws. We taped the straw onto the rubber sheeting, which covered the mouth of the milk bottle. Changes in the air pressure pushed the rubber membrane up and down and made the straw move.

My teachers also encouraged my creativity. When I was in the fifth grade I helped make many of the costumes for the school play. I was good at painting and art. Both at home and at school I was praised and encouraged to work on this.

When I started school, I was still diagnosed with brain damage. The teachers were aware of my diagnosis and were willing to work with me even though they had had no training in special education. Two years of intensive teaching prior to kindergarten had prepared me for a normal school. I was now fully verbal, and many of the more severe autistic symptoms had disappeared. When an educational program is successful the child will act less autistic. I now would play with other children and had better control of my tantrums. However, I still had problems with them, especially when I got tired or became frustrated when a teacher didn't give me enough time to respond to a question. My mind processed information slowly, and answering a question quickly was difficult.

I was still a poor reader at age eight, when my mother tried a new approach. Every afternoon after school, I sat with her in the kitchen and she had me sound out the words in a book. After I learned the phonetic sounds and the rules, she read a paragraph out loud to me. Then I sounded out one or two words. Gradually she had me read longer and longer passages. We read from a real book that was interesting instead of a little kid's beginning book. I learned well with phonics, because I understood spoken language. It took me a long time to learn to read silently, though. Saying the words out loud helped me to keep the sequence organized. I also used to tell myself stories at night. Saying them out loud gave each story a sequence, which made them seem more real. Even in high school I would discuss philosophical concepts out loud with myself.

As I grew older, the people who were of the greatest assistance were always the more creative, unconventional types. Psychiatrists and psychologists were of little help. They were too busy trying to psychoanalyze me and discover my deep dark psychological problems. One psychiatrist thought if he could find my "psychic injury," I would be cured. The high school psychologist wanted to stamp out my fixations on things like doors instead of trying to understand them and use them to stimulate learning.

It was Mr. Carlock, one of my science teachers, who became my most important mentor in high school. After I was thrown out of regular high school, my parents enrolled me in a small boarding school for gifted students with emotional problems. Even though I had scored 137 on the Wechsler IQ test when I was twelve, I was totally bored with schoolwork, and I continued to get lousy grades. The other teachers and professionals at the school wanted to discourage my weird interests and make me more normal, but Mr. Carlock took my interests and used them as motivators for doing schoolwork. When I talked about visual symbols such as doors, he gave me philosophy books.

Likewise, the psychologist and psychiatrist wanted me to get rid of my squeeze machine, but Mr. Carlock defended it and went a step further toward helping me direct my interests and energies. He told me that if I wanted to find out why it relaxed me, I had to learn science. If I studied hard enough to get into college, I would be able to learn why pressure had a relaxing effect. Instead of taking my weird device away, he used it to motivate me to study, get good grades, and go to college.

Mr. Carlock then introduced me to the scientific indexes, such as the *Psychological Abstracts* and the *Index Medicus*. Real scientists, I learned, do not use the *World Book Encyclopedia*. Through the indexes I could find the world's scientific literature. In the mid-sixties there were no computerized scientific indexes. We didn't even have photocopy machines in the public library. Each entry from an index had to be copied into a notebook by hand. Searching the scientific literature was real work in those days. Mr. Carlock took me to the library and taught me how to do this and take the first step toward becoming a scientist. These were the books the real scientists used.

Mr. Carlock's training served me well. Later in life, when anxiety attacks were tearing me apart, I was able to research what medication I needed in the library. Through the *Index Medicus* I found the answers.

Many children with autism become fixated on various subjects. Some teachers make the mistake of trying to stamp out the fixation. Instead, they should broaden it and channel it into constructive activities. For example, if a child becomes infatuated with boats, then use boats to motivate him to read and do math. Read books about boats and do arithmetic problems on calculating boat speed. Fixations provide great motivation. Leo Kanner stated that the path to success for some people with autism was to channel their fixation into a career. One of his most successful patients became a bank teller. He was raised by a farm family who found goals for his number fixation. To motivate him to work in the fields, they let him count the rows of corn while the corn was being harvested.

Dr. Kanner also noted that an autistic person's fixations can be their way to achieve some social life and friends. Today, many people with autism become fascinated with computers and become very good at programming. An interest in computers can provide social contacts with other computer people. The Internet, the worldwide computer network, is wonderful for such people. Problems that autistic people have with eye contact and awkward gestures are not visible on the Internet, and typewritten messages avoid many of the social problems of face-to-face contact. The Internet may be the best thing yet for improving an autistic person's social life. Tom McKean said when he was a college student that computers were a godsend because he could communicate with other people and not have to concentrate on trying to talk normally.

Teachers need to help autistic children develop their talents. I think there is too much emphasis on deficits and not enough emphasis on developing abilities. For example, ability in art often shows up at an early age. At meetings, parents, teachers, and people with autism have given me astonishing drawings by very young children. Autistic children as young as seven will sometimes draw in three-dimensional perspective. One time I visited a school where a twenty-year-old autistic man was drawing beautiful airport pictures on notebook paper. Nobody was working with him to develop this talent. He should have been taking courses in drafting and computer drawing.

Tom McKean became frustrated during a college computer programming course because the professor flunked him for finding a better way to write a program. My guess is that the professor may have been offended by Tom's direct manner, not understanding that being direct to the point of rudeness sometimes is a characteristic of autism. Tom would walk up to the blackboard and erase and correct his professor's example. In his book *Soon Will Come the Light,* Tom wrote, "Look, if we did it this way instead, we could save four or five lines of code. If I was looking for a job as a programmer, I would not have been hired if I used the code he [the professor] insisted on." Tom was frustrated and confused when he failed the course. A more creative professor would have challenged him with more interesting and difficult program writing.

Teenagers and adults with autism need to build on their strengths and use their interests. They should be encouraged to develop abilities in fields such as computer programming, engine repair, and graphic arts. (Computer programming is also an excellent field because social eccentricity is tolerated.) Autistics also need mentors to explain the ways of the world. I have helped many autistic adults by explaining to them that they think differently from other people. It makes it easier to figure out what and why things are going on when one learns that other people's actual thinking processes are different. Video cameras and tape recorders can be very useful in teaching social interactions. When I look at videotapes of some of my old lectures, I can see the things I did wrong, such as using odd voice patterns. Teaching a person with autism the social graces is like coaching an actor for a play. Every step has to be planned. This is one reason that Mr.

Carlock did more for me than teach me science. He spent hours giving me encouragement when I became dejected by all the teasing by classmates. Mr. Carlock's science lab was a refuge from a world I did not understand.

When I became interested in something, I rode the subject to death. I would talk about the same thing over and over again. It was like playing a favorite song over and over on the stereo. Teenagers do this all the time, and nobody thinks that it is odd. But autism exaggerates normal behavior to a point that is beyond most people's capacity for understanding. For example, many people thought the way I perseverated on my door symbols was weird and tried to get me to get rid of them. It took someone like Mr. Carlock to help me channel such fixations.

College and Graduate School

Before I entered college, my mother informed the administration of my problems. The school was close to my old high school and I was still able to see Mr. Carlock on weekends. This was very important for my success. He provided needed support and encouragement while I adapted to life in college. I might not have been able to make it without him.

There were two kinds of college courses: easy ones, like biology, history, and English, and impossible ones, like math and French. Mr. Dion, the math teacher, spent hours with me after each class. Almost every day I went to his office and reviewed the entire day's lecture. I also had to spend hours with a tutor to get through French. For moral support there was Mrs. Eastbrook, the assistant dean's wife. She was another one of the unconventional people who helped me. She had wild hair and wore long johns under her skirt. When I got lonely or down in the dumps, I went over to her house and she gave me much-needed encouragement.

College was a confusing place, and I strove to use visual analogies to understand the rules of collegiate society. When I got into college, I made new analogies to augment the simple ideas that I had come up with in boarding school to stay out of trouble. There I had quickly learned which rules I really had to follow and which rules I could bend through careful observation and logic. I developed a simple classification system for rules, which I called "sins of the system." A rule designated as a sin of the system was very important, and breaking it would result in severe loss of privileges or expulsion. Students got into serious trouble for smoking and having sex. If a student could be totally trusted not to engage in these two activities, she could break some of the minor rules without any consequences. I designated smoking and sex as sins of the system. Once the staff realized that I would not run off into the bushes and have sex I was never punished for going out in the woods without a staff member. I was never given special permission to go hiking by myself, but on the other hand, I learned that the staff would make no attempt to stop me. I figured out that the teachers and houseparents were much more concerned about smoking and sex, and I learned how to stay out of trouble.

For people with autism, rules are very important, because we concentrate intensely on how things are done. I always took the rules seriously and won the confidence of my teachers. People who trust me have always been a big help. But many people have difficulty deciphering how people with autism understand rules. Since I don't have any social intuition, I rely on pure logic, like an expert computer program, to guide my behavior. I categorize rules according to their logical importance. It is a complex algorithmic decision-making tree. There is a process of using my intellect and logical decision-making for every social decision. Emotion does not guide my decision; it is pure computing.

Learning a complex decision-making process is difficult. I had a strict moral upbringing, and I learned as a child that stealing, lying, and hurting other people were wrong. As I grew older I observed that it was all right to break certain rules but not others. I constructed a decision-making program for whether rules could be broken by classifying wrongdoing into three categories: "really

bad," "sins of the system," and "illegal but not bad." Rules classi-
fied as really bad must never be broken. Stealing, destroying property, and injuring other people are in this category, and they were
easy to understand. The "illegal but not bad" rules can often be
broken with little consequence. Examples would be slight speeding on the freeway and illegal parking. The "sins of the system"
category covers rules that have very stiff penalties for seemingly
illogical reasons. Using my system has helped me negotiate every
new situation I enter.

My Aunt Breechen was another important mentor. She was
always very tolerant and encouraged me to work with cattle. I fell
in love with Arizona while visiting her ranch. My infatuation
with the cattle chutes there also provided the motivation that
started my career, and I returned there to go to graduate school.

I wanted to do my master's thesis in animal science on the
behavior of cattle in feedlots in different types of cattle chutes, but
my adviser at Arizona State University thought that cattle chutes
were not an appropriate academic subject. Back in 1974, animal
behavior research on farm livestock was a rarity. Once again, my
fixation propelled me. I was going to do my survey of cattle
behavior in cattle chutes even though the professor thought it was
stupid. I then had to seek out a new adviser. Most of the professors in the Animal Science Department thought my ideas were
crazy. Fortunately, I persevered and found two new professors,
Dr. Foster Burton, chairman of the Construction Department,
and Mike Nielson, from Industrial Design, who were interested.
With them I figured out my survey methods. An idea that seemed
crazy to conservative professors in animal science seemed perfectly reasonable to a construction man and a designer.

My master's thesis brought together all of my ideas about and
fixations on the way things work. I wanted to determine the effect
of different squeeze chute designs on the behavior of the animals,
the incidence of injury, and the chutes' efficiency. The variables I
looked at were the breed of the cattle, the design of the squeeze
chute, and the size of the cattle. I measured how often the cattle

balked and refused to enter the squeeze chute, speed of handling, and things that could injure the animals, such as falling on slippery surfaces and head stanchions that could choke them. To survey the cattle, I stood next to the chute with a data sheet and recorded the behavior of each animal while it was branded and vaccinated.

I then had to punch the data into IBM punch cards for analysis on the mainframe computer in the Engineering Department. When I was at Arizona State University, there were no nice little desktop computers. Keypunching five thousand IBM cards was mind-numbing work, because the data for each animal had to be punched onto an individual card. I would arrive at the keypunch lab before the engineers got there at 6:00 P.M. and punch cards until my bladder gave out. If I left to go to the bathroom, an engineering student would grab my keypunch machine. I became an expert on the keypunch and the card sorter. When the sorter jammed, the engineering students would stand by helplessly while I unjammed it. Often I fixed the machine for them so I could get their cards sorted so I could get back to running mine. I always referred to the decks of cards as my cattle. Visualizing each card as an actual animal made it easier to understand how to sort them into different groups for statistical analysis. For example, I could sort the cards into size categories to see if cattle size affected efficiency. I used to call running the card sorter "sorting cattle."

The results of my survey indicated that the design of the equipment affected its operation. Some types of squeeze chutes were more likely than others to injure the steers, and some breeds of cattle were more accident-prone in them than others. I also did a time-motion study to determine the most efficient speed for handling the animals. If a crew tried to go too fast, animals were more likely to become injured and vaccinations were given improperly. Twenty years ago I determined how much time was required to perform vaccinations and other procedures on cattle. These figures are still good today. It is simply impossible to handle the animals faster and do a decent job.

In some ways, I credit my autism for enabling me to understand cattle. After all, if I hadn't used the squeeze chute on myself, I might not have wondered how it affected cattle. I have been lucky, because my understanding of animals and visual thinking led me to a satisfying career in which my autistic traits don't impede my progress. But at numerous meetings around the country I have talked to many adults with autism who have advanced university degrees but no jobs. They thrive in the structured world of school, but they are unable to find work. Problems often occur at the outset. Often during interviews, people are turned off by our direct manner, odd speech patterns, and funny mannerisms.

Twenty years ago I did not realize how weird I seemed. One of my good friends told me that I was always hunched over, I wrung my hands, and I had an excessively loud, unmodulated voice. I've had to get everywhere I've gotten through the back door. Fortunately, I had enough money to live on while I started very slowly pursuing my career on a freelance basis. Once, at an American Society for Agricultural Engineers meeting, I was able to tell that I made a poor impression on two engineers, because they ignored me and refused to discuss engineering with me. They thought I was strange until I yanked out the drawing I had done of the dip vat at John Wayne's Red River feedlot. They said, "You drew that?"

People with autism can develop skills in fields that they can really excel in, such as computer programming, drafting, advertising art, cartooning, car mechanics, and small engine repair. Where they really need help is in selling themselves. In many cases, they have a better chance of getting hired if they are interviewed by other computer programmers or draftsmen instead of the personnel department. Likewise, showing a portfolio of work will help convince skeptical employers who are nervous about giving a job to an autistic person. I've known people who are engaged in satisfying jobs as varied as elevator repair, bike repair, computer programming, graphic arts, architectural drafting, and laboratory pathology. Most of these jobs use the visualization talents that many people with autism have. For instance, a good mechanic runs the engine in his mind to figure out what is wrong with it. People with autism who have savantlike memorization skills are good at cataloguing and reshelving books at the library. Piano tuning is another job they are good at, because many people with autism have perfect pitch.

I still remember taking that vital first step in establishing my credibility in the livestock industry. I knew if I could get an article published in the *Arizona Farmer Ranchman,* I could go on from there. While I was attending a rodeo, I walked up to the publisher of the magazine and asked him if he would be interested in an article on the design of squeeze chutes. He said he would be, and the following week I sent in an article entitled "The Great Headgate Controversy." It discussed the pros and cons of different types of chutes. Several weeks later I received a call from the magazine; they wanted to take my picture at the stockyards. I just could not believe it. It was plain old nerve that got me my first job. That was in 1972. From then on I wrote for the magazine regularly while I was working on my master's degree.

Publishing articles led to a job of designing cattle chutes at Corral Industries, a large feedlot construction company. I was still living in my visual-symbol world, and I needed concrete representations of advancement in the cattle industry. I wore a green work uniform with cattle pins on the collar like a soldier's rank insignia. I started out as a private, with bronze cattle pins, and as I became recognized in the industry I awarded myself high-ranking silver or gold cattle pins. I was totally oblivious to the fact that other people regarded my uniform as ridiculous.

Emil Winnisky, the construction manager at Corral Industries, recognized my talents, and he helped me to dress and act more appropriately. He had his secretaries take me shopping for nicer clothes and teach me better grooming. Now I wear a more appropriate western shirt, but I still award myself an advancement in cattle rank and put two silver cattle pins on my collar.

At the time, I resented Emil's intrusion into my dress and grooming habits, but today I realize he did me a great favor. With much embarrassment I remember the day that he plunked a jar of Arid deodorant on my desk and told me that my pits stank. People with autism need to be counseled on clothing and grooming. Tight or scratchy clothes make paying attention to work impossible, and many cosmetics cause allergic reactions, so each person needs to find stylish, comfortable clothes that do not irritate overly sensitive skin and deodorant and other cosmetics free from perfume (I have severe allergic reactions to perfumes). Shaving is a problem for some autistic men because of tactile oversensitivity, which makes a razor feel like a power sander. Electric razors are often easier to tolerate.

While I was working at Corral Industries I would visit the Swift meat-packing plant once a week. There I met Tom Rohrer, the manager, who was to become one of my most important mentors in the work world. The main thing Tom did for me at first was to tolerate my presence, plain and simple. I was still talking too much, but he put up with me because I figured out clever ways to solve problems, such as using plastic milk hoses to pad the edges of gates and prevent bruises. Gradually the superintendent, Norb Goscowitz, and the foremen took an interest in me. Several times Norb told me that he was advising me the same way he would advise his own daughter.

A year later, I sold Swift the contract to build a new cattle ramp for Corral Industries. During construction of this project, I learned that being technically right was not always socially right. I criticized some sloppy welding in a very tactless way, and the workers got angry. Harley Winkleman, the plant engineer, gave me some good advice. He told me, "You must apologize to the workers before a small problem turns into a big cancer." He made me go to the cafeteria and apologize, and he helped me learn to criticize more tactfully.

A year later, I got into more social hassles at the plant, and Tom defended me after I annoyed the president of Swift. I naively believed that every employee who worked there would put loyalty to the company first. The president was embarrassed when I wrote him a letter about mistakes on an equipment installation at another Swift plant. He did not appreciate my finding problems in his operation. From this I learned that loyalty to the best interests of the company was often not the primary motivator for another person's actions. I will never forget that when the going got really rough, Norb told me, "No matter what, you must always persevere."

I quit the job at Corral Industries and continued to write for the *Arizona Farmer Ranchman* while I started my design business on a freelance basis. Freelancing enabled me to avoid many of the social problems that can occur at a regular job. It meant I could go in, design a project, and leave before I got into social difficulties. I still don't easily recognize subtle social cues for trouble, though I can tell a mile away if an animal is in trouble.

When a new manager took over the *Arizona Farmer Ranchman*, I did not realize that he thought I was weird and I was in danger of being fired. A fellow employee told me that he was turned off by me. My pal Susan saw the warning signs, and she helped me assemble a portfolio of all my articles. After the manager saw how many good articles I had written, he gave me a raise. This experience taught me that to sell my services to clients, I always had to have a portfolio of drawings and photos of completed projects. I learned to avoid social problems by limiting my discussions with clients to technical subjects and avoiding gossip about the social life of the people I worked with.

Employers who hire people with autism must be aware of their limitations. Autistic workers can be very focused on their jobs, and an employer who creates the right environment will often get superior performance from them. But they must be protected from social situations they are unable to handle. An autistic man who had successfully worked at an architectural firm for many years was fired when he was promoted to a position that involved customer contact. Another man lost his job at a lab after he got drunk with other employees. Employers need to educate their employees about autism so that an autistic person is not placed in a social situation that he or she can't handle.

But for every Mr. Carlock or Tom Rohrer, there will always be people who make life difficult. I remember the time when I drove into Scottsdale feed yard and walked up to the door that led into the cattle working area, and a man named Ron put his hand on the door and said that no girls were allowed. Back in the early seventies, no women worked in feedlots. Today many do, and many yards prefer women for handling and doctoring cattle, because they are gentler than men. But back then I didn't know which was my greater handicap, being a woman or having autism.

Attempting to get into a man's world was difficult enough. When I started designing facilities at meat plants, I had my car decorated with bull testicles and was constantly given "gross-out" tours. I had to get dressed in the men's bathroom when I worked at the dairy at Arizona State University. At one plant I was shown the blood pit on three separate occasions. During the third walk through the blood, I stamped my feet and splattered it all over the plant manager. He respected me after he saw that I knew how to operate the equipment. What people call sexual harassment today is nothing compared to what I went through.

Though he will never know it, when Ron blocked the door that led to the cattle working area, he instantly transformed a small, insignificant wood door in a fence into a special symbolic door in my pantheon of door symbols. Any event that actually involved a door being blocked seemed like part of a grand plan that God had in store for me. My visual-symbol world enabled me to keep on going. A blocked door had to be conquered. True to form, I was like a bull filled with pure determination. Nothing was going to stop me.

Update: Autism/Asperger's and Careers

I am very concerned about careers for people with high-functioning autism or Asperger's syndrome. Since *Thinking in Pictures* was written, more and more really gifted students are being labeled as having Asperger's. I am worried that some of these students will have their careers hindered by the label. The students I am most concerned about are the very bright students who are not being challenged at school and who misbehave because they are bored. In some schools these students are kept out of gifted and talented classes due to the Asperger's label.

I was a miserable, bored student and I did not study until I was mentored by Mr. Carlock, my high school science teacher. Over the years I have observed that the high-functioning autistic individuals who became successful have had two important factors in their lives: *mentoring and the development of talents.* The students who failed to have a good career often had no mentors and no development of their talents. I ended up in a career where I could use my visual skills to design cattle-handling facilities.

I have observed that there are many successful undiagnosed people with Asperger's working in many jobs. One man is a plant engineer who keeps a gigantic multi-million-dollar meatpacking plant running. In another plant, I met a head maintenance man who was clearly an undiagnosed Asperger. The man who fixed my copier had Asperger traits. I have also been interviewed by several journalists who were on the spectrum. Some college professors are also Asperger. The computer industry is filled with Asperger people. These are the happy people on the spectrum. One Asperger computer programmer told me that he was happy because he was with his own people.

Many of these successful people are my generation now in their forties and fifties. How were these people able to get and keep their jobs? All of us were raised in the '50s and '60s where it was standard to teach all children social skills. When I was a child,

I was expected to sit through formal Sunday dinners and behave. Most of the time I did. Rudeness was not tolerated and I was taught to say *please* and *thank you*. Normal family activities provided structured opportunities to learn social skills. Sit-down meals and activities such as playing cards and board games like Chinese checkers taught turn-taking and patience.

Today many children lack this structure. Video games and time on the computer are spent solo. Many of my favorite childhood activities *required* participation with another child. I played with other children in board games, bike races, softball, and building tree houses. The other kids were fascinated with the kites and parachutes that I built.

Even the normal children today are growing up with more social problems. Later on they do not know how to behave at work. In the '90s, the *Wall Street Journal* started publishing more and more articles on how normal people should conduct themselves. The articles cover topics such as gossip, use of e-mail, and behavior at office parties. In the '70s and '80s these articles were rare, yet now there are one to three of them in most issues. In the '90s, MIT, the prestigious engineering school, started a course in social skills. Many engineering students have mild Asperger's. Social skills training is extremely important for people on the spectrum. I am not suggesting turning "Aspies" into social beings. People with autism and Asperger's are seldom interested in socializing for the sake of socializing. However, they need to have good manners and not be viewed as total slobs who wear the same dirty shirts for a week.

Multitasking Problems and Learning Driving

Multitasking is still very difficult for me. I would have a horrible time working as a cashier in a busy restaurant where I would have to make change and talk to people at the same time. Often I am asked how I can drive if I cannot multitask. I can drive because the operation of the car, steering and braking, has become a fully automatic skill. Research has shown that when a motor skill is first being learned, one has to consciously think about it. When the skill becomes fully learned, the frontal cortex is no longer activated and only the motor parts of the brain are turned on. I learned to drive on ranch roads in Arizona and I did not drive on the freeway or in heavy traffic for a full year. This avoided the multitasking issue because when I finally started driving in traffic, my frontal cortex was able to devote all its processor space to watching traffic. I recommend that people on the spectrum who are learning to drive spend up to a year driving on easy roads until steering, braking, and other car operations can be done without conscious thought.

Portfolios to Show Your Work

When I started freelance design work, people thought I was weird. I had to sell my work not my personality. People respected the accurate articles that I wrote for the *Arizona Farmer Ranchman* and they were impressed with my drawings and photos of completed cattle-handling facilities.

The successful people on the spectrum often get in the back door by showing a portfolio of their work to the right person. That often means avoiding the traditional front door with a job interview or the normal college admission process. One student circumvented the strict New York State testing requirements by sending a portfolio of her creative writing to an English professor. Her work was so good that he got her excused from the exams. I sold many jobs by sending portfolios of pictures and drawings to plant engineers. I contacted them after I read in a trade magazine that their plant was expanding.

Portfolios must be professionally and neatly presented. The person on the spectrum may need help choosing the best items to put in the portfolio. More information is in my careers book *Developing Talents*.

Getting in the Back Door

The computer field is full of people with Asperger's or Asperger's traits. Many of these individuals followed their parents into the field. When they were eight, their parents taught them computer programming. In other cases, the person started at an entry-level job and then worked his/her way up. This is how many of the Asperger's people who work in construction or in factories get good jobs. They start out as laborers and then they hang around the computers. *The Wall Street Journal* has many articles about people who started highly specialized niche businesses. Parents and teachers need to think creatively to find mentors and jobs. A mentor might be a retired electronics specialist who lives next door. Mentors are attracted to talent. Talents should be developed into skills that can turn into careers. Individuals on the spectrum need to learn that high standards are required to be successful but having perfect work is impossible. I remember almost quitting livestock equipment design when one of my early customers was not completely satisfied. My friend, Jim Uhl, a building contractor, explained to me that satisfying everybody is not an attainable goal. Explain to the individual that getting 90 to 95 percent of the answers right on a test is excellent, A-grade level work. In a job your work has to be at the 90 to 95 percent level. The concept of a percentage may be easier to understand with a bar graph or pie chart. The individual needs to understand that in some jobs 90 to 95 percent is an acceptable standard but in jobs such as computer programming the error rate has to be lower. However, absolute perfection is like absolute zero in physics: it is impossible to attain.

High school and college students must get work experience and learn basic skills like punctuality. They also must learn to do what the boss tells them and to be polite. Working for a seamstress helped teach me work skills when I was a teenager. When I was in college, I had summer volunteer jobs at a school for autistic children and at a research lab. The best work experiences use the individual's talent. A volunteer job in a career related field may be better preparation for adult life than a paying job that is not career related.

Other Sources of Learning

High-functioning teenagers on the spectrum often get bullied in high school. I was kicked out of a large girls' high school after I threw a book at a girl who teased me. High school was the worst time in my life. Going away to a specialized boarding school where I could pursue interests such as horseback riding, roofing a barn, and electronics lab was the best thing that happened to me. It is a shame that some high schools no longer have classes in art, auto mechanics, wood working, drafting, or welding. Some students need to be taken out of the social obstacle course of high school to attend a university, community college, or technical school. Online classes are another option. There are now some special high school programs for Asperger's that help develop strengths. Valerie Paradiz, a mother of a child with Asperger's, started one of the first programs—the Aspie School in New York. I really like their slogan, "reengaging students in learning." Their program emphasizes hands-on learning in areas such as movie making and graphic arts.

Exposing Children to Interesting Things

Students need to be exposed to many different interesting things in science, industry, and other fields so they learn that there is more to life than video games. Talents can be developed and nurtured when children have different experiences where they can use their special skills. Scientists have fabulous programs for visualizing organic chemistry molecules. At MIT, John Belcher developed a computer program that turns mathematical equations into beautiful abstract designs. Getting a student hooked on this could motivate a career in chemistry and physics. Other fascinating areas are distributed computing projects, statistics programs, and computer graphics. The journal *Science* has a section called "Net Watch." It provides descriptions and links to interesting science Web sites. Reviews of the best sites are in the magazine or on *www.sciencemag.org/netwatch*. Large bookstores have a full selection of computer programming books that can be used to educate and motivate students. Commercially available simulation software such as *Sim City* and *Spore* can stimulate an interest in science, biology, or design. Children have to use their intellect to play these video games. Parents should bring trade journals and publications about their profession or business into the school library for students to read. Every industry from construction to banking has its own journal. *The Wall Street Journal* is another good resource. Old medical and scientific journals, computer industry magazines, and general interest publications such as *National Geographic* and *Smithsonian* could also be given to the library. Parents could also direct teachers to the Web sites of their professional organizations and interesting sites related to their careers. Parents could show a PowerPoint presentation with lots of pictures of what they do at work to get students interested. Trips to fun places like construction sites, TV stations, control rooms, factories, zoos, farms, backstage at theaters, a graphic design studio, or architectural computer-aided drafting departments can help get students motivated.

When I was a child I spent lots of time outdoors watching ants and exploring the woods. Kids today miss out on these experiences. I loved collecting shells on the beach and finding different weird rocks for my rock collection that lived on a shelf in our toolshed. Another fun activity I shared with other children was stick racing in the brook. We would drop sticks off the bridge into the brook and run to the other side to see which one came out first. Richard Louv's book *Last Child in the Woods* has many practical suggestions on how to get kids engaged with nature. A strip of woods or a vacant overgrown field can be used to get kids interested in biology, insects, conservation, ecology, and many other careers. There is a big world out there of interesting things and kids need to be exposed to them.

Autism/Asperger Advocacy

Many individuals with high-functioning autism or Asperger's feel that autism is a normal part of human diversity. Roy, a high-functioning autistic, was quoted in *New Scientist,* "I feel stabbed when it comes to curing or treating autism. It's like society does not need me." There are numerous interest groups run by people on the autism/Asperger spectrum and many of them are upset about attempts to eliminate autism. A little bit of the autism trait provides advantages but too much creates a low-functioning individual who can not live independently. The paradox is that milder forms of autism and Asperger's are part of human diversity but severe autism is a great disability. There is no black-and-white dividing line between an eccentric brilliant scientist and Asperger's.

In an ideal world the scientist should find a method to prevent the most severe forms of autism but allow the milder forms to survive. After all, the really social people did not invent the first stone spear. It was probably invented by an Aspie who chipped away at rocks while the other people socialized around the campfire. Without autism traits we might still be living in caves.

6

BELIEVER IN BIOCHEMISTRY

Medications and New Treatments

PUBERTY ARRIVED when I was fourteen, and nerve attacks accompanied it. I started living in a constant state of stage fright, the way you feel before your first big job interview or public speaking engagement. But in my case, the anxiety seized me for no good reason. Many people with autism find that the symptoms worsen at puberty. When my anxiety went away, it was replaced with bouts of colitis or terrible headaches. My nervous system was constantly under stress. I was like a frightened animal, and every little thing triggered a fear reaction.

For the next twenty years I tried to find psychological reasons for the panic attacks. I now realize that because of the autism, my nervous system was in a state of hypervigilance. Any minor disturbance could cause an intense reaction. I was like a high-strung cow or horse that goes into instant antipredator mode when it is surprised by an unexpected disturbance. As I got older, my anxiety attacks got worse, and even minor stresses triggered colitis or panic. By the time I was thirty, these attacks were destroying me and causing serious stress-related health problems. The intensification of my symptoms over time was similar to the well-documented worsening of symptoms that occurs in people with manic-depression and is common in other people with autism.

In my younger years, anxiety fueled my fixations and acted as a motivator. I probably never would have started my business or developed my interest in animal welfare if I had not been driven by the heightened arousal of my nervous system. At some point I realized that there were two ways to fight the nerves, either by fighting fire with fire or by retreating and becoming a housebound agoraphobic who was afraid to go to the shopping center. In high school and college I treated panic attacks as a kind of omen signifying that it was now time to reach the next door and take the next step in my life. I thought that if I faced my fears, the panic attacks would go away. Milder anxiety attacks propelled me to write pages and pages in my diary, though the more severe ones paralyzed me and made me not want to leave the house for fear of having an attack in public.

In my late twenties, these severe attacks became more and more frequent. The jet engine was blowing up, exploding instead of propelling me. My visual mind was going into overdrive, since I was desperate to find a psychological explanation for the worsening attacks. I even started classifying different anxiety symptoms as having special meanings. I thought that diffuse anxiety was more psychologically regressive than anxiety-induced colitis, because when I was sick from colitis, I did not feel nervous and fearful. While I was having bouts of colitis that lasted for months, I lost my fear of seeking out new things. The hyperaroused state of my nervous system seemed to manifest itself in different ways. The most severe anxiety left me housebound, whereas during colitis attacks I became fearless and would go out to conquer the world, following my internal map of visual symbols.

The more nervous I became, the more I would fixate, until the jet engine of anxiety started tearing me up. Visual symbols were not working, so I turned to medical science. I went to every doctor in town, but they found no physical cause for the headaches that accompanied my anxiety. I even went for a brain scan, but it did not provide an explanation either. Medical science was failing me, and I just took each day at a time and tried to get through it. My career was going reasonably well, and I had just been elected as the first woman board member of the American Society of Agricultural Consultants. But I could barely function. I remember one horrible day when I came home sweating and in a total state of fear for absolutely no reason. I sat on the couch with my heart pounding and thought, "Will the nerves ever go away?" Then somebody suggested that I try having a quiet period every afternoon. So for one hour every day, from 4:00 to 5:00 P.M., I watched *Star Trek*. This routine did help to calm my anxiety.

When I turned thirty-four I needed an operation to remove a skin cancer from my eyelid. Inflammation from the procedure triggered the most terrifying and explosive attacks I had ever experienced. I woke up in the middle of the night with my heart pounding. My fixation had suddenly switched from cattle and finding the meaning of my life to a fear of going blind. For the next week I woke up every night at 3:00 A.M. and had nightmares about not being able to see. Headaches, colitis, and plain old anxiety were now replaced with an overwhelming fear of blindness. To a visual thinker, blindness is a fate worse than death. I knew I had to do something drastic to prevent a full-scale nervous breakdown. It was then that I turned to biochemistry to help me with the anxiety disorder I had lived with my whole adult life.

Discovering Biochemistry

Six months prior to my eye surgery I had read an article titled "The Promise of Biological Psychiatry" in the February 1981 issue of *Psychology Today*. It described the use of antidepressant drugs to control anxiety. Using the library skills that Mr. Carlock had taught me, I found an important journal article by Dr. David Sheehan and his colleagues at the Harvard Medical School, with the big, impressive title "Treatment of Endogenous Anxiety with

Phobic, Hysterical and Hypochondriacal Symptoms," published in the January 1980 issue of *Archives of General Psychiatry.* This paper described research with the drugs imipramine (brand name Tofranil) and phenelzine (brand name Nardil) for controlling anxiety. When I read the list of symptoms, I knew I had found the Holy Grail. Over 90 percent of Dr. Sheehan's patients had symptoms of "spells of terror or panic," were "suddenly scared for no reason," or had "nervousness or shaking inside." Seventy percent had pounding hearts or a lump in the throat. There was a long list of twenty-seven symptoms, and I had had many of them.

Even though I suspected that the medications described in the article were the answers to my problems, I put off getting them. I did not like the idea of biochemistry. But the attacks following my eye surgery finally did me in. I took the paper out of my files and read it over and over. Like me, the patients in the study had failed to respond positively to tranquilizers such as Valium and Librium. I marked my symptoms on the symptom list, and I talked my doctor into giving me a 50-milligram dose of Tofranil per day. The effects were quick and dramatic. Within two days I felt better.

I had a great survival instinct; otherwise I would not have made it. The instinct to survive, along with my interest in science, helped me to find treatments such as the antidepressant and the squeeze machine. My technical education also helped me. To get my degrees in psychology and animal science, I had taken many veterinary and physiology courses. Reading complex medical articles was like reading a novel, and my training in library research taught me that the library was the place to look for answers.

My body was no longer in a state of hyperarousal. Before taking the drug, I had been in a constant state of physiological alertness, as if ready to flee from nonexistent predators. Many nonautistic people who are depressed and anxious also have a nervous system that is biologically prepared for flight. Small stresses of daily life that are insignificant to most people trigger anxiety attacks. Research is showing that antidepressant drugs such as Tofranil are helpful because they mimic adaptation to stress. After I had been on Tofranil for three years, I switched to desipramine (Nor-pramin), a chemical cousin of Tofranil, which was slightly more effective and had fewer side effects.

Taking these drugs caused me to look at myself in a whole new light. I stopped writing in my diary, and I found that my business started going much better because I was no longer in a driven frenzy. I stopped creating an elaborate visual symbolic world, because I no longer needed it to explain my constant anxiety. When I go back and read my diary, I miss the passion, but I never want to go back to those days. In my predrug days, anxiety drove my fixations. Interestingly, fixations I had before taking the med-ications have made a deep imprint on my emotions. Projects I created before taking these drugs still arouse more passion than those I started afterward.

The nerve attacks returned after I had been on Tofranil for three months, but they were less severe than before. I figured out that my nerve attacks came in cycles, so I resisted the urge to increase the dose of Tofranil. I also knew from past experience that the attacks would eventually subside and that they tended to get worse in the spring and fall. The first relapse occurred during a new equipment startup at a meat plant. Stress can trigger a relapse. I just toughed out the nerve attack, and it finally went away. It took willpower to stay on the same dose when the relapses came, but my 50 milligrams have kept working for all these years. I have taken antidepressants for thirteen years, and now I'm a true believer in biochemistry.

Taking the medication is like adjusting the idle adjustment screw on an old-fashioned automobile engine. Before I took Tofranil, my "engine" was racing all the time, doing so many rev-olutions per minute that it was tearing itself up. Now my nervous system is running at 55 mph instead of 200 mph, as it used to. I still have nerve cycles, but they seem to go between 55 and 90 mph instead of 150 and 200 mph. Before I took the medication, using the squeeze machine and heavy exercise calmed down my anxiety, but as I got older my nervous system became more difficult to tune. Eventually, using the squeeze machine to calm my nerves was like attempting to stop a blast furnace by spitting on it. At that point medication saved me.

When I think back to the nerve attacks in my predrug days, I realize that I often had periods of several months when my anxiety was quite low, and then suddenly a panic attack would flip a metabolic switch and my nerves would go from a tolerable 75 mph to a horrible 200 mph. It would then take several months for them to subside to 75 mph. It was like switching the speed on an industrial-strength fan by pushing a button. My nervous system instantly jumped from a brisk breeze to a roaring hurricane. Today it never gets beyond the brisk breeze level.

Panic attacks and anxiety occur in both people with autism and normal people. About half of high-functioning autistic adults have severe anxiety and panic. Lindsey Perkins, an autistic mathematician, states that when he tries to communicate with people, he begins to gag and feel panicky. Dr. Jack Gorman and his associates at Columbia University describe a process called kindling, which may explain such sudden increases in anxiety. In kindling, repeated stimulation of neurons in the limbic system of the brain, which contains the emotion centers, affects the neurons and makes them more sensitive. It's like starting a fire in kindling wood under the big logs in the fireplace. Small kindling fires often fail to ignite the logs, but then suddenly the logs catch on fire. When kindling occurred in my nervous system, I was on hair trigger. Any little stress caused a massive fear reaction.

Even though I felt relief immediately after I started the drug, however, my behavior changed slowly. There were obvious improvements that everybody noticed immediately, but over the years there have been more subtle gains. For instance, many people who have attended my lectures for some time have noticed that they keep getting smoother and better. An old friend whom I hadn't seen in seven years, since I started taking medication, informed me that I now walked with my back straight rather than hunched up. I had stopped walking with a limp and seemed like a completely different person to her. I knew that I had sometimes hunched, but I never realized that I used to sound like I was always trying to catch my breath or that I was constantly swallowing. My eye contact had also improved, and I no longer had a shifty eye. People report that they now have a more personal feeling when they talk to me.

I had another rude encounter with the effects of biochemistry after I had a hysterectomy for a giant fibroid tumor in the summer of 1992. Removal of an ovary greatly reduced the estrogen levels in my body. Without estrogen, I felt irritable and my joints ached. I was horrified to discover that the soothing, comforting effect of the squeeze machine had disappeared; the machine no longer had any effect. My feelings of empathy and gentleness were gone, and I was turning into a cranky computer. I started taking low doses of estrogen supplements. This worked very well for about a year, and then the nerve and colitis attacks returned as they had been in the old predrug days. I had not had a colitis attack for more than ten years. The panic was like the hypervigilance I had felt before. A dog barking in the middle of the night caused my heart to race.

Remembering my pre-Tofranil days, I realized that I was almost never nervous when estrogen levels were at the lowest point, during menstruation, and I figured out that I had been taking too high a dose of estrogen. When I stopped taking the estrogen pills, the anxiety attacks went away. Now I fine-tune my estrogen intake like a diabetic adjusting insulin doses. I take just enough so I can have gentle feelings of empathy but not enough to drive my nervous system into hypersensitivity and anxiety attacks. I think the reason my panic attacks started at puberty was that estrogen sensitized my nervous system. I also speculate that some of the unexplained cycles of nerves were caused by natural fluctuations in estrogen. Maybe in some months my ovaries just put out more of this hormone, and that was all it took to trigger a giant nerve attack. Now that I am closely regulating my estrogen intake, the nerve cycles are gone. The amount of estrogen I have to take sometimes varies because I still have one partially functioning ovary.

Manipulating my biochemistry has not made me a completely different person, but it has been somewhat unsettling to my idea of who and what I am to be able to adjust my emotions as if I were tuning up a car. However, I'm deeply grateful that there is an available solution and that I discovered better living through chemistry before my overactive nervous system destroyed me. Most of my problems were not caused by external stresses such as a final exam or getting fired from a job. I am one of those people who are born with a nervous system that operates in a perpetual state of fear and anxiety. Most people do not get into this state unless they go through extremely severe trauma, such as child abuse, an airplane crash, or wartime stress. I used to think it was normal to feel nervous all the time, and it was a revelation to find out that most people do not have constant anxiety attacks.

Medications for Autism

Today there are many new drug treatments that can be really helpful to people with autism. These medications are especially useful for problems which occur after puberty. Unfortunately, many medical professionals do not know how to prescribe them properly. At autism meetings I have heard countless horror stories of how giving the wrong drug to an autistic with epilepsy can cause grand mal seizures or how doctors make zombies out of people by giving them enough neuroleptics to put a horse to sleep. Parents have also told me about serious side effects; one autistic adult went berserk and wrecked a room because of an excessive dose of an antidepressant, and another slept all day because he was put on a cocktail of high doses of six different drugs.

The proper use of medications is part of a good autism program, but it is not a substitute for the proper educational or social programs. Medication can reduce anxiety, but it will not inspire a person the way a good teacher can. It seems that some people with autism are given so many powerful drugs that they act as a chemical straitjacket. An effective medication should work at a reasonable dose, and it should have a fairly dramatic obvious effect. If a drug has a negligible effect, it's probably not worth taking. Likewise, medications that work should be used and drugs that don't work should be discontinued. Since autism has such a wide range of symptoms, a drug that works for one person may be worthless for somebody else.

Research studies show that new antidepressant drugs such as clomipramine (Anafranil) and fluoxetine (Prozac) are often effective for people with autism. These are usually better first choices than the medicine I take. They have the added benefit of reducing obsessive-compulsive disorders and the racing thoughts that often afflict people with autism. Anafranil, a close chemical cousin of Norpramin and Tofranil, also boosts brain levels of serotonin, a substance that calms down the nervous system. Anafranil, Tofranil, and Norpramin must be used with extreme caution in persons with EEG abnormalities, because they sensitize the brain to epileptic seizures. Other antidepressants, such as Prozac, are safer for epileptics. All autistics must consult a physician who is knowledgeable in the use of medications for people with autism before they use any prescription medication.

Both Dr. Paul Hardy, an autism specialist in Boston, and Dr. John Ratey at the Harvard Medical School state that people with autism often require lower doses of antidepressants than nonautistic people. Doses that are effective for autism are often much lower than the doses used to treat depression, and those recommended in the *Physicians' Desk Reference* are too high for many autistics. Some only need one fourth to one third of the normal dose, although others require the full amount. Too high a dose will result in agitation, insomnia, aggression, and excitement. Dosages should be started very low and raised slowly until an effective amount is found; the dose should be stabilized at the lowest possible level. Increasing it beyond that point can have disastrous results, causing extreme aggression, touching off an epileptic seizure, or, in a few cases, triggering manic psychosis. If aggression, insomnia, or agitation occurs when the dose is increased, it must be immediately lowered. The first sign of an excessive dose is often insomnia.

This paradoxical effect may occur with all antidepressant drugs because they work on two different biochemical pathways in the brain. One pathway stimulates a person out of depression, and the other calms anxiety. Finding the right dose is a delicate balancing act, and unfortunately, many people with autism have difficulty communicating the subtle reactions they have.

At a recent Autism Society of America convention, I talked to four people who have had good results with Prozac. Prozac has received a lot of unfair bad publicity; most problems with the drug are caused by high doses. If a person starts to feel like he has drunk twenty cups of coffee, he is taking too much. Immediately lowering the dose will stop serious problems before they start. Kathy Lissner-Grant, a highly verbal, articulate person with autism, said that Prozac has really improved her life. It stopped racing obsessive thoughts, which other antidepressants had failed to stop. Twenty milligrams in the morning was effective. Two teenage autistic boys are doing well on 40 milligrams of Prozac. In some cases, the effective dose is extremely low. One twenty-six-year-old low-functioning man started socializing more after he started taking only two 20 mg capsules twice a week. Since Prozac metabolizes slowly, it is possible to prescribe low doses by giving a single 20 mg capsule every other day; Dr. Hardy reports that this works for many of his patients. A person can't skip days with other drugs, such as Tofranil and Anafranil, because they are cleared from the body quickly. Discussions with people with autism and their doctors also indicate that new drugs such as paroxetine (Paxil), fluvoxamine (Luvox), and sertraline (Zoloft) are also effective.

I have taken Norpramin continuously for over ten years without a drug holiday. I became scared of taking a break after reading that when some people with manic-depression resumed taking lithium after a hiatus, it was no longer effective. This occurs in some people and not in others, according to Dr. Alan C. Swann at the University of Texas Medical School, though there are no predictors as to which people will become immune to the drug. During my travels, I have observed two cases in which Anafranil and Tofranil stopped working when they were resumed after the patient had stopped taking them. The first case involved an autistic woman who had successfully graduated from college but whose endless obsessions had been wrecking her life. Anafranil had changed that. Her doctor discontinued the drug, but when her symptoms returned, the drug no longer worked for her. In another case, a woman with a brain stem injury became supersensitive to light, sound, and touch. Tofranil greatly reduced her sensitivities. She was taken off the drug, and it too no longer worked. However, this problem may only apply to certain drugs, such as the tricyclic antidepressants, and only under specific conditions. In the case of many other drugs, stopping and starting does not compromise the effectiveness.

There is much that is not known about medications for autism. I am one of the few people in whom successful use of the same dose of antidepressants has been maintained for over ten years. Reports from parents indicate that many serious side effects occur when the dose is raised after a relapse of anxiety or behavior problems after months of successful treatment. Some of these relapses will subside by themselves if the dose is not raised.

If I hadn't been able to apply my scientific approach to problems, I would never have discovered the medications that have saved my life. There is so much misinformation about using medication to treat autism because of all the varieties of the illness. For instance, if an autistic person has abnormalities on his or her EEG, it may be hazardous to take those antidepressants that can cause an epileptic seizure. In such people, other medications, including buspirone (Buspar), clonidine (Catapres), or beta-blockers such as Inderal (propranolol hydrochloride), have been helpful.

Buspar is a tranquilizer, and beta-blockers and clonidine are blood pressure medications. According to Dr. Ratey, beta-blockers greatly reduce aggressive behavior. Dee Landry, a high-functioning autistic woman in Colorado, told me that beta-blockers reduced her anxiety and sensory overload. She has been successfully using them for many years. I've also met two nonverbal autistic teenagers who were saved from a fate in the back ward with beta-blockers. At puberty the boys became aggressive and started knocking holes in the walls of their house. Beta-blockers enabled them to continue to live at home. Dr. Ratey informed me that he has had good success with Buspar. When Buspar is used, the low-dose principle should be followed. When beta-blockers are used, they are given at the doses that normally control blood pressure. To prevent excessive decreases in blood pressure, the dosage must be raised very slowly. The person's blood pressure should be monitored every day to make sure it does not get too low.

Another blood pressure medication that is very useful in reducing sensory oversensitivity is clonidine. Both scientific research and reports from people with autism indicate that it has improved behavior and social interaction in both children and adults. Clonidine was the highest-ranking drug for overall improvement in behavior in a parent survey conducted by Dr. Bernard Rimland for Autism Research International. Out of 118 cases, 51 percent reported that it had a beneficial effect. If the clonidine patch is used, it should not be cut in half. One parent reported that her child got a dangerous overdose when a cut patch got wet.

Tranquilizers such as diazepam (Valium) and alprazolam (Xanax) should be avoided if possible, according to Dr. Ratey. Other medications are better for long-term treatment. Methylphenidate (Ritalin) will make most people with autism much worse, but in a few known cases it has helped. Dee Landry told me that taking Ritalin has stabilized her sensory perceptions. The natural substance melatonin may help some autistic children and adults to sleep at night. Dr. Rimland's 1994 parent survey also indicated that calcium supplements were helpful in 58 percent of ninety-seven autism cases.

Each case is different. Discussions with parents, professionals, and people with autism indicate that some autistics need medications to control anxiety, panic, and obsessions, while others have mild symptoms that can be controlled with exercise and other nondrug treatments. All medications have some risk. When the decision is being made to use a medication, the risk must be weighed against the benefit.

Epileptic-like Conditions

Some autistic symptoms may be caused by epileptic-like conditions. Tiny mini-seizures that are difficult to detect on an EEG can create sensory scrambling problems, self-injurious behaviors, and outbursts of aggression. Substances that normalize electrical activity in the brain sometimes reduce autistic symptoms and improve a child's ability to understand speech.

In some cases, sudden outbursts of rage are actually frontal-lobe epilepsy. If temper tantrums or aggression appear totally out of the blue, this condition should be suspected and anticonvulsant medication might be helpful. Frontal-lobe epilepsy can be present even if an EEG test gives normal results, since it will not show up unless the person has an attack in the doctor's office.

Some of the people affected respond well to vitamin B_6 and magnesium or dimethylglycine (DMG), according to Dr. Rimland. Studies in France have shown that these supplements improve behavior and help normalize brain electrical activity in hospitalized patients with autism. They appear to be most effective for people who have epileptic-like symptoms, such as sudden outbursts of rage or laughing one minute and crying the next. They have also been effective in young children who start to develop normal language and then lose their ability to speak and understand speech.

In severely impaired nonverbal children, the use of anticonvulsants early in life may improve speech by reducing auditory processing problems that make understanding speech nearly impossible. Parents have reported in a few cases that vitamin B_6 and magnesium supplements improved speech. New medications for epilepsy are a very promising area of research. A new epilepsy drug called felbamate (Felbatol) has recently been cleared by the Food and Drug Administration. This drug has helped two young children with severe impairments. One had no ability to understand speech, and the other was very aggressive and so impulsive that she was uncontrollable. Felbatol brought speech back to the first and drastically improved the behavior of the second. However, this drug must be used with great caution, because it can cause aplastic anemia. Frequent blood testing may be required to prevent possibly fatal complications.

Christopher Gilberg, a noted researcher in Sweden, has reported that an epilepsy drug called ethosuximide (Zarontin) stopped autistic symptoms and made speech return in a severely autistic child. Dr. Andrius Plioplys, at Mercy Hospital in Chicago, has found that autistic symptoms were reduced in three children aged three to five when they were given the anticonvulsant drug valproic acid (Depakene). They had no seizures, but there were some abnormalities on their EEGs. These treatments are most likely to have the best effect in young children. Besides improving auditory processing so that the child can hear speech accurately, the drugs may improve speech if given at a young age, when the brain is most receptive to learning language.

There is a great need for detailed research to find the specific autism subtypes in which anticonvulsant drugs are most effective. I speculate that they may be of most help for the kind of autistic child who appears to develop normally until eighteen to twenty-four months and then loses both speech and social interaction. This kind of child is more likely than others to have epileptic seizures and abnormalities that are easily detected on neurological tests. Neurological examination often indicates that such children give more evidence of central nervous system impairment than highly verbal autistic children. However, some children who have normal results on neurological tests may also benefit from anti-convulsant drugs. The tests may not be sensitive enough to detect their abnormalities. I had the kind of autism in which there was no period of normal language development. Unfortunately, the present diagnostic system lumps all autism types into the same diagnosis. From a medication standpoint, this is like mixing apples and oranges.

When loss of language occurs after age three, the disorder is usually called not autism but either acquired aphasia disintegrative disorder or Landau-Kleffner syndrome. One boy with Landau-Kleffner syndrome told his mother that there was something wrong with his ears and that his brain was not working right. He could not hear speech because of a buzzing noise in his ears. Children with full-blown Landau-Kleffner syndrome often show autistic behavior, and if they do not lose all their speech, it is greatly impaired, consisting of only a few nouns and verbs. They also speak in a monotone.

Dr. Pinchas Lerman in Israel has found that treatment with corticosteroids sometimes improves language. Prednisone has been used, but it has very severe side effects and should only be given if it has a dramatic positive effect on a child with severe autistic behavior. Dr. Lerman believes that treating the symptoms when they first appear improves the drug's effectiveness. The longer the brain is bombarded with epileptic activity, the more difficult the child may find it to recover speech. This is an area that needs further research. Since loss of language may be due to immaturity of the nervous system, it is possible that the steroids should be given for only a short period.

Treatment for Self-Abuse

A few people with autism engage in self-injury by either hitting their heads or biting themselves. There has been considerable research on the drug naltrexone (Trexan) for stopping such self-abuse. This drug, which is normally used for treating heroin over-doses, works by blocking the action of the brain's own opiates. Several different research studies have shown that it is often highly effective in stopping severe self-abuse in which an autistic person bangs his head, bites himself, or hits his eyes. In a study by Rowland Barrett and his colleagues at Emma Pendleton Bradley Hospital in Rhode Island, naltrexone was successfully used on a short-term basis to break the cycle of self-abuse.

When naltrexone is first given, self-abuse may temporarily escalate as the person attempts to get his opiate fix. The drug has the same effect on stallions that bite their own chests: the biting temporarily gets worse and then stops when the horse realizes it can no longer get its endorphin fix. In both animals and people, sensory integration methods such as massage, brushing the skin, and deep pressure can sometimes stop self-abuse without the use of drugs. A vibrator applied to the body part that is attacked is often helpful. Follow-up of a short series of naltrexone doses with sensory integration may help prevent a return of the problem.

Lorna King, an occupational therapist in Phoenix, Arizona, has observed that children who are self-abusive do not appear to feel pain. To reduce self-abuse, she does sensory integration exercises such as applying deep pressure by rolling the child up in a heavy mat and swinging on a swing. As the abusive behavior decreases, the ability to feel pain returns. Lorna emphasizes that sensory integration procedures must never be administered immediately after someone has hit himself, because they would inadvertently reward the self-abuse. It is best to do the exercises at set times each day so they will not be associated with self-injury.

Jack Panksepp, at Bowling Green University, has found that naltrexone has also helped autistic children become more social, though finding the right dose is critical. The main reason this drug has not been used much in the United States is its extremely high cost. It has been marketed as a one-dose treatment for heroin overdose. However, a new version used for treating alcoholism may be less expensive.

An alternative for self-injury is Prozac. At a meeting I learned that one man completely stopped abusing his body when he took Prozac in combination with tryptophan (a natural substance in milk, meat, and tropical fruits that increases serotonin levels and enhances the effect of Prozac). These two substances must be used together with great caution to prevent serotonin overdose. Unfortunately, tryptophan supplements are not available in the United States, because the substance was banned by the FDA after some people died from taking supplements from a contaminated batch. The FDA has been overzealous in regulating alternative treatments, and removal of tryptophan from the market has hurt people with autism. The FDA is also attempting to regulate other supplements that are useful to autistic people, such as melatonin, DMG, B_6, and magnesium.

Similarly, some medical professionals are hostile toward so-called natural treatments, which have often failed to work in controlled studies. The most sensible explanation for some of these failures is that autism is a very wide-ranging disorder with many subtypes involving different biochemical abnormalities. A supplement such as tryptophan will work on one autistic person and have no effect on another. Some of these supplements may work on only 10 percent of the autistic population, but for these people they are very helpful.

Neuroleptics

Some professionals may criticize me for writing about highly controversial experimental treatments, but experimentation with anticonvulsant drugs is far less dangerous than the high doses of neuroleptic drugs that some doctors give out like candy. Drugs such as haloperidol (Haldol) and thioridazine (Mellaril) are sometimes used in institutions to turn autistic people into zombies.

Neuroleptic drugs are very toxic to the nervous system, and staying on high doses of these drugs will almost always damage the nervous system and cause a movement disorder called tardive dyskinesia, similar to Parkinson's disease. The intended purpose of neuroleptic drugs is to treat hallucinations in schizophrenics. For schizophrenics, taking Haldol can mean the difference between having a relatively normal life and being totally out of control. That choice makes the risk of serious side effects acceptable.

Some people with autism also have Tourette's syndrome, a disorder in which the person makes repeated involuntary movements (tics) or says a short word involuntarily many times a day. These persons often respond well to a very low dose of Haldol. Haldol and Catapres are two medications that work for Tourette's. But people with autism who do not have Tourette's should usually avoid Haldol. Anyone in whom Tourette's is suspected or who has a family history of Tourette's should also avoid Ritalin, which can make Tourette's syndrome worse.

There will always be claims for magic breakthroughs and setbacks in the treatment of such a confounding disorder as autism. Most important for the autistic child or adult is a knowledgeable, open-minded physician who will try different medications, carefully observe their effect, and try new approaches if the first doesn't work. It is best to avoid mixing a whole bunch of drugs and suddenly stopping treatment. Dosages should be decreased gradually after long-term use, since abrupt withdrawal of certain drugs can have serious consequences. Some drug combinations also have strange interactions. Two parents of autistic children have reported that Prozac mixed with the anticonvulsant drug carbamazepine (Tegretol) made their children too sleepy to function well, although Prozac normally acts as a stimulant. Giving an autistic person two or three drugs in the same medication category makes no sense at all, but giving up to three drugs from different categories—beta-blockers, anticonvulsants, neuroleptics, tricyclic antidepressants, serotonin reuptake inhibitors, and antidepressants—may be an effective treatment in certain cases. Nonetheless, I have seen too many autistic people who have been overmedicated. Parents and teachers who see a person with autism for many hours each day are often in the best position to determine whether a medication is effective, though intelligent, verbal patients should be actively involved in evaluating their own drug treatments.

Many doctors also dismiss the idea that allergies and food intolerances can have an effect on autistic symptoms. These problems tend to be worse in more severe cases. Hundreds of parents have informed me that removing foods such as milk, wheat, corn, chocolate, and tomatoes from a child's diet has greatly improved behavior. There have been no cures, but there have been improvements. The foods that are most likely to cause allergic reactions are ones that formed a major part of the diet for the very young child. Often the foods that cause an increase in bad behavior are the ones that the child likes, and sometimes a child will crave the forbidden foods. Standard skin scratch tests for allergies are often unreliable and may fail to detect food allergies. One way to check is to put the child on a diet that temporarily eliminates two of the worst sources of allergies, milk and grain gluten. If milk and dairy products are removed, however, the child must be given calcium supplements for bone growth and nerve function.

Parents and teachers should join support groups such as the Autism Society of America to obtain the latest information on treatments. Through newsletters and other communications, these groups often provide information about new treatments before the professionals do. Autism is a field in which there have been many treatment fads and wild claims about cures. Each new development has been helpful, but there is not going to be an instant, magic treatment that will cure autism as if it were a broken leg.

Many desperate parents spend thousands of dollars and much heartache on endless medical tests at different hospitals. After a few basic tests are done, including a good neurological exam to rule out treatable medical conditions such as a brain tumor, epilepsy, thyroid problems, hydrocephaly, and metabolic problems such as undiagnosed phenylketonuria, tests are a big waste of money. It is better to spend limited financial resources on getting the child into a good educational program by age two or three. The drugs described in this chapter all require a doctor's prescription. As mentioned before, the care of a physician who is both knowledgeable about autism and open-minded about its treatment is essential. My message for parents is simple, and it's advice that a good doctor gave my mother over forty years ago: trust your instincts about doctors, about medications, about yourself, and, most important, about your child.

Believer in Biochemistry

Even though the medical information in *Thinking in Pictures* is over ten years old, it is still accurate. The principle of using lower than normal doses of SSRI (selective seratonin reuptake inhibitors), antidepressants such as Prozac (fluoxetine), Zoloft (sertraline), Paxil (paraxetine), and Celexa (citalopram) is still correct. Many parents keep telling me the same story. "He did really well on a low dose, but he became agitated and could not sleep on a higher dose." The biggest mistake made with all types of antidepressants is that the dose gets raised when it should be lowered. Due to serotonin abnormalities in the brain, people on the spectrum often need lower doses of antidepressants. Sometimes one half to one third of the normal starter dose is all that is needed. Many people on the spectrum have told me that SSRIs are effective for reducing anxiety.

There are many SSRIs on the market. Dr. Max Wiznitzer, Rainbow Children's Hospital in Cleveland, Ohio, Dr. Ed Cook from Chicago, and Dr. Eric Hollander from Mt. Sinai Hospital in New York often use Prozac in high-functioning teenagers and adults. I know many professional people taking Prozac. When they were put on the correct dose they told me they felt great and it had no effect on their intellectual ability. Prozac is the only SSRI that is fully approved by the Food and Drug Administration (FDA) for individuals under eighteen years of age. Zoloft has limited FDA approval for treating obsessive-compulsive disorder in children. Doctors are allowed to prescribe other nonapproved medications to children by going "off-label." This means that the doctor prescribes the drug for a purpose that is not on the drug's label. Off-label prescribing of drugs is done for many diseases. Some effective cancer treatments are "off-label" prescriptions.

Brains are different and some people will do better on one of the other SSRIs such as Zoloft. Try something that worked well in a genetically related relative. Japanese researchers report that differences in how well an individual with autism responds to SSRIs is affected by differences in serotonin genetics. Discussions with both doctors and individuals with autism have indicated that in some people, Paxil caused memory problems. However, if Paxil is working well for an individual, it would probably be best to keep taking it.

How to Make Medication Decisions

All medications have risks. One must weigh the risk against the benefit. A basic principle is to try one thing at a time. If a child enrolls in a new school or starts some other therapy at the same time a medicine is tried, it will be difficult to determine if the medicine is effective. If possible, wait two to five weeks between trying different things. Do not start a diet or supplement at the same time a medication is started.

To make a drug worth the risk, it must have an obvious benefit. One should say, "Wow, this stuff works!" Giving a child a powerful drug to make him slightly less hyper is probably not worth the risk. Giving a teenager or an adult who has uncontrollable rage a powerful medication to stop rage is probably worth the risk, if the drug prevents him from being kicked out of his school program or group home. When medications are used properly, they help to normalize function. Drugs must never be used to control a person by oversedation.

Drug interactions *must* be looked up. Prescription drugs have many interactions with over-the-counter and herbal remedies. For example, sinus or allergy medicine may reduce the effectiveness of antidepressants. One drug may either block or speed up the metabolism of another drug. When this occurs, doses will have to be lowered or raised. Some interactions are very dangerous. St. John's Wort may make HIV/AIDS drugs less effective. Taking St. John's Wort and antidepressants at the same time may cause mania. Other drug interactions can cause risky increases in blood pressure. Grapefruit juice interacts badly with many drugs. Dr. Joe Huggins, an autism specialist in Canada, explains that it can have an unpredictable enhancement effect on many drugs. Orange juice does not have this same effect. Some nutritional supplements are blood thinners. Taking too many blood thinning supplements or combining them with aspirin may be hazardous. I made this mistake and had severe nosebleeds.

One must also be careful switching brands of drugs. When I tried switching my antidepressant to a generic, it did not have the same effect. A good friend of mine had a similar problem. Differences in the way a pill is manufactured may affect the rate it is absorbed. This may require adjustment of the dose. If a generic is being used, it is best to keep using the same brand.

New Drugs Are Not Always Better

I am still taking the same low dose of Norpramin (desipramine) antidepressant. I have been on this drug for twenty-five years. Reports from parents indicate that switching an individual who is stable on an old drug to something different sometimes has bad results. If the individual is doing well and is stable on a reasonable dose of something old, it may be best to keep taking it. My old drug is probably not a good first choice for a new patient but it is working well for me. I forgot to take it one time for three days and I felt depressed. Unfortunately drug studies in most scientific papers are short-term studies of a few months. So when a new drug is marketed, little is known about long-term risks. There are almost no studies on long-term patients like me and I do not dare stop taking the drug. I have seen too many disasters when a person who was stable stopped taking their medication.

Atypical Antipsychotics

The atypical class of medications was not available when I wrote *Thinking in Pictures.* Treatment of schizophrenia was the original reason these drugs were developed. Atypicals work on both the serotonin system and the dopamine system in the brain. The main use of these drugs for individuals on the autism spectrum is to control rage in teenagers and adults. In some cases, they may be given to older children. Dr. Christopher McDougal at Indiana University School of Medicine uses atypicals for severe cases of self-injury, but Dr. Max Witznitzer reports success with treating self-injury with naltrexone. The five atypical medications that were available when this update was written are Risperdal (risperidone), Zyprexa (olanzapine), Geodon (ziprasidone), Seroquel (quetiapine fumerate), and Abilify (aripiprazole).

Risperdal was one of the first atypicals that was developed. Scientific studies show that it is a very effective drug for severe rage and aggression in older children and adults with autism. Compared to other medications such as Prozac, Zoloft, beta-blockers or Naltrexone, atypical drugs have *severe* long-term side effects. Since they have greater risks, a greater benefit is required to make them worth the risk.

There are reports in the scientific literature that tardive dyskinesia (a Parkinson's-like condition) has occurred in some individuals who take Risperdal. Weight gain is another major serious side effect of Risperdal and Zyprexa because they stimulate appetite. Some individuals have gained over one hundred pounds and the drugs may also increase the risk of getting diabetes. Seroquel and Geodon cause less weight gain and they can be substituted for Risperdal. However, Dr. McDougal reports that Seroquel may be less effective than Risperdal for controlling rage.

Side effects can be reduced by using very low doses of the atypicals. These doses may be lower than the starter doses recommended on the label. Dr. Joe Huggins uses low doses of less than 2 mg per day of Risperdal. Dr. Bennett Leventhal, a Chicago autism specialist, states that he uses very low doses of Abilify. He says it works like two different drugs depending on the dose. He recommends using low doses. The pharmaceutical companies have also developed medications that combine an SSRI with an atypical. Some autism specialists do not recommend these combination drugs and state that it is better to use the two agents separately.

Black Box Warnings

The Food and Drug Administration has placed "black box" warnings on drugs that may have greater risks. Many drugs have these "black box" warnings but very careful monitoring reduces risks. Dr. Michelle Riba and Dr. Steven Sharfstein, past presidents of the American Psychiatric Association, are deeply concerned that the black box warning label on SSRI and tricyclic antidepressants that warn of suicidal thoughts in children and adolescents "may have a chilling effect on appropriate prescriptions for patients." They are concerned that individuals who need these drugs will not get them. An article in *Science* indicates that doses that are too high may be the cause of some of the problems with suicidal thoughts. Some patients reported they felt like they were jumping out of their skin. Dr. Martin Teachers of McLean Hospital in Boston states some of the doses of SSRIs were too high. The slight increase in suicidal thinking may occur during the first few weeks when the correct antidepressant dose is being determined. The risks of suicidal thinking are low. Paxil (paroxetine) may be associated with greater risks. The last two sentences of the Food and Drug Administration's black box warning reads, "The average risks of such events in patients receiving antidepressants was 4 percent, twice the placebo risk of 2 percent. No suicides occurred in these trials." Trials were conducted on 4,400 patients. However, risks from atypicals, such as weight gain and tardive dyskinesia, may worsen the longer the individual is on the drug. Problems with antidepressants usually occur during the first few weeks and then the risk is reduced. Compared to antidepressants, atypicals have more serious long-term risks.

It is important to read the actual wording in a black box warning in order to make a wise decision. Many things have risks. Both cars and stairs are dangerous, but we use them every day.

Nothing is risk-free. My old antidepressant now has a black box warning and I am going to continue to take it.

ADHD and Asperger's

Some individual with Asperger's may also receive a diagnosis of Attention Deficit Hyperactivity Disorder. Some Asperger individuals have good results with stimulant drugs such as Ritalin. With high-functioning people with either autism or Asperger's, stimulants or other ADHD drugs may have either a beneficial effect or a really bad effect. A person with autism who works in the computer industry has found that Prozac and Ritalin have been effective. However, individuals on the lower end of the autism spectrum often have bad results with ADHD medications. Stimulants must be used very cautiously in individuals with possible heart (cardiac) abnormalities. The long-acting formulations of stimulants may have greater risks. Parents have told me that in some children, switching to a long acting formulation caused problems.

Medications for Nonverbal Adults

Dr. Joe Huggins treats the most difficult low-functioning cases, people who have been thrown out of sheltered workshops or group homes due to rage or self-abuse. For this population, Dr. Huggins avoids the SSRIs such as Prozac and uses Risperdal, beta-blockers, and the anticonvulsant valproic acid. He uses Risperdal to control rage and keeps the dose under 2 mg per day. The anticonvulsant valproic acid is used to control aggression that occurs randomly and Risperdal works best for rage that is directed at people. Valproic acid controls rages that are caused by tiny seizures. If rage attacks that are not related to a specific place, per-

son, or task occur, try valproic acid. Anticonvulsants such as valproic acid have to be given at the regular high adult dose. Valproic
acid and some of the older anticonvulsants have a severe black box
warning about liver and blood damage. Blood tests *must* be done
to monitor for problems so that the drug can be stopped before
permanent damage occurs. Problems are most likely to occur in
the first six months and then the risk is reduced. Newer anticonvulsants are safer and can be used as a substitute but it may be less
effective. However, Dr. Huggins has found that valproic acid is a
very effective medication. Research has also shown that a similar
drug called Depakote (divalproex) is effective for controlling
explosive temper.

Dr. Huggins recommends beta-blockers such as propranolol
for hot and sweaty undirected rage. The individual may sound out
of breath and the rage is often not directed at a particular person.
Dr. Max Wiznitzer calls beta-blockers underappreciated drugs
that can be useful. They must not be used in people who have
asthma.

Diet and Vitamin Supplements for Autism

Discussion with many parents has indicated that the casein (dairy)
free and gluten (wheat) free diet has improved language and
reduced behavior problems in some children and adults. The best
results often occur in children who appear normal and then
regress at eighteen to twenty-four months and lose language. A
very simple but strict dairy- and gluten-free diet would consist of
rice, potatoes, beef, chicken, fish, pork, eggs, fruits, and vegeta-
bles. Olive oil can be substituted for butter. In the beginning it is
best to use all fresh, unprocessed meats and produce. Soy products
must be avoided and drinks loaded with sugar should be reduced.
If the diet is going to work, the good effects should become
apparent within two to four weeks. Individuals who stay on this

diet must take vitamins and calcium supplements. If the diet works, there are special casein- and gluten-free breads and cookies that will add variety. Dr. Max Wiznitzer stated that parents have reported that the supplement DMG appeared to have beneficial results. Studies conducted in Norway by Dr. Knivsbreg and his colleagues indicated that the diet was helpful. Children on the spectrum are highly variable. Treatments such as the diet may really help one child and have little effect on others. The highly variable symptoms in individuals with autism make valid scientific studies difficult because some individuals will respond to the diet while others do not. In very young children age two to six, it may be better to avoid drugs and try the diet and some of the vitamin supplements first. Some children have good responses from some of the nutritional supplements which provide omega-3 fatty acids. One study showed that fish oil and evening primrose supplements reduced ADHD symptoms and improved both reading and spelling in children. More information is available from the Autism Research Institute in San Diego, California. Gastrointestinal problems are more common in autistic compared to normal children. Autistic children who have these problems should be treated by a specialist.

Choosing Treatments

People often get into arguments about alternative versus conventional treatments. Sometimes a combination works best. Donna Williams has found that a tiny ¼ mg-per-day dose of Risperdal combined with the casein- and gluten-free diet worked better than either thing by itself. Prior to taking the Risperdal, she was unable to attend meetings in a large convention center due to sensory overload. In another adult, Zoloft combined with a gluten-free diet has reduced both headaches and sensory sensitivity problems. For both conventional medications and nutritional/biomedical approaches, avoid making the mistake of taking too many things. Adding more and more medications or supplements is a mistake and the risks of harmful interactions increase. Use careful logical evaluation to find the items that work and to stop using things that do not work.

7

DATING DATA

Autism and Relationships

MANY PEOPLE with autism are fans of the television show *Star Trek*. I have been a fan since the show started. When I was in college, it greatly influenced my thinking, as each episode of the original series had a moral point. The characters had a set of firm moral principles to follow, which came from the United Federation of Planets. I strongly identified with the logical Mr. Spock, since I completely related to his way of thinking.

I vividly remember one old episode because it portrayed a conflict between logic and emotion in a manner I could understand. A monster was attempting to smash the shuttle craft with rocks. A crew member had been killed. Logical Mr. Spock wanted to take off and escape before the monster wrecked the craft. The other crew members refused to leave until they had retrieved the body of the dead crew member. To Spock, it made no sense to rescue a dead body when the shuttle was being battered to pieces. But the feeling of attachment drove the others to retrieve the body so their fellow crew member could have a proper funeral. It may sound simplistic, but this episode helped me finally understand how I was different. I agreed with Spock, but I learned that emotions will often overpower logical thinking, even if these decisions prove hazardous.

Social interactions that come naturally to most people can be daunting for people with autism. As a child, I was like an animal that had no instincts to guide me; I just had to learn by trial and error. I was always observing, trying to work out the best way to behave, but I never fit in. I had to think about every social interaction. When other students swooned over the Beatles, I called their reaction an ISP—interesting sociological phenomenon. I was a scientist trying to figure out the ways of the natives. I wanted to participate, but I did not know how.

In my high school diary I wrote: "One should not always be a watcher—the cold impersonal observer—but instead should participate." Even today, my thinking is from the vantage point of an observer. I did not realize that this was different until two years ago, when I took a test in which a piece of classical music evoked vivid images in my imagination. My images were similar to other people's, but I always imagined them as an observer. Most people see themselves participating in their images. For instance, one musical passage evoked the image of a boat floating on a sparkling sea. My imagery was like a postcard photograph, whereas most other people imagined themselves on the boat.

All my life I have been an observer, and I have always felt like someone who watches from the outside. I could not participate in the social interactions of high school life. First of all, I could not understand why clothes were so important when there were much more interesting things to think about and do in the science lab. Electronics and experimental psychology were much more intriguing than clothes. My peers spent hours standing around talking about jewelry or some other topic with no real substance. What did they get out of this? I just did not fit in. I never fit in with the crowd, but I had a few friends who were interested in the same things, such as skiing and riding horses. Friendship always revolved around what I did rather than who I was.

Even today, personal relationships are something I don't really understand. And I still consider sex to be the biggest, most important "sin of the system," to use my old high school term. It has caused the downfall of many reputations and careers. From reading books and talking to people at conventions, I have learned that the autistic people who adapt most successfully in personal relationships either choose celibacy or marry a person with similar disabilities. By successful adaptation, I mean being able to lead a productive, satisfying life. Marriages work out best when two people with autism marry or when a person with autism marries a handicapped or eccentric spouse. The two partners get together because they have similar interests, not because of physical attraction. They are attracted because their intellects work on a similar wavelength.

I've remained celibate because doing so helps me to avoid the many complicated social situations that are too difficult for me to handle. For most people with autism, physical closeness is as much a problem as not understanding basic social behaviors. At conventions I have talked to several women who were raped on dates because they did not understand the subtle cues of sexual interest. Likewise, men who want to date often don't understand how to relate to a woman. They remind me of Data, the android on *Star Trek*. In one episode, Data's attempts at dating were a disaster. When he tried to be romantic, he complimented his date by using scientific terminology. Even very able adults with autism have such problems.

In *News from the Border*, Paul McDonnell describes an experience with dating, explaining that "things were going fine between us until I started being obsessed with seeing her very often." Paul realized that he was pushing the woman to spend more and more time with him when she just wanted to be friends. He was not able to recognize that his girlfriend didn't want constant togetherness. Autistic adults with more rigid thinking have even worse problems when they attempt to date. They have no idea of appropriate behavior. One young man became interested in a girl and went to her house wearing a football helmet to disguise himself. He thought that it would be all right to look in her windows. In his literal, visual mind he thought that since he would not be recognized, it was okay to stand outside and watch for her.

Although business relationships can easily be learned by rote, dating is difficult. The social skills one needs to rent an apartment and keep a job were easier for me to learn than the social skills for dating, because I have very few emotional cues to guide me during complex social interactions. After one of my lectures, I received a totally inappropriate Valentine from a young man with autism. It was the kind of Valentine that third-graders give to each other. He expected me to consider it as a serious proposal and was disappointed when I ignored him. I did not write back, because I have learned from experience that responding to this kind of mail just encourages it. His teachers need to explain to him that making a proposal to someone you have just met is not acceptable. Like me, he has to be taught the rules of social interaction just as he is taught spelling. When I have to deal with family relationships, when people are responding to each other with emotion rather than intellect, I need to have long discussions with friends who can serve as translators. I need help in understanding social behavior that is driven by complex feelings rather than logic.

Hans Asperger stated that normal children acquire social skills without being consciously aware because they learn by instinct. In people with autism, "Social adaptation has to proceed via intellect." Jim, the twenty-seven-year-old autistic graduate student I have mentioned in previous chapters, made a similar observation. He stated that people with autism lack the basic instincts that make communication a natural process. Autistic children have to learn social skills systematically, the same way they learn their school lessons. Jim Sinclair summed it up when he said, "Social interactions involve things that most people know without having to learn them." He himself had to ask many detailed questions about experiences other people were having to figure out how to respond appropriately. He describes how he had to work out a "separate translation code" for every new person. Similarly,

Tony W. had an intellectual awareness of how other people felt, but he did not experience those feelings himself. Donna Williams described how she copied emotions so that she acted normal, but it was a purely mechanical process, like retrieving files from a computer.

I do not read subtle emotional cues. I have had to learn by trial and error what certain gestures and facial expressions mean. When I started my career, I often made initial contacts on the telephone, which was easier because I did not have to deal with complex social signals. This helped me get my foot in the front door. After the initial call, I would send the client a project proposal and a brochure showing pictures of previous jobs. The call enabled me to show my qualifications without showing my nerdy self—until I was hired to design the project. I was also good at selling advertising for the Arizona Cattle Feeders' Association annual magazine on the telephone. I just called up a big company and asked for its advertising department. I had no fear of anyone's rank or social position. Other people with autism have also found that becoming friends with somebody on the phone is easier than building a face-to-face relationship, because there are fewer social cues to deal with.

Autistic people tend to have difficulty lying because of the complex emotions involved in deception. I become extremely anxious when I have to tell a little white lie on the spur of the moment. To be able to tell the smallest fib, I have to rehearse it many times in my mind. I run video simulations of all the different things the other person might ask. If the other person comes up with an unexpected question, I panic. Being deceptive while interacting with someone is extremely difficult unless I have fully rehearsed all possible responses. Lying is very anxiety-provoking because it requires rapid interpretations of subtle social cues to determine whether the other person is really being deceived.

Some researchers don't believe autistics are capable of deception. They subscribe to Uta Frith's conception of autism, wherein people with the syndrome lack a "theory of mind." According to

Frith, many people with autism are not able to figure out what another person may be thinking. It is true that autistics with severe cognitive deficits are unable to look at situations from the vantage point of another person. But I have always used visualization and logic to solve problems and work out how people will react, and I have always understood deception.

As a schoolchild, I played hide-and-seek. I learned how to trick the seeker into going the wrong way by stuffing my coat with leaves and putting it in a tree. I also had my entire boarding school believing that they had seen a flying saucer when I swung a cardboard saucer containing a flashlight in front of another girl's window. When she asked me about it, I told her she had probably seen a piece of insulation falling from the roof of our unfinished dormitory. I had rehearsed a whole bunch of explanations for the sighting, including the falling insulation, so she wouldn't connect my absence with the appearance of the saucer. My ploy was successful. Within two days, most of the students thought that a real flying saucer had been sighted. This deception was easy because I had gone over in my imagination all the stories I was going to tell.

I've always enjoyed these kinds of tricks, because they require a vivid imagination, which I have in abundance. I'm motivated by the same challenge that makes hackers break into computers. I really identify with clever hackers. If I were fourteen years old today, I'm sure I'd be hacking away just for the thrill of seeing whether I could do it. I would never engage in harmful deceptions, though. In some ways I guess these tricks are a substitute for deeper human connection. They enable me to penetrate the world of other people without having to interact with them.

Often people with autism are taken advantage of. Paul McDonnell wrote about the painful experience of being betrayed by somebody he thought was his friend, having his money stolen and his car damaged. He didn't recognize the social signals of trouble. It is easy for me to understand the concept of deception when it involves playing tricks with flying saucers or stuffing coats with leaves, but understanding the social cues that indicate an insincere person is much more difficult. In college I was betrayed by students who pretended to be my friends. I told them my innermost thoughts, and the next thing I knew they were laughing about them at a party.

Over time, I have built up a tremendous library of memories of past experiences, TV, movies, and newspapers to spare me the social embarrassments caused by my autism, and I use these to guide the decision process in a totally logical way. I have learned from experience that certain behaviors make people mad. Earlier in my life, my logical decisions were often wrong because they were based on insufficient data. Today they are much better, because my memory contains more information. Using my visualization ability, I observe myself from a distance. I call this my little scientist in the corner, as if I'm a little bird watching my own behavior from up high. This idea has also been reported by other people with autism. Dr. Asperger noted that autistic children observe themselves constantly. They see themselves as an object of interest. Sean Barron, in his book *There's a Boy in There,* describes having conversations with himself to figure out social mistakes. He divides himself into two people and acts out the conversation.

According to Antonio Damasio, people who suddenly lose emotions because of strokes often make disastrous financial and social decisions. These patients have completely normal thoughts, and they respond normally when asked about hypothetical social situations. But their performance plummets when they have to make rapid decisions without emotional cues. It must be like suddenly becoming autistic. I can handle situations where stroke patients may fail because I never relied on emotional cues in the first place. At age forty-seven, I have a vast databank, but it has taken me years to build up my library of experiences and learn how to behave in an appropriate manner. I did not know until very recently that most people rely heavily on emotional cues.

After many years I have learned—by rote—how to act in different situations. I can speed-search my CD-ROM memory of videotapes and make a decision quite quickly. Doing this visually may be easier than doing it with verbal thinking. And, as I have said, I try to avoid situations where I can get into trouble. As a child, I found picking up social cues impossible. When my parents were thinking about getting divorced, my sister felt the tension, but I felt nothing, because the signs were subtle. My parents never had big fights in front of us. The signs of emotional friction were stressful to my sister, but I didn't even see them. Since my parents were not showing obvious, overt anger toward each other, I just did not comprehend.

Social interaction is further complicated by the physiological problems of attention shifting. Since people with autism require much more time than others to shift their attention between auditory and visual stimuli, they find it more difficult to follow rapidly changing, complex social interaction. These problems may be a part of the reason that Jack, a man with autism, said, "If I relate to people too much, I become nervous and uncomfortable." Learning social skills can be greatly helped with videotapes. I gradually learned to improve my public speaking by watching tapes and by becoming aware of easily quantifiable cues, such as rustling papers that indicate boredom. It is a slow process of continuous improvement. There are no sudden breakthroughs.

Figuring out how to interact socially was much more difficult than solving an engineering problem. I found it relatively easy to program my visual memory with the knowledge of cattle dipping vats or corral designs. Recently I attended a lecture where a social scientist said that humans do not think like computers. That night at a dinner party I told this scientist and her friends that my thought patterns resemble computing and that I am able to explain my thought processes step by step. I was kind of shocked when she told me that she is unable to describe how her thoughts and emotions are joined. She said that when she thinks about something, the factual information and the emotions are combined into a seamless whole. I finally understood why so many people allow emotions to distort the facts. My mind can always separate the two. Even when I am very upset, I keep reviewing the facts over and over until I can come to a logical conclusion.

Over the years, I have learned to be more tactful and diplomatic. I have learned never to go over the head of the person who hired me unless I have his or her permission. From past experiences I have learned to avoid situations in which I could be exploited and to stroke egos that may feel threatened. To master diplomacy, I read about business dealings and international negotiations in the *Wall Street Journal* and other publications. I then used them as models.

I know that things are missing in my life, but I have an exciting career that occupies my every waking hour. Keeping myself busy keeps my mind off what I may be missing. Sometimes parents and professionals worry too much about the social life of an adult with autism. I make social contacts via my work. If a person develops her talents, she will have contacts with people who share her interests.

During the past twenty years, for example, I've worked with Jim Uhl. He has constructed more than twenty of my projects, and he is one of my closest friends. Construction is his life. His business started in a tiny toolshed at the back of his home and has grown into a major company that does big jobs for the Arizona Department of Transportation and the mines. We just love to talk about contracting. Some of the best times of my life have been working on construction projects. I can relate to people who produce tangible results. Seeing my drawings turn into steel and concrete turns me on. Construction workers love to complain about stupid people in the front office, and I fit right in when they bitch about the "suits and ties" from the office who don't understand equipment or construction. Over the years I have worked with many crews and many different contractors. They all like to complain and tell construction war stories. I have no trouble being with them, and I become one of the guys. Another reason I fit in with construction workers and technical people is that we are mostly visual thinkers.

I am told by my nonautistic friends that relationships with other people are what most people live for, whereas I get very attached to my projects and to certain places. Last year Jim and I drove out to Scottsdale Feedyard, which is now closed and partially torn down. All that was left were a few posts, some tanks at the feed mill, and a deserted, wrecked office. The pens had been sold for scrap steel. It upset me very much and I didn't know if we should have come. The windows in the manager's office were broken, and the rain had warped the wood paneling. One of the few posts still standing was from the door in the fence where twenty years ago I had been blocked by the cowboy foreman.

Watching the Swift plant slowly self-destruct and knowing it was going to close was very upsetting for me. I guess my relationships with Tom Rohrer and Norb Goscowitz and the other people there were the closest I've had. The Swift plant was the place where I had had some of my deepest thoughts about the meaning of life. Memories of its closing are much more devastating than any other memory. I still can't write about it without crying.

My sense of identity was tied up with that plant, just as the things I had in my high school room were my identity. Then, when I went away for the summer, I did not want to pack any of my wall decorations away because I felt I would somehow lose myself. I had a special attic room in the dormitory where I went to think and meditate. Going to the special room, known as the Crow's Nest, was essential to my sense of well-being. When the construction of the dorm was finished, I no longer had free access to it; a locked door prohibited me from entering. I was so upset that the headmaster gave me a key.

I also remember becoming upset when my Aunt Breechan died, but I was even more distraught when I found out that her ranch was for sale. The idea of the loss of the place made me grief-stricken. Hans Asperger also observed a strong attachment to places in autistics, noting that autistic children take longer to get over homesickness than normal children. There is an emotional bonding to the routines and objects at home. Maybe this is because of the lack of strong emotional attachments to people. I think Mr. Spock would understand.

Update: Learning Social Skills

Over the last ten years I have gained additional insights into how people relate to each other. I learned that I am *what I do* instead of *what I feel*. In my life I have replaced emotional complexity with intellectual complexity. People on the spectrum who are happy have friends with their same interests. Computer programmers are happy when they are with other programmers and they can talk about programming. I talked to one lady on the spectrum who met her husband at a science fiction book club. She writes technical manuals and he works in the computer industry. They love fine food and their idea of a wonderful romantic evening is to go to a really nice restaurant and spend time talking about computer data storage systems. Normal people have a hard time understanding why this special interest is so absorbing.

Develop Shared Interests

Social interaction revolves around shared interests. When I was in high school being teased by the other kids, I was miserable. The only place I was not teased was during horseback riding and model rocket club. The students who were interested in these special interests were not the kids who did the teasing. These activities were a shared interest for us.

I strongly recommend hobbies and careers where common interests can be shared. Mentors who can nurture talent can help students become successful. Students on the spectrum should be encouraged to participate in activities such as robotics club, choir, poetry group, scouting, or chess club. My '50s upbringing helped me because turn taking and sharing was drilled into me. Today some Asperger's students have difficulty working as a team to build a robot. Working with another person should be part of the activity. Little kids need to be taught turn taking because this will make it easier to work with another person when they get older. Too many activities today are solitary. Special interest groups such as *Star Trek* conventions or historical societies are great places to network and find other people with similar interests. The people on the spectrum who are depressed and unhappy often have no interests they can share with another person.

There are some really smart Asperger's and high-functioning students who need to be removed from the social pressure cooker of high school. After all, socializing with teenagers is not an important life skill. I am a strong believer in mainstreaming elementary school students so they can socialize with normal children. Lower-functioning students often do fine in high school because it is obvious to the other students that they are handicapped and should not be teased. But for some high-functioning high school students, it might make sense for them to take classes online or at a community college.

Learning Manners and Social Survival

I think some of the high-functioning Asperger's people are having serious employment problems because today's society fails to teach social skills. A brilliant man with Asperger's was fired from a library job for making comments to fat patrons. Mother taught me that these kinds of comments are rude. Even though honesty is the best policy, my opinion about other people's appearance was usually not welcome. Through many specific examples, I developed a category of "rude honesty" when I needed to keep my mouth shut. All social skills were learned by being given many specific examples that I could put into categories such as "rude honesty," "introduction routines with a new client," "how to deal with coworker jealousy," etc. As I gained more and more experience I placed each new social experience in the appropriate social file. Coworker jealousy was difficult to deal with. At one plant, a jealous engineer damaged some of my equipment. Today I have learned how to bring him into the project to make him feel a part of it. This will reduce jealousy. I have also learned to compliment the jealous person when they do good work. Today I just accept the fact that jealousy is a lousy human trait. To get a project done it has to be defused.

Social Skills Versus Social Relatedness

Learning social skills is like learning how to act in a play. Social skills can be taught but social emotional relatedness cannot be taught. Social skills and emotional relatedness are two different things. Often parents ask me, "Will my child have a true emotional relationship with me?" It is sometimes difficult for parents to accept that the brain of their child is wired differently. A social emotional relationship that is purely emotional may be of little interest to the child. Autism varies widely, and some individuals will be more emotionally related than others.

Modulating emotions is difficult for me. One time on a plane I laughed so hard at a movie that many people started staring at me. When I cry at a sad movie, I cry more than most people. My emotion is either turned on or all turned off. I have the four simple emotions of happy, sad, fearful, or angry. I never have mixtures of these emotions, but I can rapidly switch emotions.

After I was kicked out of a large girls' school for throwing a book at a girl who teased me, I learned to change anger to crying. I was unable to change the intensity of the emotion but I could switch to a different emotion. At my boarding school, horseback riding was taken away after I got into several fist fights due to teasing. Since I wanted to ride the horses, I immediately switched to crying. Switching to crying enabled me to not lose a job due to either hitting or throwing things. At the Swift Plant, I often retreated to the cattle yards to cry. Today any kind of violent behavior would not be tolerated in the workplace.

Subtle Emotional Cues

I was in my early '50s when I first learned about small eye signals. I did not understand why eye contact with so important. There was a whole secret world of eye movements that were unknown to me until I read Simon Baron-Cohen's book *Mind Blindness*. Tone of voice was the only subtle signal I picked up. Obviously I recognized strong emotion in other people when they expressed anger by yelling, sadness by crying, or happiness by laughing.

Mother has written about the difficulties with her marriage in her book *A Thorn in My Pocket*. When I was a child, I did not pick up on the emotional turmoil between my mother and father. I failed to recognize the signs of conflict because they were subtle. They seldom yelled at each other and they never hit each other or threw things.

What Does Research Show?

Hundreds of scientific papers have been written on abnormalities in face perception in autism. The bottom line is that in autistic people the amygdala (emotion center) is abnormal and people with autism use different brain circuits when they recognize faces. I still have embarrassing moments when I do not recognize the face of a person I met five minutes ago. I am able to recognize people I have been around for a long time. If a face has a really unique feature like a giant nose, I can remember that. The number of studies on face recognition and eye signals greatly outnumber papers on how people with autism think or perceive sensory input. Normal people are more interested in studying emotions rather than studying sensory problems or how savant skills work. I wish the scientists would spend more time on sensory problems. Severe problems with sensory oversensitivity wrecks the lives of many people on the spectrum. The most miserable individuals are the ones with such severe sensory problems that they cannot tolerate a restaurant or office. Socializing is impossible if your ears hurt from normal noise in movie theaters, sporting events, or busy streets.

8

A COW'S EYE VIEW

Connecting with Animals

ONE THIRD of the cattle and hogs in the United States are handled in facilities I have designed. Throughout my career I have worked on systems to improve the treatment of livestock. The principle behind my designs is to use the animals' natural behavior patterns to encourage them to move willingly through the system. If an animal balks and refuses to walk through an alley, one needs to find out why it is scared and refuses to move. Unfortunately, people often try to correct these problems with force instead of by understanding the animal's behavior. My connection with these animals goes back to the time I first realized that the squeeze machine could help calm my anxiety. I have been seeing the world from their point of view ever since.

People ask me all the time whether the cattle know they are going to be slaughtered. What I have observed over the years and at many meat plants is that the things that frighten cattle usually have nothing to do with death. It is the little things that make them balk and refuse to move, such as seeing a small piece of chain hanging down from an alley fence. For instance, a lead animal will stop to look at a moving chain and move his head back and forth in rhythm with its swing. He isn't concerned about being slaughtered; he's afraid of a small piece of chain that jiggles and looks out of place.

Most people do not observe these simple things because they get the cattle too excited by poking and prodding them when they refuse to move through an alley or out of a pen. When cattle are excited, it is impossible to determine what is bothering them. They go into antipredator mode and push themselves together in a boiling ball of circling, agitated animals, with their heads toward the center of the group. The smallest distraction can stop a group of cattle moving through an alley. I remember one time when a meat plant became totally chaotic because a plastic juice bottle had fallen into the entrance where the cattle lined up to walk into the plant. They absolutely refused to walk over the white plastic bottle. Anything that causes visual contrast will attract the animals' attention. They fear a drain gate across a concrete floor or a sparkling reflection from a puddle. Sometimes moving an overhead lamp to eliminate a reflection on a floor or wall will make it easier to move cattle and hogs. Poor lighting can cause many problems. Cattle and hogs will not walk into a dark place, so installing a lamp to illuminate the entrance to an alley will entice them to enter. Animals, like people, want to see where they are going.

When I put myself in a cow's place, I really have to be that cow and not a person in a cow costume. I use my visual thinking skills to simulate what an animal would see and hear in a given situation. I place myself inside its body and imagine what it experiences. It is the ultimate virtual reality system, but I also draw on the empathetic feelings of gentleness and kindness I have developed so that my simulation is more than a robotic computer model. Add to the equation all of my scientific knowledge of cattle behavior patterns and instincts. I have to follow the cattle's rules of behavior. I also have to imagine what experiencing the world through the cow's sensory system is like. Cattle have a very wide, panoramic visual field, because they are a prey species, ever wary and watchful for signs of danger. Similarly, some people with autism are like fearful animals in a world full of dangerous predators. They live in a constant state of fear, worrying about a change in routine or becoming upset if objects in their environment are moved. This fear of change may be an activation of ancient antipredator systems that are blocked or masked in most other people.

Fear is a universal emotion in the animal kingdom, because it provides an intense motivation to avoid predators. Fear is also a dominant emotion in autism. Therese Joliffe wrote that trying to keep everything the same helped her avoid some of the terrible fear. Tony W. wrote that he lived in a world of daydreaming and fear and was afraid of everything. Before I started taking antidepressants, minor changes in my daily routine caused a fear reaction. There were times that I was dominated by fear of trivial changes, such as switching to daylight savings time. This intense fear is probably due to a neurological defect that sensitizes the nervous system to stimuli that are minor to normal people.

In order to survive, members of a prey species such as cattle or sheep have to be ever vigilant and flee when they spot a predator. Cattle and sheep have supersensitive hearing, an acute sense of smell, and eyes on the sides of their heads so they can scan the landscape while grazing. They are much more sensitive to high-pitched sounds than people and can hear sounds that are outside the range of human hearing.

High-pitched sounds tend to be more disturbing to them than low-pitched sounds. Tom Camp, a USDA researcher in Texas, found that a loud bell on an outdoor telephone caused a calf's heart rate to jump suddenly by fifty to seventy beats per minute. It's unlikely that anyone but me would have noticed that the sounds that upset cattle are the same kinds of sounds that are unbearable to many autistic children with overly sensitive hearing. A sudden hissing similar to that caused by the air brakes on a semi truck will trigger a strong startle reaction in both calves and cattle. When calves hear this sound, they instantly lay their ears against their heads and back up to get away from the source of the noise. Like cattle, a person with autism has hypervigilant senses.

Even today, a person whistling in the middle of the night will cause my heart to race. High-pitched sounds are the worst. High, rapidly repeated sounds are stimulating to the nervous system. P. B. McConnell and his colleague J. R. Baylis, in Germany, found that dog trainers use high-pitched intermittent sounds to stimulate a dog to do something like fetch, while low sounds are used to make it stop, such as saying "Whoa" to a horse. In tame animals the high-pitched sounds have a mild activating effect, but in wild animals and autistic children they set off a massive fear reaction.

Contrary to popular belief, cattle and other livestock can see color, but their visual system is most attuned to detecting novel movement. Cattle vision is like having wide-angle camera lenses mounted on the sides of your head. The animals have 360 degree vision and can see all around themselves, except for a small blind spot behind their rear ends. However, the price they pay for wide-angle vision is a very narrow field where they can perceive depth. To do that, cattle have to stop and put their heads down. Predatory species, such as lions, dogs, cats, and tigers, have their eyes on the front of their heads, which enables them to perceive depth and accurately judge distances when they leap and bring down their prey. Eyes on the front of the head provide superior binocular vision, whereas eyes on the sides of the head provide the ability to scan the environment and be constantly vigilant.

In the old American West, novelty sometimes triggered stampedes during the great cattle drives. A hat blowing in the wind or a horse bucking would set off the instinct to flee. It is possible to desensitize cattle to novelty, however. For example, calves in the Philippines are grazed along the highways from birth. They learn that all the sights and sounds of the highway will not hurt them. These tame, halter-broken animals are not perturbed by anything.

Most cattle on American ranches are exposed to far less novelty. Coats and hats left on fences will often cause them to balk and refuse to walk by. When a steer is calm in its familiar home feedlot pen, the same hat or coat left on a fence may evoke first fear and then curiosity. The steer will turn and look at the coat and then cautiously approach it. If the coat does not move, he will eventually lick it. A coat that is flapping in the wind is more likely to make animals fearful, and they will keep their distance. In the wild, sudden movement is a sign of danger; it may be a lion in a bush or an animal fleeing from a predator.

The reaction of cattle to something that appears out of place may be similar to the reaction of autistic children to small discrepancies in their environment. Autistic children don't like anything that looks out of place—a thread hanging on a piece of furniture, a wrinkled rug, books that are crooked on the bookshelf. Sometimes they will straighten out the books and other times they will be afraid. Their fear reaction may be similar to a cow's reaction to a coffee cup in an alley or a hat on a fence. Autistic children will also notice minor discrepancies that normal people ignore. Could this be an old antipredator instinct that has surfaced? In the wild, a broken branch on a tree or disturbed earth is a possible sign of predator activity in the vicinity. The animal that survives and avoids the lions is the one that has developed the finest abilities in detecting warning signs of changes.

Cattle, deer, and antelope will turn and face a source of potential danger that is not immediately threatening. Cows on a pasture will turn and face an approaching person, and antelope on the African plains will turn toward and sometimes follow a lion. After all, the lion they can see is less of a threat than a lion they cannot see. The animals will follow the lion but remain at a safe distance, which enables instant flight. This is known as the animal's flight zone.

People working with cattle reared on the open range can use the principles of the flight zone to move groups of animals efficiently and quickly. The size of the flight zone will vary depending on how tame the cattle are. Tame dairy cattle may have no flight zone, and they will approach people for petting. Beef cattle raised on western ranches are not completely tame, and they will move away if people go too close to them. The flight zone can vary from five feet to over one hundred feet. Excited cattle will have a larger flight distance than calm cattle. H. Hedigar stated in his book *The Psychology and Behavior of Animals in Zoos and Cir-*

cues that taming is the artificial removal of the flight distance between animals and people.

It is fairly easy to move groups of cattle in a quiet and orderly manner if people work on the edge of the herd's collective flight zone. Deep invasion of the flight zone, however, may cause cattle to panic. If they are cornered in a pen, they may attempt to jump a fence to increase the distance between themselves and a threatening person.

Therapists have observed that autistic children often lash out when they stand close to other children while waiting in a line. They become tense when other children invade their personal space. Having another child accidentally brush up against them can cause them to withdraw with fear like a frightened animal. A light unexpected touch triggers flight, and a firm touch, similar to the pressure of a tightly bunched herd of cattle, is calming.

A great deal of my success in working with animals comes from the simple fact that I see all kinds of connections between their behavior and certain autistic behaviors. Another example is the fact that both cattle and people with autism can become very set in their habits. A change in a daily routine can cause an autistic person to have a tantrum. Such changes used to make me very anxious. Ranchers have discovered that cattle placed on a new pasture must be encouraged to graze the entire area when they are first put there. I observed a lazy group of bulls that refused to walk less than a quarter of a mile to a good pasture. Why do cattle do this? It may have something to do with instincts to avoid predators. When cattle learn that a certain area is safe, they become reluctant to move to a new area, which may contain danger.

An experiment that Ken Odde and I conducted at Colorado State University indicated the great strength of a bovine's reluctance to change a previously learned safe route. Cattle were given a choice between an alley that led to a squeeze chute and an alley that they could just walk through. The animals quickly learned to avoid the side where they would be restrained in the squeeze chute. When the alleys were switched, most of the cattle refused to switch sides to avoid restraint. Being held in a squeeze chute is slightly uncomfortable, but not so aversive that the animals were willing to change from the previously learned safe route. When something really painful or disagreeable happens, though, most animals will quickly change to avoid it. Mary Tanner, a student at Colorado State University, found that most cows at a dairy were willing to enter both sides of a milking parlor, but a few were very rigid and always entered on the same side.

Preliminary evidence indicates that the more nervous and excitable cows are the ones that are the most reluctant to change a previously learned safe route. Resistance to change may be partially motivated by attempts to reduce anxiety. In my own experience, minor changes in my high school class schedule or switching from daylight savings time to standard time caused severe anxiety. My nervous system and the nervous systems of some other people with autism are in a state of hyperarousal for no good reason. Before I took antidepressant drugs, my nervous system was constantly ready to flee predators. Insignificant little stresses caused the same reaction as being attacked by a lion. These problems were created by abnormalities in my nervous system. Now that the medication has calmed my nerves, I can take small changes in routine in stride.

One of the most stressful events for semiwild cattle is having people deeply invade their flight zone when they are unable to move away. A person leaning over the top of an alley is very threatening to beef cattle that are not completely tame. Cattle will also balk and refuse to walk through an alley if they can see people up ahead. This is one of the reasons that I designed curved single-file alleys with solid sides. They help keep cattle calmer. The solid sides prevent the animals from being frightened by people and other moving objects outside the alley. A curved alley also works better than a straight one because the cattle are unable to see people up ahead, and each animal thinks he is going back where he came from.

Understanding these kinds of sensitivities made it possible for me to figure out ways to calm flighty antelope at the zoo when other people were convinced that it was impossible to train them to cooperate during veterinary procedures. These procedures were often very stressful, because the animals had to be either shot with a tranquilizer dart or grabbed by people. Antelope can be trained to accept new procedures and novel sights and sounds if those things are introduced gradually and quietly, while the animals are fed treats. I worked with students Megan Phillips, Wendy Grafham, and Mat Rooney to train nyala and bongo antelope to enter a plywood box willingly and stand still during veterinary procedures such as blood testing and injections. The solid sides on the box provided the animals with a sense of safety and security. While they munched on treats, the veterinarian worked on them. During training, we had to take care to avoid triggering a massive fright reaction in these prey-species animals. They had to be carefully desensitized to the sound and movement of the doors on the box, and to people reaching into the box and touching them.

The crafty animals quickly learned to enter the box to get the treats and then kick the moment a blood test was attempted. To stop this, we withheld the treat until the animal stood still and cooperated. Trainers have to discriminate between kicking because of fear and kicking simply to avoid doing something the animal doesn't want to do. Withholding a feed reward will stop learned kicking, but it will have no effect on kicking or thrashing due to fear.

People who work with nonverbal, low-functioning people with autism must similarly be able to determine whether a tantrum or other bad behavior is caused by fear or pain or is a learned avoidance response. Sometimes it's because of pain from sounds that hurt their ears or fear of an unexpected change in routine. Like the cattle and the antelope, autistics are afraid of the unexpected. But sometimes they throw tantrums simply to get attention or to avoid doing a certain activity or school lesson. In one study, aggression and outbursts were greatly reduced in very severely handicapped autistic adults by giving them an object to hold fifteen minutes before they were scheduled to have lunch or ride on the bus. A spoon was used before lunch, and a toy bus was used before riding on the bus. Touch was the only sense that was not confused by sensory jumbling, and holding the object let these people get mentally ready for the next event in their daily routine. There were times when I threw a big tantrum just to watch the grownups react. Observant teachers can tell the difference between a massive fear reaction and the calculated use of bad behavior to avoid tasks the person does not want to do.

People Problems

Mistreatment by people is the number-one cause of animals becoming frightened. The best equipment in the world is worthless unless management controls the behavior of plant employees. When I first started designing equipment, I naively believed that if I could design the perfect system, it would control employee behavior. This is not possible, but I have designed equipment that requires very little skill to operate, provided employees are gentle. Good engineering is important, and well-designed facilities provide the tools that make low-stress, quiet handling at slaughter possible, but employees must operate the system correctly. Rough, callous people will cause distress to animals even if they use the best equipment.

Management attitude is the most important variable that determines how animals are treated. I wouldn't be surprised if this were true of any organization. Livestock handling has greatly improved during the past ten years, and managers are becoming more sensitive about animal welfare, but there still needs to be improvement. It is very painful for me to watch somebody abuse an animal, especially when it happens in one of my systems. Some people buy new equipment and think that it is a substitute for good management. Over the years I have seen animal handling improve with a change in management, and I have seen it get rough and nasty when a good manager left. A good manager serves as a conscience for the employees. He has to be involved enough to care but not so involved that he becomes numb and desensitized. One cannot rely on the foreman to enforce good behavior. This person often becomes immune to animal suffering on the slaughter floor. The manager who enforces good animal handling is usually most effective if he is at the plant-manager level. Someone in a distant headquarters office is often too detached from the reality of the slaughter floor to be concerned.

Plants that have high standards of animal welfare enforce strict codes of conduct. One manager built his office so that he could see the stockyards and the cattle ramp that led into the plant. If he saw employees hitting or whipping the cattle, he called the foreman. Employees who handle thousands of animals often become careless and hard. The people who actually kill the animals should be rotated, and complete automation of the actual killing procedure is good for employee well-being. Automation of killing is especially important in very high-speed plants, with rates of over 150 cattle per hour. A person becomes a zombie when he has to shoot thousands of cattle every day. At slower speeds one can take pride in doing the job humanely and treat each animal with respect, but at high speeds it's all one can do to keep up with the relentless movement of the line.

Management also has to be willing to take the time and make the effort to improve handling methods. Employees have to be trained to understand cattle behavior and use the natural instincts of the animals to assist movement. Trained employees learn to time groups of animals so that they will follow the leader. Each group must be driven up to the single-file alley just as the last animal from the previous group is walking into it. If the next group is driven up too quickly, the cattle or hogs will turn around, because there is no place to go. I love nothing more than to watch a plant I've designed run smoothly and efficiently, knowing that the animals are being treated with decency.

I'm always surprised at the number of people who think that the "jungle" still exists at the Chicago stockyards. The Chicago stockyards have been gone for more than thirty years. When I discuss my job with fellow travelers on airplanes, many ask if a sledgehammer is still used. That was banned by the Humane Slaughter Act in 1958 in all meat plants that sold to the U.S. government. In 1978 the act was strengthened to cover all federally inspected plants that sell meat in interstate commerce. The Humane Slaughter Act requires that cattle, pigs, sheep, and goats must be instantaneously rendered insensible to pain prior to slaughter. The act does not cover poultry or ritual slaughter by any religious faith. The law requires that animals are rendered insensible to pain by either captive bolt stunning, electrical stunning, or CO_2 gas. Captive bolt kills the animal instantly by driving a steel bolt into the brain. It has the same effect as a gun. Electrical stunning causes instantaneous unconsciousness by passing a high-amperage electrical current through the brain. It works the same way as electroconvulsive shock treatment in people. If the procedure is done correctly the animal becomes instantly unconscious.

People often ask me if animals are afraid of blood. Again it's the small distractions that scare the animals more than blood. Blood or urine from relatively calm cattle appears to have no effect, but blood from cattle that have become very frightened may contain a "smell of fear" substance. If the cattle remain relatively calm they will voluntarily walk into a chute with blood on it. But if an animal becomes severely stressed for over five minutes the next animal will often refuse to enter.

Design of Restraint Equipment

Many people who design systems to restrain animals don't think about what the device will feel like to the animal. Some engineers are strangely unaware that a sharp edge will dig and hurt. They build devices that mash the animal or dig into it. Restraint equipment used to hold cattle or hogs for either veterinary work or slaughter often squeezes the animal too hard or holds it in an uncomfortable position. One of the reasons I am good at designing this equipment is that I can visualize what the device will feel like. I can put myself into a twelve-hundred-pound steer's body and feel the equipment. What would it be like with a gentle person operating it? What would it be like with a rough person operating it? When I see somebody squeeze an animal too hard in a squeeze chute, it makes me hurt all over.

One of my crusades in the meat industry has been to eliminate shackling and hoisting as a method of restraint in kosher slaughter plants. The main animal welfare problem with kosher slaughter is the dreadful methods of restraint used in some plants. The variable of the restraint method must be separated from the variable of the actual shehita kosher cut, which is performed on a fully conscious animal. In kosher slaughter, a special, razor-sharp, long straight knife is used. When the cut is made correctly according to the rules outlined in the Talmud, the animal does not appear to feel it. The Talmud states that there cannot be any hesitation during the cut and the incision must not close back over the knife. The knife must have a perfect blade and be free of nicks, because a nick would cause pain.

I will never forget having nightmares after visiting the now defunct Spencer Foods plant in Spencer, Iowa, fifteen years ago. Employees wearing football helmets attached a nose tong to the nose of a writhing beast suspended by a chain wrapped around one back leg. Each terrified animal was forced with an electric prod to run into a small stall which had a slick floor on a forty-five-degree angle. This caused the animal to slip and fall so that workers could attach the chain to its rear leg. As I watched this nightmare, I thought, "This should not be happening in a civilized society." In my diary I wrote, "If hell exists, I am in it." I vowed that I would replace the plant from hell with a kinder and gentler system.

Ten years ago I was hired by the Council for Livestock Protection in New York to develop a humane upright restraint system for kosher calves. The council was a consortium of major animal advocacy groups such as the Humane Society of the United States, the American Society for the Prevention of Cruelty to Animals, the Fund for Animals, the Massachusetts SPCA, the American Humane Association, and others. It was formed in the early seventies to replace shackling and hoisting with more humane methods of restraint. At this time, upright restraining equipment existed for kosher slaughter of large cattle, but no equipment was available for calves or sheep. When the Humane Slaughter Act was passed in 1958, kosher slaughter was exempted, because no humane alternatives to shackling and hoisting of fully conscious animals existed.

Walter Giger, Don Kinsman, and Ralph Prince, at the University of Connecticut, had demonstrated that a calf can be restrained in a comfortable manner when it straddles a moving conveyor. The animal rides the conveyor like a person riding a horse, supported under the belly and chest. Solid sides on each side of the conveyor prevent it from tilting off. The Connecticut researchers had a good idea, but I had to invent many new components to construct a system that would work in a commercial slaughter plant. To make the new system work, I had to eliminate all pressure points which caused discomfort to the animals. For example, uncomfortable pressure on the leg joints caused calves to struggle and fight the restrainer. Elimination of the pressure points resulted in calm, quiet calves.

One of the advantages of a conveyor restraint system for both conventional slaughter, where cattle are stunned, and ritual slaughter is that the cattle move through it in a continuous line. Each animal has its head on the rear of the animal in front of it. Having observed cattle, I realized that they remain calmer when they can touch each other. Since the cattle were in continuous contact with each other, they remained calmer at the slaughter plant than at the squeeze chute at the Colorado State University Experiment Station. I've also observed that cattle are accustomed to walking in single file. An overview of a cow pasture shows the small, twelve-inch-wide cowpaths. Walking in single file is part of the nature of cattle. This is why a system that handles cattle moving through in single file works well.

Many people do not believe me when I tell them that cattle

slaughter can be really calm, peaceful, and humane. In some plants, the cattle remain absolutely calm and the employees are very conscientious. At one large plant, 240 cattle per hour quietly walked up the ramp and voluntarily entered the double-rail conveyor restrainer. It was as if they were going in to get milked. Each fat steer walked into the restrainer entrance and settled down on the conveyor like a little old lady getting on the bus. Most animals entered the restrainer when they were patted on the rear end. Since the cattle move through the system in a continuous line, they are never alone and separated from their buddies. At this plant, the system had been beautifully installed and was brightly illuminated. When slaughter is conducted properly, the cattle experience less stress and discomfort than they experience during handling procedures in the veterinary chute.

Being autistic has helped me to understand how they feel, because I know what it is like to feel my heart race when a car horn honks in the middle of the night. I have hyperacute senses and fear responses that may be more like those of a prey-species animal than of most humans. People often fail to observe animals. Recently I visited a slaughter plant where the cattle were terrified of air that hissed from a pneumatically powered gate. Every time the gate opened or closed, the cattle recoiled and backed down the chute. They reacted as if they had seen a rattlesnake. It was obvious to me that the hissing air scared them but other people failed to see it. Purchase of a few air silencers solved the problem. With the hissing gone, the animals were no longer afraid of the gate. All it took was a cow's eye view.

Update: Troubleshooting Challenging Behavior

The best place to look for an update on my work with animals is in my book, *Animals in Translation*. I do have a few words on troubleshooting challenging behavior. In both the field of animal behavior and in autism education, the number one mistake is misunderstanding the motivation of behavior. In animal behavior, fear and aggression are often mixed up. Punishing behavior caused by fear often makes it worse. Some people with autism experience massive fear when they experience sensory overload. Yelling at the person is the wrong thing to do when the individual's sensory system is already in a state of overload. The person's fear is going to get worse.

When working with nonverbal people with autism you have to be a good detective to figure out the cause behind a challenging behavior like throwing things or biting people. The first thing that must be ruled out is a hidden medical problem that the person cannot tell you about. If an individual who used to be calm and cooperative suddenly turns violent, pain may be the cause. Heartburn or acid reflux is a common problem in adults with autism. Try some simple remedies such as elevating the head of the bed six inches, not laying down after eating, and medicine for heartburn. Constipation is another common problem. Other painful conditions that can cause behavior problems are dental problems, ear infections, or sinus infections. One quiet little boy had pushed a bean up his nose and he disrupted his class until the bean was removed.

Sensory issues are another trigger of problem behaviors. Suspect sensory sensitivity if the behavior problem occurs right after the individual is moved to a new environment. The fear of getting one's ears blasted by the smoke alarm can trigger a tantrum. If a smoke alarm has previously gone off in the room, the individual may be afraid to go back into that room. The sight of a mobile phone may cause panic because it can ring at any time. Changing the ring tone may help. Fluorescent lights or some other stimuli that the person cannot tolerate are other possibilities.

Troubleshooting Guide for Challenging Behavior in Nonverbal Individuals

Step 1. Look for a painful, hidden medical problem.
Step 2. Look for a sensory reason.

Step 3. If 1 and 2 can be ruled out, look for the behavioral reasons for the challenging behavior.

There are three major behavioral motivators.

1. The person is attempting to communicate.
2. He/she is trying to get attention.
3. The person wants to escape from a task that he/she dislikes.

There are many good books available to help remedy problems with challenging behavior such as the *Treasure Chest of Behavioral Strategies.* Once you have figured out the motivation, you can develop a behavioral program. If communication is a problem, then the individual may need a communication system such as "Picture Exchange" or a picture board. If a desire for attention is the cause, then ignoring the behavior sometimes works. If the individual is attempting to escape from a task, you must make sure that a sensory sensitivity issue is not the true cause. If there is no sensory issue, then try quietly to direct the person back to the task or change the task to make it more appealing.

Other interventions that can be used are working with an occupational therapist to calm the nervous system and special diets and supplements. Some teenagers and adult individuals will need medication. Doctors must not make the mistake of giving more and more medication every time there is a crisis. A program of vigorous exercise also helps to calm the nervous system. A combination of medical, behavioral, and nutritional/biomedical approaches is usually best.

Fear Associations

A person with autism may panic when he/she sees some common, ordinary thing. Maybe a blue coat evokes fear because the fire alarm went off at the exact moment the blue coat was being put on. The coat then becomes associated with the fire alarm. Sensory-based fear associations are common in animals. I saw a horse that was afraid of black cowboy hats. White cowboy hats and ball caps caused no reactions. The horse feared black hats because he was looking at a black hat when he was abused. Another animal became afraid of the sound of a nylon jacket because it was associated with abuse. These fear memories are stored as pictures, sounds, smells, or touches. Since nonverbal people with autism are sensitive to smells, it is likely that a smell could become associated with an aversive stimulus such as sensory overload at a supermarket. The smell of a new detergent brought into the home could possibly become associated with a "meltdown" in the detergent aisle of a local supermarket.

The problem with severe fear memories is that they can never be erased from the person's memory. A person or animal can learn to overcome a fear. The brain does this by sending a signal down to the amygdale (emotion center) to close the "computer file" of the memory. The file can be closed but it cannot be deleted. In animals, fear memories have a nasty habit of popping back even after the animal has learned to get over its fear. This is especially a problem in high-strung, nervous animals. Sensitive nervous animals that get frightened easily such as Arabian horses can become so traumatized by severe abuse that they may never completely learn to get over their fears. Animals with calmer genetics have an easier time learning to close the file on a fear memory. Making fear memories permanent helps animals to survive in the wild. The ones that forget where they met a lion will not survive.

9

ARTISTS AND ACCOUNTANTS

An Understanding of Animal Thought

MANY PEOPLE have been fascinated by the terrific feats of memorization of savants. According to Bernard Rimland, of the Autism Research Institute in San Diego, approximately 9 or 10 percent of people with autism have savant skills. Some are like calendar calculators who can tell you the day of the year for any date; others can perfectly play a piece of music they have heard only once. Another type can memorize every street in a city or every book in a library. There are also savants who can rapidly identify all the prime numbers in a list of numbers, even though they are incapable of doing basic arithmetic calculations. Hans Welling, a researcher in Portugal, speculates that mathematically weak savants may have a method for visually analyzing the symmetry of numbers, which would enable them to distinguish prime from nonprime numbers.

Savants are usually very impaired in learning other skills, such as socializing. One mother told me about her teenage savant son, who could do extraordinary computer programming but simply could not learn the meaning of money. Savants memorize huge amounts of information but have difficulty manipulating the material in meaningful ways. Their memory skills far exceed those of normal people, but their cognitive deficits are great. Some are incapable of making simple generalizations that cattle and other animals make easily.

It is no mystery how the autistic savant depicted in the movie *Rain Man* beat the casinos in Las Vegas and counted cards in the game of twenty-one. It was simply intense visualization and concentration. The only reason I can't count cards is that I can no longer concentrate intensely enough. My visualization skill has not changed, but I can no longer hold a single image steady for a long enough period of time. When I visualize equipment, I edit the images like a feature movie. I may visualize the system from a vantage point on the ground, but in the next instant I see it from another perspective. I am no longer able to hold a continuous video in my imagination. I would speculate that the true card-counting savant mind works like a video camera that is fixed to a tripod and continuously records the same scene. The vantage point of the savant's mind camera remains fixed for relatively long intervals. When the savant's concentration is locked onto one thing, it is difficult for him to shift attention. If a VCR could be plugged into his brain and his visual memories could be played on a TV, his memory would likely resemble a very long home movie taken from a single, stationary vantage point. This intense ability to hold an image constant may also contribute to the rigid and inflexible behavior of most savants.

What interests me most about autistic savants of the extreme type is that they do not satisfy one of Marian Stamp Dawkins's chief criteria for thinking. Dawkins, a researcher at the University of Oxford, is one of the few specialists who studies thinking in animals. She makes a clear distinction between instinctual behavior and true thinking. Similar to the main operating programs of a computer, instincts are behavior patterns that are programmed in the animal. Some instincts are hard-wired like computer hardware, and others can be modified by experience. An example of instinctual behavior is a calf following its mother. Animals are also capable of learning behavior that is not governed by instincts. For example, cows can quickly learn to line up for milking at 4:00 P.M.

But cows lining up at milking time or running after a feed truck are simply responding to straightforward stimulus conditioning. Animals are also capable of learning simple rules of thumb. An animal can remember that he gets food when a green light turns on or he must jump a barrier to avoid a shock when a red light turns on. But to determine whether or not the animal is really thinking requires testing under novel conditions where he cannot use a simple rule of thumb. Numerous studies reviewed by Dawkins clearly indicate that animals can think and are capable of using previously learned information to solve problems presented under novel conditions. Animals have the ability to generalize, even though they do not use language.

Dawkins's work begs the deeper question of whether a child with autism who is unable to generalize can think. For example, a person with classic Kanner autism can be taught not to run out into the busy street in front of his house because it is dangerous. Unfortunately, he often fails to generalize this knowledge to a street at somebody else's house. In another scenario, the autistic person may learn the procedure for buying a candy bar at Safeway but have difficulty figuring out how to buy a candy bar at Walgreen's. Such people are not able to comprehend any deviations from the pictures in their memory.

According to Dawkins's criteria, then, savant autistics are not capable of true thought. Autistic people like myself are able to satisfy her criteria for thinking, but I would be denied the ability to think by scientists who maintain that language is essential for thinking.

When a well-respected animal scientist told me that animals do not think, I replied that if this were true, then I would have to conclude that I was unable to think. He could not imagine thinking in pictures, nor assign it the validity of real thought. Mine is a world of thinking that many language-based thinkers do not comprehend. I have observed that the people who are most likely to deny animals thought are often highly verbal thinkers who have poor visualization skills. They excel at verbal or sequential thinking activities but are unable to read blueprints.

It is very likely that animals think in pictures and memories of smell, light, and sound patterns. In fact, my visual thinking patterns probably resemble animal thinking more closely than those of verbal thinkers. It seems silly to me to debate whether or not animals can think. To me it has always been obvious that they do. I have always pictured in my mind how the animal responds to the visual images in his head. Since I have pictures in my imagination, I assume that animals have similar pictures. Differences between language-based thought and picture-based thought may explain why artists and accountants fail to understand each other. They are like apples and oranges.

Studies by Jane Goodall, Dian Fossey, and many other researchers have shown very clearly that primates such as chimpanzees and gorillas can think, though few scientists would also concede that farm animals have thinking abilities. Yet anyone who has spent any time working with cattle knows that they are able to recognize familiar objects when they see them in a new location. My experience suggests that these animals think in discrete visual images. They are able to make an association between a visual image stored in their memory and what they are seeing in the present. During an experiment on the farm at Colorado State University, for example, cattle were handled in a squeeze chute for blood testing once a month for five months. Most cattle willingly reentered the squeeze chute during each blood test after the first one, but a few refused to enter. These animals were very discriminating as to which part of the squeeze chute they disliked, often refusing to put their heads in the stanchion though voluntarily entering the body-squeezing part.

Apparently when the person operating the lever closed the stanchion too quickly, the animal got banged on the head. Animals that had been accidentally struck were more likely to balk at the head stanchion. Most of them marched right up to the squeeze chute and willingly walked into the body squeeze section, but they stopped short of the stanchion because they feared getting banged on the head. Some animals poked their head toward the stanchion and then quickly jerked it back before the operator could close the stanchion around their neck. They acted like sissy swimmers who put a toe in the cold water and then jerk it out.

Over the five-month period the animals grew too large for the manually operated chute, so they were taken to a hydraulically operated squeeze chute for the fifth and final blood test. The hydraulic chute was painted a different color and looked somewhat different from the manually powered squeeze chute. Likewise, the alleys and corrals leading up to the hydraulic chute were totally different. When the cattle approached the hydraulic squeeze chute, many of them balked and refused to put their heads into the stanchion. They recognized the squeeze chute in spite of the different design and new location. They had generalized their knowledge of squeeze chutes and stanchions to a new place.

Cattle I have worked with have had the ability to apply previously learned skills to new situations, which also indicates a capacity for thought. Cattle with large horns, such as Texas longhorns, have good spatial sense and will turn their heads to walk up a thirty-inch-wide truck loading ramp. But young cattle that have had no prior experience with narrow chutes and ramps will hit their horns on the entrance and be unable to enter. Turning the head to pass through a narrow place is not governed by instinct. Experienced animals learn to turn their heads. After they have learned, they will turn their heads before they enter a chute they have never seen before. When an experienced animal approaches the chute entrance, he turns his head and enters effortlessly.

Some very elegant research with birds has shown that even our feathered friends can think. Herb Terrace, the famous chimpanzee trainer, trained pigeons to peck at a series of lighted buttons in a specific order to obtain food. The task was designed to make it impossible for the pigeon to use a simple rule of thumb such as "red light equals food." All of the experiments were conducted in an enclosed box and controlled by a computer to insure that the pigeons did not receive cues from the trainer. (Whenever animal thinking is being evaluated, the "Clever Hans effect" must be taken into account. Hans was a famous horse that had been trained to count by tapping his hoof. Many people were very impressed and thought the horse really could count. Hans did not know how to count, but he was a very perceptive horse who picked up subtle cues from his trainer.) Terrace designed a whole series of trials to show that the pigeons could apply previously learned knowledge about the button order to new button-pushing problems.

Irene Pepperberg has slowly and laboriously taught an African gray parrot named Alex to use language beyond mere repetition by having him watch two people talking to each other. One person would hold up an object such as a cork and ask, "What is this?" If the second person gave the correct name for the cork, she would be praised by the first person and given the cork. However, if the second person gave the wrong name for the object, she was told "no" very firmly. After Alex watched many of these conversations, he started to use words in appropriate ways. Each small step was mastered before he went on to the next step.

For a reward, the parrot would be given the object. He had to learn that the correct word could get him things he wanted. People teaching language to severely autistic children use similar methods. The Lovaas language-teaching method requires seeing the object, hearing the word, and pairing the word with both the object and reward. After a child learns the objects, he is given pictures of objects. For some children severely afflicted with autism, relating to such pictures is difficult.

More evidence to support the idea of animal thought can be found in Benjamin Beck's extensive review of the published scientific literature. While it is well known that monkeys and chimpanzees can use tools, Beck found many reports of tool use in birds and nonprimate mammals. Tool use is another sign that animals can really think. Elephants will push uprooted trees onto electric fences to break them, and one elephant even used a bamboo stake to scrape off a leech. Eskimo lore is full of accounts of polar bears throwing chunks of ice at seals. I have watched seagulls carry shellfish up over the roof of a steel boathouse and then drop them to break them open. The gulls also dropped clams on the road and waited for cars to run over them, exposing the tasty morsels. Beck's review of the literature indicated that birds can learn tool use by observation. When one bluejay in a captive colony had learned to use reaching tools, five other jays also learned. A Galapagos finch that does not usually use sticks for probing learned to use them after observing another species of bird using this tool.

At the University of Illinois farm where I worked as a graduate student, the pigs in one pen learned to unscrew the bolts that held the fence to the wall. As fast as I could screw the bolts back in, their little tongues were unscrewing them. All five pigs in that pen learned to unscrew bolts. My aunt had a horse that learned to put its head through a gate to lift it off the hinges; and at every large cattle feedlot, there are always one or two cattle who rival the techniques of the great escape artists among us. One time I witnessed a twelve-hundred-pound crossbred Brahman steer jump six six-foot gates. He just levitated over them. A horse has to run to jump a gate, but this big Brahman rose up like a leaping whale and effortlessly cleared the top of the gates. The vast majority of cattle are content to stay in the pens and don't try to get out, but a bull that has learned how to break barbed-wire fences is impossible to keep in, because he has learned that he will not get cut if he presses against the posts. Fences only work because cattle do not know that they can break them.

Dolphins at the University of Hawaii are being taught to understand symbolic sign language. Initial training is conducted by a person who makes hand signals that represent a simple sequence of commands. After the dolphin learns how to do a series of these tasks with a person, the next step is to have it look at a videotape of the person. This helps to prevent the Clever Hans effect. The simple command sentences are rearranged into hundreds of different combinations so the dolphins cannot memorize a set routine. Dolphins can easily transfer instructions from a real person to a videotape of the person. A third step further prevents possible cuing from the trainer. The trainer is now dressed in black and videotaped against a black curtain. The only thing the dolphin can see is the trainer's white gloves making the signs against a black backdrop. The dolphins are able to understand the videotaped hand signals, too. At this point, the images are more abstract, and the dolphins are taking the first steps toward understanding symbolic representation of words.

My experience as a visual thinker with autism makes it clear to me that thought does not have to be verbal or sequential to be real. I considered my thoughts to be real long before I learned that there was a difference between visual and verbal thinkers. I am not saying that animals and normal humans and autistics think alike. But I do believe that recognizing different capacities and kinds of thought and expression can lead to greater connectedness and understanding. Science is just beginning to prove what little old ladies in tennis shoes have always known: little Fifi really does think.

Bird Savants

The ability of birds to migrate is based on capabilities that resemble savant skills. It is possible that savant skills are part of an older memory-imaging system that is masked by higher thinking skills. Professor Floriano Papi, in Italy, has written an important book, titled *Animal Homing,* on the abilities of animals and birds to migrate and home. Since the ancient Romans, carrier pigeons have been used to carry messages. How does a pigeon find its way home after it has been taken far away in a cage?

Birds navigate by using a combination of an innate sense that enables them to detect the earth's magnetic field and memories they have acquired. In some birds, the innate magnetic detection system is coupled with genetic programming that forms the basis of an instinct to migrate. This will get the bird headed in the right general direction, but information from memory is also essential for accurate homing and migration. If a young bird migrates with its flockmates, it simply learns visual landmarks and other information, such as constellations and orientation of the sun. Some birds, such as the European teal, can distinguish and memorize the constellations. Papi reports that some birds can make visual calibrations of constellations, correcting for the earth's rotation during different times of the year, which doesn't seem all that different from the intense savantlike visual memory.

Clara Parks, whose autistic daughter has great artistic talents, noted that when her daughter painted a picture of their house, the constellations she included were very accurate. Mrs. Parks has commented that her daughter's eye is like a camera. Possibly, her visual skill and birds' navigational skills have similarities. This explains migration, but it fails to explain how a carrier pigeon can find its way home over a landscape it has never seen before. The pigeons rely on visual landmarks when they fly over familiar territory, but when they fly over unknown territory, they rely on smell. When a pigeon is transported from its home loft to the release point, it remembers smells along the way, and it uses these smell cues to get back home. Pigeons deprived of their sense of smell will become lost. Those with their sense of smell intact will also get lost if they are transported in a container that blocks smell. It appears that visual landmarks are the preferred method of homing, but a bird will switch gears and use olfactory cues when it finds itself over strange territory where familiar visual landmarks are absent. It may be using "smell pictures."

A fairly high percentage of people with autism have a very acute sense of smell and become overwhelmed by strong odors. I am embarrassed to admit it, but when I was a young child, I liked to sniff people like a dog. The scents of different people were interesting. Some animals have highly developed senses which are more acute than ours. Bloodhounds can track a fugitive for miles by smell, and predatory birds have greater visual acuity than humans. Many animals have very sensitive hearing and can hear high-frequency noises that are out of the range of human hearing. Many people with autism share these hyperacute senses. They are unable to concentrate in the classroom because they can hear talking in three other rooms. I have often observed that the senses of some people with autism resemble the acute senses of animals.

Emotions in Farm Animals

The manager of a very large swine farm once asked me in all seriousness, "Do pigs have emotions?" To him, pigs were simply pork-producing entities. We have seen that their ability to think and learn exceeds conditioned stimulus response, but do they experience true emotions? Are the feelings of a sow defending her piglets or an antelope running in fear from a lion similar to feelings in people under similar circumstances? Even a chicken can be highly motivated; Ian Duncan, at the University of Guelph, found that a hen would push open a very heavy door to reach a nest box, though she was not motivated to push open a lightweight door to reach a rooster. Is this behavior driven by emotion?

Early in my career I befriended two pet steers at the Kelly feedlot in Maricopa, Arizona, while I was doing a photography assignment for a company that made meat packaging equipment. The advertising agency wanted a photo of a great majestic Angus steer against the blue Arizona sky. To get the picture I had to lie down on the ground and wait for the cattle to come up to me. Cattle are less afraid of people when they reduce their size by kneeling or lying down. These two black steers let me touch them, and by the end of the afternoon they would allow me to pet them. At first they seemed to be afraid, but then they started to like it. They stretched out their necks to get stroked under the chin.

About two weeks later I returned to the feedlot, and I wanted to see if the steers would remember me. I stopped my truck in front of the pen, and the black steers immediately ran over to the fence and stuck their heads out to be petted. They wanted to be petted even though I did not offer them food. They simply wanted to be stroked.

There are many other examples of both farm animals and wild animals seeking pleasurable contact with people. Sows that have become pets will turn their bellies toward people so the people will scratch them. At one farm, a pet sow would squeal and become agitated if people walked by and failed to stop and rub her belly. When they stopped and rubbed, she would lie down, stretch out, and appear to be in bliss. Rhinos in a game park in Texas also solicited petting. When people walked up to their enclosure, one fellow would push his body up against the fence so that visitors could rub a soft spot where his rear leg joined his body. After he was petted and fed a few oranges, he would run along the fence and jump up and down like a calf on a spring day. To me, he appeared to be happy.

To the scientist who wants objective data, these anecdotes do not prove that animals have emotions. But scientists have proved that laboratory rats are capable of recognizing a familiar person and seeking him out. Psychologist Hank Davis found that lab rats will bond with a person who has petted, handled, and fed them. When a rat is placed on a table between a familiar caretaker and a stranger, it will investigate both of them and choose the familiar person most of the time. In most mammals and birds, the young will become very upset when they are separated from their mother. When calves are weaned, both the cows and the calves bellow for about twenty-four hours. Some calves bellow until they are hoarse.

Cattle will also bellow for departed penmates. This is most likely to occur with Holsteins, which are very calm cattle. Their social behavior is easy to observe because the presence of an observer is not likely to disturb them. I have seen Holstein steers bellowing to penmates that were departing in a truck. The cattle that were left behind watched as their fat penmates walked up the ramp to get on the truck that would take them to Burgerland. Two steers stared at the truck as it turned out of the parking lot. One stretched out his neck and bellowed at the truck, and his penmate on the truck bellowed back. The nice feedlot manager was worried that his cattle knew they were going to die. They had no way of knowing this; they just didn't like being separated from their buddies. Research by Joe Stookey and his colleagues at the University of Saskatchewan confirms that cattle do not like being alone; the cattle in their study would stand more quietly during weighing on a scale if they could see another animal in front of them.

Studies of animal responses to stress and fear may provide more reliable evidence that human and animal emotions are similar. Hundreds of studies of rats, cats, cattle, pigs, monkeys, and many other animals have shown that when animals encounter something that scares them, the levels of cortisol (stress hormone) in their blood rise. Adrenalin is pumped throughout the body, and both heart rate and breathing greatly increase to prepare the animal for fight or flight from danger. Research has shown that fear is a universal emotion in mammals and birds. Of course, people have these same physiological responses. A person mugged on a city street and an animal chased by a predator have the same increases in adrenalin, heart rate, and breathing rate. In both animals and people, fear causes fight or flight.

Fear can have very bad effects on the productivity of farm animals. The Australian scientist Paul Hemsworth found that when sows were afraid of people, they had fewer piglets. Fear was measured by determining how quickly a sow would approach a strange person. Each pig was tested by placing it in a small arena with a stranger. Pigs that had been mishandled by workers took longer than other pigs to walk up and touch the strange person. They also had lower weight gains.

Further studies indicated that tender loving care improved both reproductive performance and weight gain. Many large Australian swine farms started a training program to improve employees' attitudes toward pigs. As the workers learned more about pig behavior and became more interested in why pigs act the way they do, productivity increased. Farms where the attitude of the employees improved showed an increase of 6 percent more piglets born per sow. Employees who had a good attitude toward pigs engaged in more positive behaviors, such as petting, and fewer aversive behaviors, such as slapping. Hemsworth also found that pigs that had been slapped regularly had learned to stay away from people and still had sufficient anxiety to cause a chronic elevation of stress hormone and decreased weight gain. They clearly felt threatened when people were around.

Other animals also have the ability to anticipate an unpleasant experience. In one study, dairy cows that had been shocked in a restraining chute had a much higher heart rate when they approached the same restraining chute six months later than cows that had been restrained in the same chute with no shock.

Anatomical and Neurological Measures

The best hard scientific evidence that animals have emotions may come from the study of brain anatomy and neurophysiology. This evidence will help convince the skeptics. I had the opportunity to audit an anatomy class on the human brain at the University of Illinois Medical School. I had dissected many cattle and pig brains, but this was the first time I was going to see what a human brain actually looked like. When the brain was sliced down the middle, I was astounded to learn that the limbic system, which is the part of the brain associated with emotion, looked almost exactly like the limbic system in a pig's brain. At the gross anatomical level, the single major difference between a human brain and a pig's brain is the size of the cortex. The limbic system in both is very similar in size, but the human's is covered by a great massive cortex, like an overgrown cauliflower that engulfs the brain stem. The cortex is the part of the brain that gives people their superior thinking powers. The seat of emotion is buried deep beneath it.

The major difference between the human brain and the brains of other higher mammals, such as dogs, cats, cattle, and horses, is the size of the cortex. Both animal and human brains may get emotional signals from the limbic system, but since people have greater abilities to process information, their expression of emotions is more complex. A sad person may write a beautiful piece of poetry, while a sad dog may whine and scratch on the door when he is left alone. The emotion may be similar, but the expression of the emotion is vastly different.

The chemical messenger systems in the brains of people and higher mammals are the same. Messages between brain cells are transmitted by substances called neurotransmitters. High levels of the neurotransmitter serotonin are associated with calmness and reduced aggression. Prozac makes people feel better because it increases serotonin levels. Some of the other neurotransmitters are norepinephrine, GABA, dopamine, and endorphins. GABA is the brain's own natural tranquilizer, similar chemically to Valium. Endorphins are the brain's own opiates. Drugs such as Naltrexone, which block the action of endorphins, are used in the treatment of heroin overdose and alcohol abuse. Dopamine and norepinephrine have an activating effect. The wild delusions and hallucinations of a schizophrenic are often stopped by drugs that block the action of dopamine.

The best evidence that human and animal emotions are similar is the study of the effect of antidepressant and tranquilizing drugs on animals. Modern veterinarians are treating dogs, cats, and horses with the same drugs that are used to treat anxiety and obsessive-compulsive disorder in humans. A recent seminar by Dr. Karen Overall, from the veterinary school at Pennsylvania State University, sounded like a session at the American Psychiatric Association.

The drug Anafranil, which has actions similar to those of Prozac, is being used to treat obsessive-compulsive behavior in both horses and dogs. A person with this disorder may wash his hands for two hours a day. In dogs, excessive grooming and licking causes open sores. In many cases, a dose of Anafranil will stop the behavior. Judith Rapoport, M.D., an expert on obsessive-compulsive behavior who works at the National Institute of Mental Health, speculates that symptoms in people may come from the older areas of the brain, which we share with animals.

The drug Naltrexone, which blocks endorphins, will stop self-injurious behaviors in both autistic children and horses. Just as a few very severely autistic people will cause self-injury by biting or hitting themselves, high-strung stallions confined to stalls will occasionally engage in chest biting. Dr. Nick Dodman at the Tufts Veterinary School, in Massachusetts, found that Naltrexone will reduce or stop this behavior. He is also successfully using Prozac, beta-blockers, BuSpar (busperone), and Tegratol (carbenmazepine) to control aggression in dogs. Beta-blockers such as Inderal (propranolol) are sometimes used by musicians and actors to reduce anxiety and fear before a performance. Inderal has similar fear-reducing effects in dogs. Dogs are even being treated for hyperactivity with Ritalin (methylphenidate). Both hyperactive dogs and hyperactive children become calmer on the drug.

I would speculate that the most basic emotions in people and animals have similar neurological mechanisms and that the difference between human and animal emotion is the complexity of emotional expression. Emotions help animals survive in the wild, because they provide intense motivation to flee from a predator or protect newborn offspring. Instinct refers to fixed behavior patterns in animals, such as mating rituals, but they are fueled by emotion. It is likely that an animal is motivated by fear to find a secluded place to nest that is safe from predators, but fear would not be the primary emotion in a hungry animal. Hunger and fear are both intense motivators.

Like a prey-species animal, many people with autism experience fear as the primary emotion. When I was charting my life in the visual symbol world, I did not know that most people are not driven by constant fear. Fear fueled my fixations, and my life revolved around trying to reduce it. I delved deeper into my visual symbols because I thought I could make the fear go away if I could gain an understanding of the significance of my life. It got to the point that everything I did assumed symbolic significance on my visual map. I thought that an intellectual understanding of life's great philosophical questions would turn off the anxiety. My emotions were primal and simple, but the symbolism of my visual symbol world was extremely complex.

I replaced emotional complexity with visual and intellectual complexity. I questioned everything and looked to logic, science, and intellect for answers. As a visual thinker, I could understand the world only in that way. I kept striving to turn off the fear until I discovered the powers of biochemistry.

Both people and animals have temperament traits that are genetic and inborn. A fearful animal and a fearful autistic person are both stressed and upset by new routines and strange things. Training and taming can mask flighty temperament traits, but they are still there under the surface, waiting to explode. A bull from a nervous genetic line may be placid and calm on his familiar ranch but go berserk when he is confronted with new surroundings and new people. Likewise, some autistic people are very calm when they adhere to familiar routines, but an outburst of temper or aggression can occur if something unexpected happens.

Dr. Jerome Kagan and his associates at Harvard University have found that inborn temperament traits first start to show up in children at age two. Their categories of inhibited and uninhibited children are very similar to those of calm and excitable cattle or horses. These basic traits become apparent during very early childhood. Shy or inhibited children are wary of others, and they tend to be cautious and avoid strangers. Uninhibited children are more outgoing and social and less afraid of new experiences. Learning and social influences mask and override most of these differences, but children at the extremes of the spectrum retain the differences.

In Kagan's study, the extremely shy, inhibited children had greater physiological reactivity. When they were exposed to new tasks and strange people, their heart rate increased. They also had higher cortisol levels than uninhibited children. Kagan speculates that shy children have a more sensitive sympathetic nervous system, which reacts quickly and intensely, so that novel situations are more likely to cause them to panic. Possibly they are like high-strung, excitable animals. In other words, they are shy to avoid danger. The ancient systems that protected us from predators are working overtime in these children. It is interesting that temperament testing in people and animals is yielding results that have many similarities.

My ability to think visually has helped me to understand how an animal could think and feel in different situations. I don't have any difficulty imagining myself as the animal. But to be able to do this without being anthropomorphic, I have spent years observing animals behaving in different situations. I'm always adding additional information to my library of information by reading books and articles about animal behavior. I use the same thinking process I use for designing equipment to visualize how these animals think.

As Elizabeth Marshall Thomas, author of *The Hidden Life of Dogs,* would say, "Dogs have dog thoughts." I would apply that to farm animals, too. One of my students remarked that horses don't think, they just make associations. If making associations is not considered thought, then I would have to conclude that I am unable to think. Thinking in visual pictures and making associations is simply a different form of thinking from verbal-based linear thought. There are advantages and disadvantages to both kinds of thinking. Ask any artist or accountant.

Update: Animal Behavior and Autism

You can read *Animals in Translation* to see my full views on how autistic thinking and animal thinking are similar. Briefly, the most important similarity is that both animals and people with autism can think without language. They think by associating sensory-based memories such as smells, sounds, or visual images into categories. My categorical method of thinking is explained in the Chapter 1 update.

The second similarity is that both animals and people with autism possess savant-type skills. This idea was first introduced in *Thinking in Pictures*. Animals and autistic savants can do feats of great memory. Squirrels can remember where they hid hundreds of nuts and birds remember a migration route after traveling it only once. After a squirrel hides a nut he rears up and "takes a picture" of the location. This is the same way I find my car in parking lots without numbering or lettering for spaces. I look at the buildings, trees, and poles and then "download" an image into my brain of what the angle of certain buildings looks like. To find my car when I return I walk back through the lot following the same path I used when I left and I stop when the images I am seeing as I walk match the "snapshot" stored in memory.

The third similarity is that both think in details. As described in the Chapter 1 update, my thinking involves putting details together to form concepts. A normal person forms a concept first and tends to ignore details. Animals and individuals with autism notice details that normal people may not perceive. In my work with slaughter plants, I have learned that cattle are afraid of lots of little visual details like reflections on a wet floor, a wriggling chain, or high-contrast colors such as a yellow ladder against a gray wall. If these distractions are removed the cattle quietly walk up the chute.

The fourth similarity between animals and autism is extreme sensitivity to tone. I did not perceive eye signals from other people but I did attend to tone of voice. Tone was the only subtle social signal that I perceived. Everybody who has a dog knows that he is very responsive to the intent in tone of voice. From tone of voice both a dog and myself can determine if a person is pleased or angry. People with autism who learned to speak late have told me that they thought that tone was the meaning instead of the words. This is another indicator of primal importance of tone. Animals can also have similar problems with sensory over sensitivity. Dogs that are scared of fireworks may be sound sensitive. Sound sensitivity in both autism and animals can be very pitch specific. A collie was afraid of the vacuum cleaner and barked loudly when it was set for rugs and he had no response when it was set for floors. At different settings the sound had a different pitch. Individuals with autism have similar reactions to different sounds.

Emotionally, there are both similarities between animals and people with autism and big differences. Dogs are highly social and are easy to train because they want to please their master. The sociability of dogs is totally different from autism, but other aspects of emotion are similar. Among the aspects of emotions that are similar is less complexity. Animals and people with autism have simpler emotions. They are either happy, angry, fearful, or sad. They do not have complicated mixtures of emotion. Another similarity is that fear is the primary emotion in both autism and animals. This idea has already been discussed in detail.

To finish this summary I would like to answer to people who might be offended by comparing autism to animals. Modern neuroscience and genetics is showing that there is no black-and-white divide between people and animals. Research on sequencing the genome of people and animals is blurring the line. Long stretches of DNA in the human genome and the genome of animals such as dogs is either the same or similar.

As a person with autism, I do not feel offended when I compare myself to an animal. In some ways animals such as cattle or dogs have traits that are to be greatly admired. They do not get into horrible wars where large numbers of their species are killed or tortured. I have observed that the animals with the most complex brains, such as chimps and dolphins, engage in some of the nastiest behavior toward each other. They are fully described in *Animals in Translation*. As brains become more complex, the possibilities of wiring errors may increase. I speculate that wiring errors may create great genius but they may also create individuals who are capable of horrific acts unless they are brought up in a caring environment where they are taught right from wrong.

10

EINSTEIN'S SECOND COUSIN

The Link Between Autism and Genius

AT AN AUTISM CONFERENCE I attended eight years ago, I met Einstein's second cousin. We had lunch in the hotel restaurant, and I can remember the great difficulty she had in finding something on the menu that she would not be allergic to. She then proceeded to tell me that she had one musically talented autistic child and an intellectually gifted child. As we continued to talk, she revealed that her family history contained many individuals with depression, food allergies, and dyslexia. Since then I have talked with many families and discovered that the parents and relatives of autistic children are often intellectually gifted.

In the *Journal of Autism and Developmental Disorders,* Sukhdev Narayan and his colleagues wrote that the intelligence and educational achievements of the parents of an autistic child with good language skills are often greater than those of similar parents without any autistic children. I was not surprised when I learned that two Nobel prizewinners have autistic children. Even in families with low-functioning autistic children I have found a high incidence of intellectually gifted parents and relatives. Research studies have not yet shown a definitive relationship between low-functioning autism and increased intellectual ability in family histories. But this may be due to a number of factors, including the high incidence of low-functioning autism caused by factors such as a high fever at age two, premature birth, Fragile X syndrome, or some other readily diagnosable neurological problem. Numerous discussions with such families more often than not do reveal that intellectual ability is present, however.

Looking at my own family history reveals at least one pattern that has now been well documented. Three different studies reported in the *Journal of Autism and Developmental Disorders* and one in the *American Journal of Medical Genetics* indicate that there is a relationship between autism and depression, or affective disorder, in families. My grandfather on my mother's side was a brilliant, shy engineer who invented the automatic pilot for airplanes. For over forty years his invention kept every airplane on course. He worked toward developing this compass in a loft over a streetcar maintenance building, patiently pursuing his theories even though the scientists at all the big aviation companies thought he was wrong.

My grandmother on my mother's side and my mother both have good visualization skills and are intellectually talented. Granny was always bothered by loud noise. She told me that when she was a little girl, the sound of coal sliding down the chute was torture. Throughout her life she had bouts of depression, which were effectively treated in her later years with the drug Tofranil.

On my father's side of the family, there was the infamous Grandin temper. Dad would blow up in restaurants if the food took too long to arrive. He also had a tendency to fixate on a single subject. One time he got obsessed with shutting down the riding stable next door to his house. He spent days and days writing letters to the city officials and measuring the amount of manure that was thrown in the dumpster. My father had a lonely boyhood, and it is very likely that he had a mild form of autism.

Fortunately, none of my siblings are autistic. I have two sisters and a brother. One of my sisters is a visual thinker who is very artistic and extremely good at redecorating old houses. She can look at a dumpy old house and see in her mind the cute place she can turn it into. She had learning problems in school, possibly owing to mild auditory processing problems that made it difficult for her to understand speech in a noisy classroom. Mathematics was difficult for her. My other two siblings are both normal, although my youngest sister has a slight tendency to suffer from sensory overload when too many different noisy activities occur at once. Her eight-year-old son has no signs of autism, but he has had difficulty learning to read and problems understanding some speech sounds. My other nieces and nephews are normal.

Mild autistic traits often show up in the parents and relatives of children with autism. Another study published in the *Journal of Autism and Developmental Disorders,* by G. R. Delong and J. T. Dwyer, indicated that over two thirds of families with a high-functioning autistic child had a first- or second-degree relative who had Asperger's syndrome, the mild form of autism. Based on hundreds of discussions with families I've met at conferences, it is clear that many parents of autistic children are visual thinkers with talents in computers, art, and music. Other common traits in the family histories of autistics are anxiety disorder, depression, and panic attacks. Narayan found that the parents of autistic children, especially the fathers, had a tendency to pursue a special interest singlemindedly, and they were likely to have poor social skills. Parents who were not autistic themselves had some of the traits of their autistic children. In a study conducted by Rebecca Landa and other researchers at Johns Hopkins School of Medicine, where parents were asked to make up a story, 34 percent made up a rambling, plotless story without a clear beginning, middle, and end. That is the nature of associational visual thinking. It is like putting a jigsaw puzzle together. It is not done in any particular order.

There is good evidence that autism has a strong genetic basis. Folstein and Rutter reported that in identical twins, when one twin was autistic, the other twin was autistic 36 percent of the time. Nonautistic twins had a higher percentage of learning problems than normal twin pairs had. Identical twins have the same genetic makeup, whereas fraternal twins have completely different genes. When one fraternal twin was autistic, the other was almost never autistic. But the inheritance of autism is complex. There is no single autism gene. Robin Clark speculates in the journal *Personal Individual Differences* that the disorder may occur if a person receives too big a dose of genetic traits which are only beneficial in smaller amounts. For example, a slight tendency to fixate on a single subject can enable a person to focus and accomplish a great deal, whereas a stronger tendency to fixate prevents normal social interaction.

People with autism run a greater risk than others of having a child with autism, learning difficulties, or developmental problems. However, family history studies by Edward Ritvoe and his colleagues at UCLA have shown that the siblings of an autistic have almost no increased risk of having an autistic child, although they do run an increased risk of having children with learning disabilities or mild autistic traits.

Many researchers speculate that a cluster of interacting genes may cause a variety of disorders such as depression, dyslexia, schizophrenia, manic-depression, and learning disabilities. Dr. Robert Plomin and his colleagues at Pennsylvania State University state that autism is one of the most inheritable psychiatric diagnoses. They also maintain that many disorders such as depression represent extremes of a continuum of behavior from normal to abnormal. The same genes are responsible for both normal variations and the abnormal extremes. It is likely that this same principle applies to autism. People labeled autistic have an extreme form of traits found in normal people. Leo Kanner found that in four out of nine cases, depression or anxiety occurred in the parents of autistic children. Recent studies by Robert Delong, at Duke University in North Carolina, found there is often a history of manic-depression in the families of children with autism.

Genius Is an Abnormality

It is likely that genius is an abnormality. If the genes that cause autism and other disorders such as manic-depression were eliminated, the world might be left to boring conformists with few creative ideas. The interacting cluster of genes that cause autism, manic-depression, and schizophrenia probably has a beneficial effect in small doses. In her book *Touched with Fire,* Dr. Kay Redfield Jamison reviewed studies that showed a link between manic-depression and creativity. Manic-depressives experience a continuum of emotions, from moody to full-blown mania and deep, dark depression. When writers experience a mild form of the condition, they often produce some of their best work. When the disorder becomes full-blown, they are no longer able to function. There is a tendency for the mood swings to worsen with age, and this may explain why famous writers such as Ernest Hemingway committed suicide relatively late in life. Studies have shown that artists, poets, and creative writers have higher rates of manic-depression or depressive disorder than the general population.

A study done at the University of Iowa by N. C. Andreason showed that 80 percent of creative writers have had mood disorders at some time during their life. A high percentage of artists, poets, and writers have to be medicated to control their condition. Thirty-eight percent of writers and artists have had to take medication, and 50 percent of poets have had to receive treatment. The University of Iowa study also showed that parents and siblings of writers have a high rate of mood disorders.

Dean Simonton, at the University of California at Davis, has studied the factors that make a person a great politician, such as leadership, charisma, and boundless energy or drive. People with these qualities often have had problems with depression and alcohol abuse. Simonton concludes that "in order to be creative, it seems you have to be slightly crazy."

A study of mathematical giftedness further reinforces the idea of abnormality and genius. A paper by Camilla Persson Benbour, at Iowa State University, provides strong evidence that mathematical genius and giftedness are highly correlated with physical abnormalities. Three things that occur more frequently in people with high mathematical ability than in the population at large are lefthandedness, allergies, and nearsightedness. Both learning disability in mathematics and math talent are associated with lefthandedness. Young children who show very high ability in verbal reasoning and mathematics are twice as likely to have allergies as the rest of the population. Students with extremely high ability are also more likely to be nearsighted. The old stereotype of a little genius with thick glasses may be true.

Obviously, not all geniuses are abnormal, but the genes that produce normal people with certain talents are likely to be the same genes that produce the abnormalities found at the extreme end of the same continuum. Back in the 1940s researchers recognized that elimination of the genes that cause manic-depression would have a terrible cost. Researchers at McLean Hospital near Boston concluded,

> If we could extinguish the sufferers from manic-depressive psychosis from the world, we would at the same time deprive ourselves of an immeasurable amount of the accomplished and good, of color and warmth, of spirit and freshness. Finally, only dried-up bureaucrats and schizophrenics would be left. Here I must say that I would rather accept into the bargain the diseased manic-depressives than give up the healthy individuals of the same heredity cycle.

Twenty years earlier, John W. Robertson wrote in his book *Edgar A. Poe, A Psychopathic Study,*

> Eradicate the nervous diathesis, suppress the hot blood that results from the over-close mating of neurotics, or from that unstable nervous organization due to alcoholic inheritance, or

even from insanity and the various forms of parental degeneracy, and we would have a race of stoics—men without imagination, individuals incapable of enthusiasms, brains without personality, souls without genius.

As I have said, it has only been recently that I realized the magnitude of the difference between me and most other people. During the past three years I have become fully aware that my visualization skills exceed those of most other people. I would never want to become so normal that I would lose these skills. Similarly, being childlike may have helped me to be creative. In his book *Creating Minds,* Howard Gardner outlined the creative lives of seven great twentieth-century thinkers, including Einstein, Picasso, and T. S. Eliot. One common denominator was a childlike quality. Gardner describes Einstein as returning to the conceptual world of a child, and says that he was not hampered by the conventional paradigms of physics. It is interesting that autism is caused by brain immaturity. In many ways I have remained a child. Even today I do not feel like a grownup in the realm of interpersonal relationships.

Some scientists are strictly analytical thinkers. The physicist Richard Feynman denied the validity of poetry and art. In his biography of Feynman, *Genius,* James Gleick wrote, "He would not concede that poetry or painting or religion could reach a different kind of truth." Of course, many scientists do value poetry and share traits from both the creative and scientific end of the continuum, just as some scientists, artists, and highly analytical philosophers have some autistic traits. Albert Einstein, Ludwig Wittgenstein, and Vincent van Gogh all exhibited developmental abnormalities during early childhood. By definition, autism is an early-onset disorder, and problems such as delayed speech and odd behavior must show up at an early age for a person to be labeled as having autistic traits.

As a child, Einstein had many of these traits. He did not learn to speak until he was three. In a letter to a mother of an autistic child, he admitted to not being able to learn to speak until late and that his parents had been worried about it. Bernard Patten reports in the *Journal of Learning Disabilities* that Einstein silently repeated words to himself until age seven and did not freely associate with his peers. Whereas some prodigies develop at an early age, Einstein did not exhibit any great genius as a young child. Some people thought he was a dullard. He was a bad speller and did poorly in foreign languages. Like many autistic-type children, he was very good at jigsaw puzzles and spent hours building houses from playing cards. He had a singlemindedness of purpose and a poor memory for things that did not interest him, especially things of a personal nature. In *Einstein: The Life and Times,* the biographer Ronald W. Clark wrote that Einstein's backwardness may have helped guide him in his field. Einstein himself said, "I sometimes ask myself, how did it come that I was the one to develop the theory of relativity? The reason, I think, is that a normal adult never stops to think about problems of space and time." He had tremendous ability to concentrate and could work for hours or days on the same problem.

In *Einstein Lived Here,* Abraham Pais wrote, "To be creative in establishing lasting deep human relations demands efforts that Einstein was simply never willing to make." Like me, he was more attached to ideas and work. I don't know what a deep relationship is. His deep passion was for science. Science was his life. One of his graduate students said, "I have never known anybody who enjoyed science so sensuously as Einstein." According to Howard Gardner, Einstein was interested in the relationships between objects far more than in relationships between people.

In their book, *The Stigma of Genius,* the biographers Joe L. Kincheloe, Shirley R. Steinberg, and Deborah J. Tippins puzzled over the dichotomy between Einstein's public charm and charisma and his private life as a loner. He was an aloof observer of people and a solitary child. In *The Private Lives of Albert Einstein,* Roger Highfield and Paul Garter wrote, "Einstein described his dedication to science as an attempt to escape the merely personal by fixing his gaze on the objective universe. The desire to locate a reality free of human uncertainties was fundamental to his most important work" (referring to the theory of relativity). I can relate to this. On weekends I write and draw by myself, and during the week I give talks and act very social. Yet there is something missing in my social life. I can act social, but it is like being in a play. Several parents have told me that their autistic child has done a great job in the school play, acting like somebody else. As soon as the play is over, he or she reverts to being solitary.

Like Einstein, I am motivated by the search for intellectual truth. For me, searching for the meaning of life has always been an intellectual activity driven by anxiety and fear. Deep emotional relationships are secondary. I am happiest when I see tangible results, such as giving a mother information on the latest educational programs that will enable her autistic child to achieve in school. I value positive, measurable results more than emotion. My concept of what constitutes a good person is based on what I do rather than what I feel.

Einstein had many traits of an adult with mild autism, or Asperger's syndrome. Kincheloe and his colleagues reported that Einstein's lectures were scattered and sometimes incomprehensible. Students would often be confused because they could not see associations between some of the specific examples he gave and general principles. The association was obvious to Einstein's visual mind but not to his verbal-thinking students. Students reported that Einstein would lose his train of thought while writing a theorem on the blackboard. A few minutes later he would emerge from a trance and write a new hypothesis. The tendency for scattered thought is due to associative thinking.

Einstein also did poorly in school until he was sent to one that allowed him to use his visualization skills. He told his psychologist friend Max Wertheimer, "Thoughts did not come in any verbal formulation. I rarely think in words at all. A thought comes, and I try to express it in words afterwards." When he developed the theory of relativity, he imagined himself on a beam of light. His visual images were vaguer than mine, and he could decode them into mathematical formulas. My visual images are extremely vivid, but I am unable to make the connection with mathematical symbols. Einstein's calculation abilities were not phenomenal. He often made mistakes and was slow, but his genius lay in being able to connect visual and mathematical thinking.

Einstein's dress and hair were typical of an adult with autistic tendencies, most of whom have little regard for social niceties and rank. When he worked at the Swiss patent office, he sometimes wore green slippers with flowers on them. He refused to wear suits and ties in the days when professors dressed for teaching. I wouldn't be surprised if his dislike for dress clothes was sensory. The clothes he preferred were all soft, comfortable clothes such as sweatshirts and leather jackets. Nor did Einstein's hair meet the norm for men's hair fashions. Long, wild hair that was not cut was definitely not the style. He just did not care.

It has been suggested by Oliver Sacks that the philosopher Ludwig Wittgenstein was probably a high-functioning person with autism. He did not talk until he was four years old, and he was considered a dullard with no talent. It is likely that his family history included depression, because both of his brothers committed suicide. He had great mechanical ability, and at age ten he constructed a sewing machine. Young Wittgenstein was a poor student, and he never wore a tie or hat. He used formal, pedantic language and used the polite form of "sie" in German to address his fellow students, which alienated them and caused them to tease him. Overly formal speech is common in high-functioning autistics.

Vincent van Gogh's artwork reveals great emotion and brilliance, but as a child and a young man he had some autistic traits. Like Einstein and Wittgenstein, van Gogh showed no outstanding abilities. Biographers describe him as an aloof, odd child. He threw many tantrums and liked to go in the fields alone. He did not discover his artistic talents until he was twenty-seven years old. Prior to establishing a career in art, he had many of the characteristics of an adult with Asperger's syndrome. He was ill groomed and blunt. In his book *Great Abnormals,* Vernon W. Grant describes his voice and mannerisms, which also resemble those of an adult with autistic tendencies: "He talked with tension and a nervous rasp in his voice. He talked with complete self-absorption and little thought for the comfort or interest in his listeners." Van Gogh wanted to have a meaningful existence, and this was one of his motivations for studying art. His early paintings were of working people, to whom he related. According to Grant, van Gogh was forever a child and had a very limited ability to respond to the needs and feelings of others. He could love mankind in the abstract, but when forced to deal with a real person, he was "too self-enclosed to be tolerant."

Van Gogh's art became bright and brilliant after he was admitted to an asylum. The onset of epilepsy may explain his switch from dull to extremely bright colors. Seizures changed his perception. The swirls in the sky in his painting *Starry Night* are similar to the sensory distortions that some people with autism have. Autistics with severe sensory processing problems see the edges of objects vibrate and get jumbled sensory input. These are not hallucinations but perceptual distortions.

Bill Gates, the head of Microsoft and the inventor of Windows, is another person who has some autistic traits. *Time* magazine was the first to make the connection, comparing Oliver Sacks's *New Yorker* article about me with John Seabrook's article on Gates in the same magazine. Some of the traits that were similar were repetitive rocking and poor social skills. Gates rocks during business meetings and on airplanes; autistic children and adults rock when they are nervous. Other autistic traits he exhibits are lack of eye contact and poor social skills. Seabrook wrote, "Social niceties are not what Bill Gates is about. Good spelling is not what Bill Gates is about." As a child, Gates had remarkable savant skills. He could recite long passages from the Bible without making a single mistake. His voice lacks tone, and he looks young and boyish for his age. Clothes and hygiene are low on his list of important things.

Mild autistic traits can provide the singlemindedness that gets things done. Hans Asperger stresses the value of people with Asperger's syndrome, recognizing that they often achieve success in highly specialized academic professions. Individuals with Asperger's syndrome who are not retarded or afflicted with extreme rigidity of thinking can excel. Asperger concludes that narrowmindedness can be very valuable and can lead to outstanding achievement.

There are few Einsteins today. Maybe they all flunk the Graduate Record Exam or get poor grades. I had to get through school by going through the back door, because I failed the math part of the Graduate Record Exam. My grades in high school were poor until I became motivated in my senior year. In college I did well in biology and psychology but had great difficulty with French and math. Most of the great geniuses have had very uneven skills. They are usually terrible in one subject and brilliant in their special area. Richard Feynman had very low scores on the Graduate Record Exam in English and history. His physics score was perfect, but his art score was in the seventh percentile.

Even Einstein, after graduating from the Zurich Federal Institute of Technology, was not able to obtain an academic appointment. He annoyed big important professors when he told them that their theories were wrong. He had to take a job at the Swiss patent office. While he was a patent clerk, he wrote his famous theory of relativity and got it published in a physics journal. Today it would be extremely difficult for a patent clerk to get a paper published in a physics journal. If Einstein had lived today, his paper probably would have been rejected and he would have stayed in the patent office.

There are many examples of great scientists, artists, and writers who were poor students. Charles Darwin, the father of evolutionary theory, was not able to master a foreign language. When he left school, he was considered only an ordinary student. Darwin wrote in his autobiography, *Life and Letters,* which was edited by his son Francis, "I was considered by all my masters and by my father as a very ordinary boy, rather below the common standard of intellect." He found life at Cambridge University dull and did poorly in mathematics. Darwin's saving grace was his passion for collecting. This provided the motivation to go on his famous voyage on the *Beagle,* where he first formulated the theory of evolution.

Gregor Mendel, the father of modern genetics, was unable to pass the exam to get a high school teaching license, according to Guinagh Kevin in his book *Inspired Amateurs.* Mendel failed the exam several times. He conducted his classic experiments in the corner of a monastery garden with pea plants. When he presented the results at his university thesis defense, he failed to get his degree. Nobody paid any attention to his wild theories, but fortunately 120 copies of his paper survived and were recognized as the works of genius that they are after his death. Today his principles are taught in every high school science class.

During my career, I have met many brilliant visual thinkers working in the maintenance departments of meat plants. Some of these people are great designers and invent all kinds of innovative equipment, but they were disillusioned and frustrated at school. Our educational system weeds these people out of the system instead of turning them into world-class scientists.

Autistic savants who can accomplish amazing feats of memory, drawing, calculation, or reproduction of musical compositions usually have almost no social skills. Until recently, many professionals assumed that savants could not be creative. They thought that their brains acted as tape recorders or photocopiers. But close examination of savant drawings and music shows that there can be true creativity, and these skills can be developed. In *Extraordinary People,* Darold A. Treffert cites two cases in which savants' social skills and musical and artistic talents have both improved. These abilities will grow if the person is encouraged and supported in this work by a good teacher. Stephen Wiltshire, the famous autistic savant from England, draws fabulously detailed pictures of buildings and also has great musical ability. In his book *An Anthropologist on Mars,* Oliver Sacks describes how Wiltshire's ability to improvise musically has steadily improved and how when he sings all signs of autism disappear, only to reappear when the music stops. Music transforms him and may temporarily open the door to emotion. When he does his detailed beautiful drawings of buildings he acts autistic. Contrary to popular belief, savants do not always have an absolute photographic memory. When Dr. Sacks asked him to make several drawings of his house there were mistakes such as an added chimney or a window in the wrong place. This was partly due to not having enough time to fully study the house. When Stephen makes drawings of imaginary cities he takes bits and pieces of building from his memory and puts them together in new ways. This is the same way I do design work.

It's clear that the genetic traits that can cause severe disabilities can also provide the giftedness and genius that has produced some of the world's greatest art and scientific discoveries. There is no black-and-white dividing line between normal and abnormal. I believe there is a reason that disabilities such as autism, severe manic-depression, and schizophrenia remain in our gene pool even though there is much suffering as a result. Researchers speculate that schizophrenia may be the evolutionary price that has to be paid for abilities in language and social interactions. Tim Crow, of the Clinical Research Centre in London, points out that the incidence of schizophrenia is the same in most societies and that it is not decreasing, even though schizophrenics are less likely than others to have children.

The genes that cause schizophrenia may confer advantages in a milder form. This may also be true for manic-depression and autism. In my own case, I believe my contributions to humane slaughtering of cattle and improved treatment of animals have been facilitated by my abnormality. But none of my work would have been possible had I not developed a correlative system of belief.

Update: Thinking with the Subconscious Mind

The Asperger's Syndrome diagnosis was not used much in the United States when *Thinking in Pictures* was written. One of my biggest concerns today with the Asperger's diagnosis is that students who should be in gifted and talented programs get shunted off into the special education track where they do not belong. I have seen students with IQs of 150 where nothing was being done to develop their intellects and prepare them for careers. Dr. Simon Baron-Cohen at the University of Cambridge in England conducted a study that showed that there were more engineers in the family histories of people with autism. Another study showed that scientists and accountants were overrepresented in autistic family histories. Many famous scientists and musicians such as Carl Sagan and Mozart were probably Asperger's. Famous people on the autism/Asperger spectrum are profiled in books and on Web sites.

Baron-Cohen asks an important question: is Asperger Syndrome a disability? Where is the dividing line between normal and abnormal? He is referring to mild Asperger's with no speech delays where the student is working at normal or above school grade levels. Brain scan studies have shown all kinds of abnormalities in the amygdale (emotion center), frontal cortex, and many other parts of the brain. At what point do these differences in the sizes of different brain structures become just variations on the more extreme end of the normal range?

In the updates of previous chapters I discussed the research on the lack of connectivity between different parts of the brain. Sections that are far apart are underconnected but local areas in the brain may have overconnectivity. Dr. S. F. Witelson in the Department of Psychiatry at McMasters University in Canada studied Einstein's brain. He found that the area responsible for mathematical reasoning was 15 percent larger. The mathematical area also had more extensive connections to the visual parts of the brain. It was like having the "math" and "art" departments fused together. Local overconnectivity may explain Einstein's genius.

I Think with My Subconscious

In most people, language covers up the primary sensory based thinking that people share with animals. Sensory based thinking is subconscious in most people. I think with the primary sensory based subconscious areas of the brain. Reading through the scientific literature on different types of memory, I came to the realization that depending on the type of psychology one was studying, there are different names for conscious and subconscious memory. There are two types of long term memory and they are probably the same thing, regardless of what they are called. Below is a chart showing the different pairs of names that mean the same thing.

Conscious memory	Unconscious memory
Verbal (word memory)	Sensory based memory (visual, motor, auditory, etc.)
Explicit memory	Implicit memory
Declarative memory	Procedural memory
More easily forgotten	Resistant to forgetting

Since I think with the subconscious, repression does not occur and denial is impossible. My "search engine" has access to the entire library of detailed sensory based memories.

My memory is not automatic. I have to push the "save" button to store a memory in my database. Things which are of little interest to me such as hotel room décor are not remembered unless the place was really unique. To push the "save" button requires either conscious effort or a strong emotion. The brain circuits that connect emotions to my "save" button are intact. However, I can search through old memories of really bad events, such as being fired from a job, with no emotion. At the time I was fired I cried for two days. The emotion was experienced in the present but the memory in my database of being fired can be accessed without emotion. It took me a long time to figure out that most normal people cannot open a "bad experience file" in their brain without experiencing emotion along with the memory.

Privileged Access

People with savant skills are often able to perform tasks better than normal people because they have direct access to primary areas of the brain and experience no interference from language. Simon Baron-Cohen's research showed that people on the autism spectrum are superior to normal people on the "hidden figure" test. In this test a person has to locate a figure such as a triangle hidden in another larger figure. When this task is done in a brain scanner, the autistic person's brain is most active in primary visual systems for object features. It is like a direct line to the "picture department." In the normal person, the frontal cortex and other areas are activated and may interfere with the visual task.

A. W. Snyder at the University of Sydney found that savantlike drawing skills emerged when the frontal cortex of a normal person was impaired with low-frequency magnetic pulses. Turning off the frontal cortex also enabled normal people to be better proofreaders. The frontal cortex is connected to everything in the brain and it interferes with perceiving details.

Work by Dr. Bruce Miller at the University of California provides hard evidence that primary visual thinking and musical parts of the brain are sometimes blocked by the frontal cortex. He studied patients who have a type of Alzheimer's disease called frontal-temporal lobe dementia. As the disease destroys language parts of the brain, art and music skills emerged in people who had no previous interest in art or music. One patient created paintings that won awards in art shows. As language deteriorated, the art became more photo-realistic and the person's behavior resembled autism. One person who lost all language designed a sprinkler head.

Since I think with my subconscious I can see the decision-making process that is not perceived by most people. One day I was driving on the freeway when an elk ran across the road. A picture flashed into my mind of a car rear-ending me. That would be the consequence for putting on the brakes. Another picture flashed up of an elk crashing through the windshield, which would be the consequence of swerving. A third picture came up of the elk passing in front of the car. That would happen if I just slowed down. Now three pictures were on the computer screen in my mind. I clicked on the slowing down choice and avoided an accident. I think what I have just described is how animals think.

II

Stairway to Heaven

Religion and Belief

AS A TOTALLY LOGICAL and scientific person, I continually add data to my library of knowledge and constantly update both my scientific knowledge and my beliefs about God. Since my thought processes use a series of specific examples to form a general principle, it makes logical sense to me that general principles should always be modified when new information becomes available. It is beyond my comprehension to accept anything on faith alone, because of the fact that my thinking is governed by logic instead of emotion. On June 14, 1968, while I was a sophomore in college, I wrote in my diary:

> I develop my views from the existing pool of knowledge and I will adapt my views when I learn more. The only permanent view that I have is that there is a God. My views are based on the basic fundamental laws of nature and physics that I am now aware of. As man learns more about his environment I will change my theory to accommodate the new knowledge. Religion should be dynamic and always advancing, not in a state of stagnation.

When I was ten or eleven, it seemed totally illogical to me that a Protestant religion was better than the Jewish or Catholic religion. I had a proper religious upbringing, with prayers every night, church on Sunday, and Sunday school every week. I was raised in the Episcopal church, but our Catholic cook believed that Catholicism was the only way to get to heaven. The psychiatrist that I started seeing in the fourth grade was Jewish. It made no sense to me that my religion was better than theirs. To my mind, all methods and denominations of religious ceremony were equally valid, and I still hold this belief today. Different religious faiths all achieve communication with God and contain guiding moral principles. I've met many autistic people who share my belief that all religions are valid and valuable. Many also believe in reincarnation, because it seems more logical to them than heaven and hell.

There are also autistic people who adopt very rigid fundamentalist beliefs and become obsessed with religion. One girl prayed for hours and went to church every day. In her case, it was an obsession instead of a belief, and she was kicked out of several churches. Low doses of the drug Anafranil allow her to practice her faith in a more moderate and reasonable manner. In another case, a young man had disturbing obsessive thoughts that ran through his head. Intensive prayer helped control them.

People at the Kanner end of the autism continuum may interpret religious symbolism in a very concrete manner. Charles Hart describes his eight-year-old son's reaction to a film in Sunday school about Abraham's being willing to sacrifice his son to God. Ted watched the film and passively said "Cannibals" at the end.

For many people with autism, religion is an intellectual rather than emotional activity. Music is the one exception. Some people feel much more religious when their participation is accompanied with extensive use of music. One autistic design engineer I know said that religious feeling is utterly missing for him, except when he hears Mozart; then he feels an electrifying resonance. I myself am most likely to feel religious in a church when the organist plays beautiful music and the priest chants. Organ music has an effect on me that other music does not have.

Music and rhythm may help open some doors to emotion. Recently I played a tape of Gregorian chants, and the combination of the rhythm and the rising and lowering pitch was soothing and hypnotic. I could get lost in it. There have been no formal studies on the effect of music, but therapists have known for years that some autistic children can learn to sing before they can talk. Ralph Mauer, at the University of Florida, has observed that some autistic savants speak in the rhythm of poetic blank verse. I have strong musical associations, and old songs trigger place-specific memories.

In high school I came to the conclusion that God was an ordering force that was in everything after Mr. Carlock explained the second law of thermodynamics, the law of physics that states that the universe will gradually lose order and have increasing entropy. Entropy is the increase of disorder in a closed thermodynamic system. I found the idea of the universe becoming more and more disordered profoundly disturbing. To visualize how the second law worked, I imagined a model universe consisting of two rooms. This represented a closed thermodynamic system. One room was warm and the other was cold. This represented the state of maximum order. If a small window were opened between the rooms, the air would gradually mix until both rooms were lukewarm. The model was now in a state of maximum disorder, or entropy. The scientist James Clark Maxwell proposed that order could be restored if a little man at the window opened and closed it to allow warm atoms to go to the one side and cold atoms to go to the other side. The only problem is that an outside energy source is required to operate the window. When I was a college sophomore, I called this ordering force God.

Many of my heroes, including Einstein, did not believe in a personal God. In 1941, Einstein wrote that the scientist's "religious feeling takes the form of rapturous amazement at the harmony of natural law, which reveals an intelligence of such superiority that compared with it, all systematic thinking and acting of human beings is an utterly insignificant reflection." When he was eleven years old, he went through a religious phase and practiced the Jewish dietary laws and adhered to a literal interpretation of Scripture. A year later this came to an abrupt end when he was exposed to science. When he read scientific books, he concluded that the Bible stories were not literally true.

In his later years, Einstein wrote: "Out yonder there was this huge world, which exists independently of us human beings and which stands before us like a great eternal riddle, at least partially accessible to our inspection and thinking. The contemplation of this world beckoned like a liberation." He felt that he was right to switch from fundamentalist beliefs to a broader view of religion. He went on to say in the same paper: "The road to this paradise was not as comfortable and alluring as the road to the religious paradise; but it has proved itself trustworthy, and I have never regretted having chosen it."

But my favorite of Einstein's words on religion is "Science without religion is lame. Religion without science is blind." I like this because both science and religion are needed to answer life's great questions. Even scientists such as Richard Feynman, who rejected religion and poetry as sources of truth, concede grudgingly that there are questions that science cannot answer.

I am deeply interested in the new chaos theory, because it means that order can arise out of disorder and randomness. I've read many popular articles about it, because I want scientific proof that the universe is orderly. I do not have the mathematical ability to understand chaos theory fully, but it confirms the idea that order can come from disorder and randomness. James Gleick, in the book *Chaos,* explains that snowflakes are ordered symmetrical patterns that form in random air turbulence. Slight changes in the air turbulence will change the basic shape of each snowflake in random and unexpected ways. It is impossible to predict the shape of a snowflake by studying the initial atmospheric conditions. This is why weather is so hard to predict. Weather patterns have order, but random changes affect the order in random, unpredictable ways.

I hated the second law of thermodynamics because I believed that the universe *should* be orderly. Over the years I have collected many articles about spontaneous order and pattern formation in nature. Susumu Ohno, a geneticist, has found classical music in slime and mouse genes. He converted the genetic code of four nucleotide bases into a musical scale. He found that the order of the bases in our DNA is not random, and when the order is played, it sounds like something by Bach or a Chopin nocturne. Patterns in flowers and leaf growth in plants develop in mathematical sequence of the Fibonacci numbers and the golden mean of the Greeks.

Patterns spontaneously arise in many purely physical systems. Convection patterns in heated fluids sometimes resemble a pattern of cells. Scientists at the University of California have discovered that silver atoms deposited on a platinum surface spontaneously form ordered patterns. The temperature of the platinum determines the type of pattern, and order can be created from random motion. A small change in temperature totally changes the pattern. At one temperature triangles are formed, and at another temperature hexagons form, and further heating of the surface makes the silver atoms revert to triangles in a different orientation. Another interesting finding is that everything in the universe, ranging from amino acids and bacteria to plants and shells, has handedness. The universe is full of self-ordering systems.

Probably within my lifetime, scientists will determine how to create life from basic chemicals. Even when they have accomplished this task, though, they will not have answered the question that has plagued people for all time: what happens when you die?

Questioning Immortality and Life's Meaning

As a young college student I had never given much thought to what happens after death, but then I started working with cattle in the Arizona feedlots. Did the animals just turn into beef, or did something else happen? This made me uneasy, and my science-based religious beliefs could not provide a satisfactory answer. I thought it must be very comforting to have the kind of blind faith that enables one to believe that one will have an afterlife in heaven.

Prior to going to Arizona State University, I had never seen the outside of a slaughterhouse and I had never seen an animal slaughtered. It wasn't until I first drove past the Swift meatpacking plant that I began to develop a concrete visual system for understanding what would become my life's work. In my diary on March 10, 1971, I wrote about a dream I had: "I walked up to Swift's and put my hands on the outside of the white wall. I had the feeling that I was touching the sacred altar." A month later I drove past Swift's again, and I could see all the cattle out in the pens, waiting for the end to come. It was then I realized that man believes in heaven, hell, or reincarnation because the idea that after the cattle walk into the slaughterhouse it is all over forever is too horrible to conceive. Like the concept of infinity, it is too ego-shattering for people to endure.

A few days later I got up the courage to go to Swift's and ask if I could go on a tour. I was told that they did not give tours. This just heightened my interest in this forbidden place. Being denied entrance made my holy land even holier. This was not a symbolic door, it was reality that had to be faced. I was attempting to answer many of life's big questions. I made many entries in my diary at that time.

April 7, 1971: "It is important that the animals not be defiled at the slaughterhouse. Hopefully they will be allowed to die with some sort of dignity. The animals probably feel more pain when they are put through the cattle chute to be branded or castrated."

May 18, 1971: "What is really significant in life? I used to think being a great scientist would be the most significant thing in the world that I could do. Now I have some second thoughts about it.

There are many different paths that I could follow right now and I do not know which one leads to significance."

For me, religion was a means of attaining a certain kind of truth. At that time I had not read any of the popular books on near-death experiences, which were not widely available until around 1975, though I still remember a vivid dream I had on October 25, 1971. Swift was a six-story building. Only the first floor of this building was a slaughterhouse, and when I found a secret elevator, it transported me to the upper floors. These upper levels consisted of beautiful museums and libraries that contained much of the world's culture. As I walked through the vast corridors of knowledge, I realized that life is like the library and the books can be read only one at a time, and each one will reveal something new.

Years later I read interviews with people who have had near-death experiences. Several people interviewed by Raymond Moody reported in his book *Life After Life* that during such an experience they saw libraries and places that contained the ultimate knowledge. The concept of a library of knowledge is also a theme in more recent books such as *Embraced by the Light,* by Betty J. Eadie.

A few days before I had my dream of the Swift plant turning into a vast library, I had visited an Arabian horse farm where great pains were taken to treat each horse as an individual. I petted the beautiful stallions, and I felt that they should never be subjected to the feedlot or the slaughterhouse. The next day I was on a feedlot operating the chute while cattle were being branded and vaccinated. When I looked at each steer, it had the same look of individuality as the stallions. For me the big question was, how could I justify killing them?

When I finally gained entry to Swift's, on April 18, 1973, it was completely anticlimactic, and I was surprised by my lack of a reaction to it. It was no longer the mysterious forbidden place; plus Swift was a very good plant where the cattle did not suffer.

Several months later, Lee Bell, the gentle man who maintained the stunners, asked me if I had ever stunned cattle—that is, killing them. After I told him I never had, he suggested that it was now time to do it. The first time I operated the equipment, it was sort of like being in a dream.

After I pulled out of the parking lot, I looked up at the sky, and the clouds were really spectacular. I understood the paradox that unless there is death, we could not appreciate life. Having first faced the paradox of power and responsibility, and coming to terms with my ambivalent feelings of controlling animals with devices such as cattle chutes, I now had to face the paradox of life and death.

The thing that was most upsetting was that there are no definitive answers to the question of what happens when one dies. Philosophers have written about it for centuries. And unanswerable questions have forced people to look to God.

Swift was a major influence on two parallel aspects of my life. It was the place where my design career started, and it was also the real-life stage where I determined religious beliefs in my unique way. Like the physicists who are trying to find the Grand Theory of Everything, I attempted to integrate all aspects of my life by using my visual mode of thinking. The night after I first killed cattle I could not bring myself to say that I had actually killed them myself. Instead, during the next two weeks I made further suggestions for simple improvements that would reduce bruises when I visited the plant.

About a year later I got my first large design project at the Swift plant, building a new cattle ramp and conveyor restrainer system. The construction crew and I named this project the Stairway to Heaven, after the Led Zeppelin song. At first the construction crew thought it was a joke, but as the stairway took shape, the name started to take on a more serious meaning to everybody who worked on it. Friends told me to make sure that Swift didn't cheat on paying me, but I felt almost mercenary in accepting money for what I had done. The changes I initiated at the plant made it more humane for the cattle. Even if I didn't get paid, I was at peace with myself knowing that twelve hundred cattle a day were less frightened.

It was difficult to handle my relations with Swift strictly as a business venture. The emotional involvement was just too great. I would remember the times when I would circle the plant in my car and look upon it as if it were Vatican City. One night when the crew was working late, I stood on the nearly completed structure and looked into what would become the entrance to heaven for cattle. This made me more aware of how precious life is. When your time comes and you are walking up the proverbial stairway, will you be able to look back and be proud of what you did with your life? Did you contribute something worthwhile to society? Did your life have meaning?

The Stairway to Heaven was completed on September 9, 1974. It was a major step in defining my purpose in life. In my diary I wrote, "I greatly matured after the construction of the Stairway to Heaven because it was REAL. It was not just a symbolic door that had private meaning to me, it was a reality that many people refuse to face." I felt I had learned the meaning of life—and not to fear death. It was then that I wrote the following in my diary:

> I believe that a person goes on to somewhere else after they die. I do not know where. How a person conducts themselves on Earth during their life will have an effect on the next life. I became convinced that some sort of an afterlife exists after I discovered God at the top of the Stairway to Heaven. The Swift plant was a place where beliefs were tested in reality. It was not just intellectual talk. I watched the cattle die and even killed some of them myself. If a black void truly exists at the top of the Stairway to Heaven, then a person would have no motivation to be virtuous. [September 1977]

For several years I was quite comfortable with my beliefs, especially concerning an afterlife, until I read Ronald Siegal's article about hallucinations in the October 1977 issue of *Scientific American*. As it turned out, many of the feelings and sights described by people who were resuscitated after they had died could be explained by hallucinations triggered in a brain deprived of oxygen. The vast majority of cases described in popular books about near-death experiences were victims of lack of oxygen. Cardiac arrest and blood loss were the most common causes of death mentioned in both Moody's books and more recent books such as *Embraced by the Light* and *Saved by the Light*. But the biggest blow to my beliefs was the discovery of the effects of biochemistry on my own brain.

In the summer of 1978 I swam through the dip vat at the John Wayne Red River feed yard as a stupid publicity stunt. Doing this provided a great boost to my career and got me several speaking engagements. However, coming in contact with the chemical organophosphates had a devastating effect. The feeling of awe that I had when I thought about my beliefs just disappeared. Organophosphates are known to alter levels of the neurotransmitter acetylcholine in the brain, and the chemicals also caused me to have vivid and wild dreams. But why they affected my feeling of religious awe is still a mystery to me. It was like taking all the magic away and finding out that the real Wizard of Oz is just a little old man pushing buttons behind a curtain.

This raised great questions in my mind. Were the feelings of being close to God caused by a chemical Wizard of Oz behind the curtain? In my diary I wrote, "To my horrified amazement the chemicals blocked my need for religious feelings." They made me very sick, but gradually the effects wore off and the feeling returned. However, my belief in an afterlife was shattered. I had seen the wizard behind the curtain. Yet there is something in me that really wants to believe that the top of the Stairway to Heaven is not just a black void.

The possibility that a void exists after death has motivated me to work hard so I can make a difference—so that my thoughts and ideas will not die. When I was working on my Ph.D., a coworker in our lab told me that the world's libraries contain our extra soma, or out-of-body genes. Ideas are passed on like genes, and I have a great urge to spread my ideas. I read an article in the newspaper about an official at the New York Public Library who said that the only place on earth where immortality is provided is in libraries. This is the collective memory of humanity. I put this on a sign and placed it over my desk. It helped me to persevere and get through my Ph.D. work. When Isaac Asimov died, his obituary contained the statement that death was not much of an issue because all his thoughts would live on in books. This gave him a kind of immortality. The ancient Egyptians and Greeks achieved immortality by leaving behind the pyramids, the Parthenon, and writings by great thinkers. Maybe immortality is the effect one's thoughts and actions can have on other people.

To destroy other people's culture is to rob them of their immortality. When I read that the Olympic stadium and the main library in Sarajevo had been destroyed, I wept. Newspaper pictures of the shattered library were most upsetting. That culture was being eliminated. The Olympic stadium, a symbol of civilization and cooperation, was in ruins. I had a difficult time reading a newspaper article describing how the stadium seats were used to make coffins—the last civilized act in a world that had become hell. I become very upset and emotional when I think about the loss of knowledge and culture, and I am unable to write about this without crying. One nation was deliberately destroying the literature, architecture, and civilization of another. A civilized city where people had cooperated for centuries was now blown to bits. This was emotion gone wild. I don't know what it is like to hate somebody so much that you would want to destroy their culture and civilization.

It was quantum physics that finally helped me believe again, as it provided a plausible scientific basis for belief in a soul and the supernatural. The idea in Eastern religion of karma and the interconnectedness of everything gets support from quantum theory. Subatomic particles that originate from the same source can become entangled, and the vibrations of a subatomic particle that is far away can affect another particle that is nearby. Scientists in the lab study subatomic particles that have become entangled in beams of laser light. In nature, particles are entangled with millions of other particles, all interacting with each other. One could speculate that entanglement of these particles could cause a kind of consciousness for the universe. This is my current concept of God.

In all the years I have worked in slaughter plants, I have intuitively felt that I must never misbehave near the kill chute. Doing something bad, like mistreating an animal, could have dire consequences. An entangled subatomic particle could get me. I would never even know it, but the steering linkage in my car could break if it contained the mate to a particle I disturbed by doing something bad. To many people this belief may be irrational, but to my logical mind it supplies an idea of order and justice to the world.

My belief in quantum theory was reinforced by a series of electrical outages and equipment breakdowns that occurred when I visited slaughter plants where cattle and pigs were being abused. The first time it happened, the main power transformer blew up as I drove up the driveway. Several other times a main power panel burned up and shut down the plant. In another case, the main chain conveyor broke while the plant manager screamed obscenities at me during an equipment startup. He was angry because full production was not attained in the first five minutes. Was it just chance, or did bad karma start a resonance in an entangled pair of subatomic particles within the wiring or steel? These were all weird breakdowns of things that usually never break. It could be just random chance, or it could be some sort of cosmic consciousness of God.

Many neuroscientists scoff at the idea that neurons would obey quantum theory instead of old everyday Newtonian physics. The physicist Roger Penrose, in his book the *Shadows of the Mind,* and Dr. Stuart Hameroff, a Tucson physician, state that movement of single electrons within the microtubules of the brain can turn off consciousness while allowing the rest of the brain to function. If quantum theory really is involved in controlling consciousness, this would provide a scientific basis for the idea that when a person or animal dies, an energy pattern of vibrating entangled particles would remain. I believe that if souls exist in humans, they also exist in animals, because the basic structure of the brain is the same. It is possible that humans have greater amounts of soul because they have more microtubules where single electrons could dance, according to the rules of quantum theory.

However, there is one thing that completely separates people from animals. It is not language or war or toolmaking; it is long-term altruism. During a famine in Russia, for example, scientists guarded the seed bank of plant genetics so that future generations would have the benefits of genetic diversity in food crops. For the benefit of others, they allowed themselves to starve to death in a lab filled with grain. No animal would do this. Altruism exists in animals, but not to this degree. Every time I park my car near the National USDA Seed Storage Lab at Colorado State University, I think that protecting the contents of this building is what separates us from animals.

I do not believe that my profession is morally wrong. Slaughtering is not wrong, but I do feel very strongly about treating animals humanely and with respect. I've devoted my life to reforming and improving the livestock industry. Still, it is a sobering experience to have designed one of the world's most efficient killing machines. Most people don't realize that the slaughter plant is much gentler than nature. Animals in the wild die from starvation, predators, or exposure. If I had a choice, I would rather go through a slaughter system than have my guts ripped out by coyotes or lions while I was still conscious. Unfortunately, most people never observe the natural cycle of birth and death. They do not realize that for one living thing to survive, another living thing must die.

Recently I read an article that had a profound effect on my thinking. It was entitled "The Ancient Contract," by S. Budiasky, and it was published in the March 20, 1989, issue of *U.S. News & World Report*. It presented a natural historical view of our evolving relationship with animals. This view presents a middle ground between the supporters of animal rights, who believe that animals are equal to humans, and the Cartesian view, which treats animals as machines with no feelings. I added the biological concept of symbiosis to Budiasky's view. A symbiotic relationship is a mutually beneficial relationship between two different species. For example, biologists have learned that ants tend aphids and use them as "dairy cows." The ants feed the aphids, and in return the aphids give a sugar substance to the ants. People feed, shelter, and breed cattle and hogs, and in return the animals provide food and clothing. We must never abuse them, because that would break the ancient contract. We owe it to the animals to give them decent living conditions and a painless death. People are often confused by the paradox of my work, but to my practical, scientific mind it makes sense to provide a painless death for the cattle I love. Many people are afraid of death and can't stand to face it.

Often I get asked if I am a vegetarian. I eat meat, because I believe that a totally vegan diet, in which all animal products are eliminated, is unnatural. Even the Hindus, traditionally vegetarian people, eat dairy products. A completely vegan diet is deficient in vitamin B_{12}, and using dairy products does not eliminate killing animals. A cow has to have a calf every year in order to give milk, and the calves are raised for meat.

But someday in the distant future, when slaughterhouses become obsolete and livestock is replaced with products of gene splicing, the real ethical questions regarding the creation of any kind of animal or plant we desire will seem far more significant than killing cattle at the local slaughter plant. Humans will have the power to control their own evolution. We will have the power of God to create totally new forms of life. However, we will never be able to answer the question of what happens when we die. People will still have a need for religion. Religion survived when we learned that the earth was not the center of the universe. No matter how much we learn, there will always be unanswerable questions. Yet if we stop evolving, we will stagnate as a species.

Bernard Rollin, a philosopher on animal rights issues at Colorado State University, points out, "It is true that free inquiry is integral to our humanity, but so too is morality. So the quest for knowledge must be tempered with moral concern." A total lack of moral concern can lead to atrocities such as the Nazi medical experiments, but medical knowledge was also delayed for a thousand years because of religious taboos about the dissection and study of human bodies. We must avoid intellectual stagnation, which retards the progress of medical knowledge, but we must be moral. Biotechnology can be used for noble, frivolous, or evil purposes. Decisions on the ethical use of this powerful new knowledge should not be made by extremists or people purely motivated by profit. There are no simple answers to ethical questions.

There is a basic human drive to figure out who and what we are. The mega-science projects of the 1990s, such as the Human Genome Project, the Hubble space telescope, and the now defunct supercollider, replace the pyramids and cathedrals of our ancestors. One of the main purposes of the Hubble space telescope was to enable us to see all the way to the beginning of the universe. It has confirmed the existence of black holes in the center of other galaxies, and its observations may radically change our theories about the origin of the universe. Some recent Hubble observations are beginning to establish the existence of other planets circling around in alternate solar systems. Years ago, scientists were burned at the stake for talking and writing about these ideas.

As a person whose disability has provided me with certain abilities, especially with regard to understanding how animals sense the world, I appreciate these difficult questions and the importance of religion as a moral ordering code for empathic, just behavior.

When the combination of organophosphate poisoning and antidepressant drugs dampened my religious emotions, I became a kind of drudge who was capable of turning out mountains of work. Taking the medication had no effect on my ability to design equipment, but the fervor was gone. I just cranked out the drawings as if I were a computer being turned on and off. It was this experience that convinced me that life and work have to be infused with meaning, but it wasn't until three years ago, when I was hired to tear out a shackle hoist system, that my religious feelings were renewed.

It was going to be a hot Memorial Day weekend, and I was not looking forward to going to the new equipment startup. I thought it would be pure drudgery. The kosher restraint chute was not very interesting technically, and the project presented very little intellectual stimulation. It did not provide the engineering challenge of inventing and starting something totally new, like my double-rail conveyor system.

Little did I know that during those few hot days in Alabama, old yearnings would be reawakened. I felt totally at one with the universe as I kept the animals completely calm while the rabbi performed shehita. Operating the equipment there was like being in a Zen meditational state. Time stood still, and I was totally, completely disconnected from reality. Maybe this was nirvana, the final state of being that Zen meditators seek. It was a feeling of total calmness and peace until I was snapped back to reality when the plant manager called me to come to his office. He had spent hours hiding in the steel beams of the ceiling, secretly watching me hold each animal gently in the restraining chute. I knew he was fascinated, but he never asked me anything about it.

When it was time to leave, I cried as I drove to the airport. The experience had been so strangely hypnotic that I was tempted to turn around and return to the plant. As I turned in the rental car and checked in at the gate, I thought about the similarities between the wonderful trancelike feeling I had had while gently holding the cattle in the chute and the spaced-out feeling I had had as a child when I concentrated on dribbling sand through my fingers at the beach. During both experiences all other sensation was blocked. Maybe the monks who chant and meditate are kind of autistic. I have observed that there is a great similarity between certain chanting and praying rituals and the rocking of an autistic child. I feel there has to be more to this than just getting high on my own endorphins.

On January 11, 1992, I returned to the kosher plant and made the following entry in my diary:

> When the animal remained completely calm I felt an overwhelming feeling of peacefulness, as if God had touched me. I did not feel bad about what I was doing. A good restraint chute operator has to not just like the cattle, but love them. Operating the chute has to be done as an act of total kindness. The more gently I was able to hold the animal with the apparatus, the more peaceful I felt. As the life force left the animal, I had deep religious feelings. For the first time in my life logic had been completely overwhelmed with feelings I did not know I had.

It was then that I realized that there can be a conflict between feeling and doing. Zen meditators may be able to achieve the perfect state of oneness with the universe, but they do not bring about reform and change in the world around them. The dreadful shackle hoist system would still exist if I had not been involved in convincing the plant to remodel. I also realized that the religious slaughter ritual was valuable, because it put controls on killing.

People who work in high-speed slaughter plants get overdosed with death, and they become numb and desensitized.

It is the religious belief of the rabbis in the kosher plants that helps prevent bad behavior. In most kosher slaughter plants, the rabbis are absolutely sincere and believe that their work is sacred. The rabbi in a kosher plant is a specially trained religious slaughterer called a hochet, who must lead a blameless life and be moral. Leading a blameless life prevents him from being degraded by his work.

Almost all cultures have slaughter rituals. When you read a modern English translation of Deuteronomy and Leviticus, it becomes obvious that the temple was also the town slaughterhouse. American Indians showed respect for the animals they ate, and in Africa the use of rituals limited the number of animals killed. In the book *The Golden Bough*, J. G. Fraser describes slaughter rituals practiced by the ancient Greeks, Egyptians, Phoenicians, Romans, and Babylonians. Both Judaism and Islam have detailed slaughter rituals. Killing is kept under control because it is done in a special place, according to strict rules and procedures.

I believe that the place where an animal dies is a sacred one. There is a need to bring ritual into the conventional slaughter plants and use it as a means to shape people's behavior. It would help prevent people from becoming numbed, callous, or cruel. The ritual could be something very simple, such as a moment of silence. In addition to developing better designs and making equipment to insure the humane treatment of all animals, that would be my contribution. No words. Just one pure moment of silence. I can picture it perfectly.

Update: Teaching Right from Wrong

Changes in my religious beliefs are too complex for a brief update. So in this section I am going to give my recommendations on how to teach children on the autism/Asperger spectrum right from wrong. The concept of right and wrong is too abstract for an autistic child to understand. They have to learn right from wrong by being given many examples of right and wrong behavior. These examples can then be placed into different categories in their brains. For example, you do not steal another child's toy because you would not like it if they stole your toy. You are polite to another child and share your toys with him because you would like to get a chance to play with his toys.

I am a person who learns by concrete examples. Depending on how I was brought up, I could be taught to be a good person or taught to be bad. When I was a child I never saw grownups behaving badly on TV and getting away with it. My heroes, Superman and the Lone Ranger, were clearly good guys who fought bad guys. These heroes never engaged in mean acts or stole things. Today heroes in movies often do bad things. This is difficult for an autistic child to categorize into good and bad. My sportsmanship was poor. By specific examples I was taught the principles of fair play. Cheating at games was not tolerated in our house. I was taught that winning by cheating was totally wrong and booing the winner was bad sportsmanship. When I stole a toy fire engine from a birthday party, my mother made me return it to its rightful owner.

When I was in elementary school, the Lord's Prayer made little sense. It was too abstract. If there is no picture in my mind, I cannot think. There were two things we did at church that had meaning to me. Every Christmas, each child had to take one of his or her really nice toys and wrap it up as a Christmas gift for a poor child. At the service the minister stood in front of a manger filled with the presents and said, "It is better to give than to receive." This made a big impression. I also never forgot the fourth grade Sunday School field trip to a local jail. This was to show us what would happen if you were bad. The worst thing in the jail was the horrible slop they served out of big kettles at lunch.

Rules of Civilized Society

When I was in high school, I categorized all of society's rules into four categories. They are:

1. Really bad things
2. Courtesy rules
3. Illegal but not bad
4. Sins of the system

I still follow these rules today. In order for a civilized society to exist, there have to be prohibitions against really bad things such as killing or injuring people, stealing, and destruction of property. Courtesy rules and manners are important because they help people to get along. However, there needs to be a category where rules sometimes can be broken. An example of illegal but not bad would be enrolling a teenager in a community college even if he was underage. To justify breaking this rule, the teenager must be well behaved and not disruptive. It must be impressed on him or her that attending the community college is a grownup privilege. The sins of the system are specific to each specific society. A sin of the system in the United States would be of no consequence in Holland. A good example would be drug offenses. In the United States the penalty for a drug offense may be worse than the penalty for murder. This makes no logical sense. The "sins" have very severe penalties that are not logical. When I was in high school, I learned I could get away with more illegals but not bads if I could be trusted never to commit a sin of the system. The high school sins were sex, smoking, and drugs. Some examples of illegals but not bads were staying outside after dark or flying my kite out on the hill without a staff member being present.

Emphasize Positive Teachings

The autism/Asperger's mind often has a tendency to get obsessed with the negative. Teach the autistic child positive religious values. Instruct the child to live a good life where others are treated with kindness and respect. Use examples where the child participates in an activity. Elementary children could help pick up trash in the neighborhood. During the holidays they could make cards and decorations for people in a nursing home. They must be taught that they should do things to make the community a better place. High school students could help teach younger children to read or paint an old lady's house. Abstract religious concepts will not be understood by many individuals on the spectrum. It is better to teach them how to be good citizens through a series of hands-on activities. Through many examples, children on the autism/Asperger's spectrum need to learn the "Golden Rule." In modern English it states, treat other people the way you would like to be treated. This principle is in all major religions.

One good teaching tool for Christians are key chains and necklaces that say, "What would Jesus do?" if he lived in today's world. He would never steal, he would be polite, he would be kind to animals, he would be honest, he would never tease, and he would help an old lady with her grocery bags. When the child does something nice, tell him, you did a Jesus good deed. In Judaism, how a person lives their life is very important. Teach children the importance of doing good deeds to help the community. In the Muslim faith, giving alms to the poor and helping people in need is one of the pillars of Islam. Get children to help in a soup kitchen or have them use some of their own money to buy food or clothing for a person in need. Some children with autism have difficulty understanding the purpose of money. To help them learn, they need to purchase the items for the poor themselves from money they have earned doing chores.

Another old-fashioned set of values that I could relate to were things like the scouting code, the 4-H pledge, and the "Rules of Living" from Roy Rogers, a children's cowboy hero in the 1950s. His rules emphasized politeness and kindness. You should drill into a young child's brain that acts such as killing or hurting other people is totally wrong. The two most important rules in the Ten Commandments for an individual on the spectrum are thou shalt not kill and thou shalt not steal. This will help prevent a child from becoming involved in gangs or other criminal activity.

I am concerned about religious obsessions especially in high-functioning autism and Asperger's. One of the most dangerous, unhealthy obsessions is the view that people from other religions are evil or bad. The worst wars in all of history have been fought between people in the name of religion. It is much better for a person on the spectrum to be obsessed with computers or sports statistics than to be obsessed with religion in a negative way. They need to be taught to live for their religion by being a good person. When I was in high school, I received a brochure from a cattle chute company that said, "thoughts with no price tags." "Men will wrangle for religion, write for it, fight for it, die for it, anything but live for it." I never forgot that quote.

REFERENCES AND SELECTED READINGS

Chapter 1   Thinking in Pictures: Autism and Visual Thought

REFERENCES

Biever, C. 2005. Lots of clues but no answers. New Scientist, May 14, pp. 14–15.

Chase, M. 1993. Inner music, imagination may play role in how the brain learns muscle control. Wall Street Journal, Oct. 13, 1993, pp. 1–8.

Courchesne, E. 2004. Brain development in autism: Early overgrowth followed by premature arrest of growth. Mental Retardation and Developmental Disabilities, Research Reviews, 10: 106–111.

Courchesne, E., Redcay, E., and Kennedy, D. P. 2004. The autistic brain: Birth through adulthood, Current Opinion in Neurology, 17: 489–496.

Farah, M. J. 1989. The neural basis of mental imagery. Trends in Neuroscience, 12: 395–399.

Freedman, D. J., Riesenhuber, M., Poggio, T., and Miller, E. K. 2001. Categorical representation of visual stimuli in the primate prefrontal cortex, Science, 291: 312–315.

Galton, F. 1911. Inquiries into human faculty and development. Dutton, New York.

Glurfa, M., Zhang, S., Jenett, A., Menzel, R., and Mandyam, V. S. 2001. The concepts of sameness and difference in an insect. Nature, 410: 930–932.

Grandin, T. 2000. My mind as a web browser: How people with autism think, Cerebrum (Winter), 13–22.

Grandin, T. 2002. Do animals and people with autism have true consciousness, Evolution and Cognition, 8: 241–248.

Hart, C. 1989. Without reason. Harper & Row, New York.

Horgan, J. 2005. Can a single cell recognize Bill Clinton?, *Discover,* June, pp. 64–69.

Huttenlocher, P. R. 1984. Synaptic elimination in the cerebral cortex. *American Journal of Mental Deficiency,* 88: 488–496.

Just, M. A., Cherkassky, J. L., Keller, T. A., and Minshew, N. J. 2004. Cortical activation and synchronization during sentence comprehension in high functioning autism: Evidence of underconnectivity, *Brain,* 127: 1811–1821.

Kosslyn, S. M., and Thompson, W. L. 2003. *Psychological Bulletin,* 129: 723–746.

Luria, A. R. 1987. *The mind of a mnemonist.* Harvard University Press, Cambridge, Mass.

Park, C. 1992. Autism into art: a handicap transfigured. In E. Schopler and G. B. Mesibov (eds.), *High Functioning Autism.* Plenum Press, New York, pp. 250–259.

Park, D., and Youderian, P. 1974. Light and number: ordering principles in the world of an autistic child. *Journal of Autism and Childhood Schizophrenia,* 4: 313–323.

Quiroga, R. Q., Reddy, L., Kreimen, G., Koch, C., and Fried, I. 2005. Invariant visual representation by single neurons in the human brain. *Nature,* 435: 1102–1107.

Thorpe, S. J., and Thorpe, M. F. 2001. Seeking categories in the brain, *Science,* 291: 260–263.

Urton, G., and Brezine, C. J. 2005. Khipu accounting in ancint Peru, *Science,* 309: 1063–1067.

Wickelgreen, I. 2005. Autistic brains out of synch. *Science,* 308: 1856–1858.

Willis, T. J., Lever, C., Cacucci, F., Burgess, N., and O'Keefe, J. 2005. Attractor dynamics in the hippocampal representation of the local environment, *Science,* 308: 873–876.

Zeki, S. 1992. The visual image in the mind and brain, *Scientific American,* September, pp. 69–76.

OTHER READINGS

Geyde, A. 1991. The neural basis of mental imagery. *Trends in Neuroscience,* 12: 395–399.

Grandin, T. 1995. How people with autism think. In E. Schopler and G. B. Mesibov (eds.), *Learning and Cognition in Autism.* Plenum Publishing, New York, pp. 137–156.

West, T. G. 1991. *In the mind's eye.* Prometheus Books, Buffalo, New York.

Chapter 2   The Great Continuum: Diagnosing Autism

REFERENCES

Allen, D. 1994. Conference. The Virginia Foundation for the Exceptional Child and Adolescent, October 8, 1994. Richmond, Virginia.

American Psychiatric Association, 1994. *Diagnostic and statistical manual IV.* Washington, D.C.

Asperger, H. 1944. Autistic psychopathy in childhood. Translated by Uta Frith. In U. Frith (ed.), *Autism and Asperger's syndrome.* Cambridge University Press, Cambridge, England, pp. 37–92.

Bauman, M. L., and Kemper, T. L. 1994. Neuroanatomic observations of the brain in autism. In M. L. Bauman and T. L. Kemper (eds.), *The neurobiology of autism.* Johns Hopkins University Press, Baltimore, Maryland, pp. 119–145.

Berger, C. L. 1992. *Facilitated communication guide.* New Breakthroughs, Eugene, Oregon.

Berk, L. 1994. Why children talk to themselves. *Scientific American,* November 1994, pp. 78–83.

Bouchard, T. J. 1994. Genes, environment and personality. *Science,* 264: 1700–1701.

Canter, D. S., Thatcher, R. W., Hrybyk, M., and Kaye, H. 1986. Computerized EEG analysis of autistic children. *Journal of Autism and Development Disorders,* 16: 169–187.

Cunningham, A. 2005. Finding autism earlier, *Scientific American Mind,* 16(1): 7.

Delacato, C. H. 1974. *The ultimate stranger.* Arena, Novato, California.

Eastham, M. 1990. *Silent words.* Oliver Pate, Ottawa.

Elliot, R. O., Dobbin, A. R., Rose, G. D., and Soper, H. V. 1994. Vigorous aerobic exercise versus general motor training effects on maladaptive and stereotypic behavior of adults with both autism and mental retardation. *Journal of Autism and Developmental Disorders,* 24: 565–576.

Folstein, S., and Rutter, M. 1977. Infantile autism: a genetic study of 21 twin pairs. *Journal of Child Psychiatry,* 18: 297–321.

Frith, U. 1989. *Autism: explaining the enigma.* Basil Blackwell, Oxford, England.

Gazzaniga, M. S. 1989. Organization of the human brain. *Science,* 243: 947–952.

Geir, M. R. and Geier, D. A. 2003. Neurodevelopmental disorders following thimerosal containing vaccines. *Experimental Biology and Medicine,* 228: 660–664.

Gilchrist, A., Green, J., Cox, A., Burton, D., Rutter, M., and LeCooteur, A.

2001. Development and cortical functioning in adolescents with Asperger's syndrome: A comparative study. *Journal of Child Psychiatry,* 42: 227–240.

Hart, C. 1989. Op. cit.

Holden, C. 2005. Mating for autism, *Science,* 308: 948.

Horney, M., Chian, D., and Lipkin, W. I. 2004. Neurotoxic effects of postnatal thimerosal mouse strain dependent. *Molecular Psychiatry,* 9: 833–845.

Kanner, L. 1943. Autistic disturbances of affective contact. *Nervous Child,* 2: 217–250.

Kennedy, D. 2002. *The ADHD Autism Connection,* Water Brook Press, Colorado Springs, Colorado.

Kirby, D. 2005. *Evidence of Harm,* St. Martin's Press, New York.

Koegel, L. and Lazebnik, C. 2004. *Overcoming Autism,* Viking (Penguin Group), New York.

Liddle, P., and Barnes, T. 1990. Symptoms of chronic schizophrenia. *British Journal of Psychiatry,* 157: 558–561.

Lovaas, I. 1987. Behavioral treatment and normal educational and intellectual functioning in young autistic children. *Journal of Consulting and Clinical Psychology,* 55: 3–9. (Long-term outcome of this treatment is discussed in a series of articles in the *American Journal of Mental Retardation,* 97: 359–391.)

Maurice, C. 1993. *Let me hear your voice.* Knopf, New York.

Muhle, R., Trentacoste, S. V. and Rapin, I. 2004. The genetics of autism, *Pediatrics,* 113: 472–486.

Plomin, R., Owen, M. J., and McGuffin, G. 1994. The genetic basis of complex human behaviors. *Science,* 264: 1733–1739.

Rimland, B., and Green, G. 1993. Controlled evaluations of facilitated communication. *Autism Research Review,* 7: 7.

Sacks, O. 1994. An anthropologist on Mars. *New Yorker,* December 27, pp. 106–125.

Sellin, B. 1995. *I don't want to be inside me anymore.* Basic Books, New York.

Silberman, S. 2001. The Geek Syndrome, *Wired,* December pp. 175–187.

Spence, S. J. 2004. The genetics of autism, *Seminar Pediatric Neurology,* 11: 196–204.

Tanguay, P. E., and Edwards, R. M. 1982. Electrophysiological studies of autism: The whisper of the bang. *Journal of Autism and Developmental Disabilities,* 12: 177–184.

Treasure Chest of Behavioral Strategies, Future Horizons, Arlington, Texas.

Volkmar, R. R., and Cohen, D. J. 1989. Disintegrative disorder or "late onset": autism. *Journal of Child Psychiatry,* 30: 717–724.

Wainwright-Sharp, J. A. 1993. Visual orienting deficits in high-functioning people with autism. *Journal of Autism and Developmental Disorders,* 23: 1–13.

Williams, D. 1992. *Nobody nowhere.* Time Books, New York.

OTHER READINGS

Coleman, R. S., Frankel, F., Ritvoe, E., and Freeman, B. J. 1976. The effects of fluorescent and incandescent illumination upon repetitive behaviors in autistic children. *Journal of Autism and Developmental Disorders,* 6: 157–162.

Lovaas, I. O. 1992. *The me book.* Pro-Ed, Austin, Texas.

Martin, R. 1994. *Out of silence: a journey into language.* Henry Holt, New York.

Osterling, J., and Dawson, G. 1994. Early recognition of children with autism. *Journal of Autism and Developmental Disorders,* 24: 247–257.

Paquier, P. F., VanDongen, H. R., and Loonen, C. B. 1992. Landau-Kleffner syndrome or "acquired aphasia with convulsive disorder." *Archives of Neurology,* 49: 354–359.

Sands, S., and Ratey, J. J. 1986. The concept of noise. *Psychiatry,* 49: 290–297.

Simmons, J., and Sabine, O. 1987. *The hidden child.* Woodbine House, Kensington, Maryland.

Walters, R. G., and Walters, W. E. 1980. Decreasing self-stimulatory behavior with physical exercise in a group of autistic boys. *Journal of Autism and Developmental Disorders,* 10: 379–387.

Chapter 3   The Squeeze Machine: Sensory Problems in Autism

REFERENCES

Asperger, H. 1944. Op. cit.

Ayres, J. A. 1979. Sensory integration and the child. *Western Psychological Services,* Los Angeles.

Barron, J., and Barron, S. 1992. *There's a boy in here.* Simon and Schuster, New York.

Bauman, M. L., and Kemper, T. L. 1994. Op. cit.

Betlison, S. 1997. The long-term effects of auditory training on children with autism. *Journal of Autism and Developmental Disorders,* 26: 361–374.

Biel, L., and Peske, N. 2004. *Raising a Sensory Smart Child, the Definitive Handbook for Helping a Child with Sensory Integration Issues.* Penguin Books, New York.

Boddaert, N., Chabane, N., Belin, P., and Bourgeois, M., et al. 2004. Perception of complex sounds in autism: Abnormal auditory cortical processing in children. *American Journal of Psychiatry,* 161: 2117–2120.

Cesaroni, L., and Garber, M. 1991. Exploring the experience of autism through firsthand accounts. *Journal of Autism and Developmental Disorders,* 21: 303–312.

Ciesielski, K. T., Courchesne, E., and Elmasian, R. 1990. Effects of focused selective attention tasks on event-related potentials in autistic and normal individuals. *Electroencephalography and Clinical Neurophysiology,* 75: 207–220.

Courchesne, E. 1991. Neuroanatomic imaging in autism. *Pediatrics* (Supplement), 87: 781–790.

Courchesne, E. 1989. *A new model of brain and behavior development in infantile autism.* Proceedings, Autism Society of America, pp. 25.

Courchesne, E., Yeung-Courchesne, R., Press, G. A., Hesselink, J. R., and Jernigan, T. L. 1988. Hypoplasia of cerebellar vernal lobules VI and VII in autism. *New England Journal of Medicine,* 318: 1349–1354.

Damasio, A. 1994. *Descartes' error: emotion, reason and the human brain.* Putnam, New York.

Damasio, A. 1994. Impaired recognition of emotion in facial expressions following bilateral damage to the human amygdala. *Nature,* 372: 669–672.

Eastham, M. 1990. Op. cit.

Edelson, S. M., Edelson, M. G., Kerr D. C., and Grandin, T. 1999. Behavioral and physiological effects of deep pressure on children with autism: A pilot study evaluating the efficacy of Grandin's Hug Machine. *American Journal of Occupational Therapy,* 53: 145–152.

Evans, B. J., and Joseph, F. 2002. The effect of coloured filters on the rate of reading in an adult student population. *Ophthalmic Physiological Optometry,* 22: 535–545.

Hashimoto, T., Tayama, M., Miyazaki, M., Sakurama, N., Yoshimoto, T. Murakawa, K., and Kurodo, Y. 1992. Reduced brain stem size in children with autism. *Brain and Development,* 14: 94–97.

Irlen, H. 1991. *Reading by the colors.* Avery, New York.

Joliffe, T., Lakesdown, R., and Robinson, C. 1992. Autism, a personal account. *Communication,* 26, 3: 12–19.

Keverne, B. 1990. Junkie monkey get quick fix from grooming. *New Scientist,* January 20, p. 32.

Kranowitz, C. S. 1998. *The Out of Synch Child,* Penguin Books, Skylight Press, New York.

Lightstone, A., Lightstone, T., and Wilkins, A. 1999. Both coloured overlays and coloured lenses can improve reading fluency, but their optimal chromaticities differ. *Ophthalmic Physiological Optometry,* 19: 274–285.

McClelland, D. C., Eyre, D., Watson, G. J., Sherrard, C., and Sherrard, E. 1992. Central conduction time in autism. *British Journal of Psychiatry,* 160: 659–663.

McDonnell, J. M. 1993. *News from the border.* Ticknor & Fields, New York.

McKean, T. A. 1994. *Soon will come the light.* Future Education, Arlington, Texas.

Muckhopadhyay, T. R. 2004. *The Mind Tree,* Arcade Publishing, New York.

Ornitz, E. 1985. Neurophysiology in infantile autism. *Journal of the American Academy of Child Psychiatry,* 24: 251–262.

Rimland, B., and Edelson, S. M. 1995. Brief report: A pilot study of auditory integration training, *Journal of Autism and Developmental Disorders,* 25: 61–70.

Rogers, S. J., Hepburn, S., and Wehner, E. 2003. Parent reports of sensory symptoms in toddlers with autism and those with other developmental disorders, *Journal of Autism and Developmental Disorders,* 33: 631–642.

Sacks, O. 1993. To see and not to see. *New Yorker,* May 10, pp. 59–73.

Sicile-Kira, C. 2004. *Autism Spectrum Disorders.* Perigree Books, New York.

Sinclair, J. 1992. Bridging the gaps on inside view of autism. In E. Schopler and G. B. Mesibov (eds.), *High-functioning individuals with autism.* Plenum, New York, pp. 294–302.

Stehli, A. 1991. *Sound of a miracle.* Doubleday, New York.

Tanquay, P. E., and Edwards, R. M. Op. cit.

Walker, N., and Whelan. 1994. Geneva Symposium on Autism. October 27, 1994. Toronto, Canada.

White, D. B., and White, M. S. 1987. Autism from the inside. *Medical Hypothesis,* 24: 223–229.

Williams, D. 1994. *Somebody somewhere.* Time Books, New York.

Willilams, D. 1996. *Autism—An Inside-Out Approach.* Jessica Kingsley, London, England.

Williams, N. G., and Borchelt, P. L. 2003. Full body restraint and rapid stimulus exposure as a treatment for dogs with defensive aggressive behavior: Three case studies. *International Journal of Comparative Psychology,* 16: 226–236.

OTHER READINGS

Bhatara, V., Clark, D. L., Arnold, L. E., Gunsett, R., and Smeltzer, D. J. 1981. Hyperkinesis treated with vestibular stimulation: an exploratory study. *Biological Psychiatry,* 61: 269–279.

Creedon, M. P. 1994. Conference. Autism Society of America. July 6–9, 1994. Las Vegas, Nevada.

Grandin, T. 1992. Calming effects of deep touch pressure in patients with autistic disorders, college students and animals. *Journal of Child and Adolescent Psychopharmacology,* 2: 63–70.

Grandin, T., and Scariano, M. 1986. *Emergence: labelled autistic.* Arena, Navato, California.

Grandin, T., Dodman, T. N., and Shuster, L. 1989. Effect of naltrexone on relaxation induced by lateral flank pressure in pigs. *Pharmacal Biochemistry of Behavior,* 33: 839–842.

King, L. 1989. Facilitating neurodevelopment. Conference Proceedings, Autism Society of America, July 19–22, Seattle, Washington, pp. 117–120.

Kumazawa, T. 1963. "Deactivation" of the rabbit's brain by pressure application of the skin. *Electroencephalography and Clinical Neurophysiology,* 15: 660–671.

McClure, M. K., and Holtz, M. 1991. The effects of sensory stimulatory treatment on an autistic child. *American Journal of Occupational Therapy,* 45: 1138–1142.

Ornitz, E. 1993. Op. cit.

Ray, T. C., King, L. J., and Grandin, T. 1988. The effectiveness of self-initiated vestibular stimulation in producing speech sounds. *Journal of Occupational Therapy Research,* 8: 186–190.

Takagi, K., and Kobagasi, S. 1956. Skin pressure reflex. *Acta Medica et Biologica,* 4: 31–37.

Zissermann, L. 1992. The effects of deep pressure on self-stimulating behaviors in a child with autism and other disabilities. *American Journal of Occupational Therapy,* 46: 547–551.

Chapter 4   Learning Empathy: Emotion and Autism

REFERENCES

Barron, J., and Barron, S. 1992. Op. cit.

Bauman, M., and Kemper, T. L. 1994. Op. cit.

Bemporad, M. L. 1979. Adult recollections of a formerly autistic child. *Journal of Autism and Developmental Disorders,* 9: 179–197.

Casler, L. 1965. Effects of extra tactile stimulation on a group of institutionalized infants. *Genetic Psychology Monographs,* vol. 71, pp. 137–175.

Chambers, W. W. 1947. Electrical stimulation of the interior cerebellum of the cat. *American Journal of Anatomy,* 80: 55–93.

Condon, W. 1981. Asyncrony. *Omni,* December, p. 18. Reported by Walli Leff.

Courchesne, E. 1988. Op. cit.

Damasio, A. 1994. Op. cit.

Grandin, T. 1984. My experiences as an autistic child and review of related literature. *Journal of Orthomolecular Psychiatry,* 13: 144–174.

Grandin, T. 1989. Effect of rearing environment and environmental enrichment on behavior and neural development in young pigs. Ph.D. thesis, University of Illinois.

Grandin, T. 2001. Welfare of cattle during slaughter and prevention of non-ambulatory cattle. *Journal of American Veterinary Medical Association,* 219:1377–1382.

Grandin, T. 2005. Maintenance of good animal welfare standards in beef slaughter plants by using auditing programs, *Journal of American Veterinary Medical Association,* 226: 370–373.

Greenough, W. T. 1984. Anatomical substrates of behavioral plasticity. In C. W. Cotman and R. F. Thompson (eds.), *Plasticity in neurobiology: Cell to behavior.* 1984 Society for Neuroscience Short Course Syllabus, Washington D.C., pp. 42–53.

Harlow, H. F., and Zimmerman, R. R. 1959. Affectional responses in the infant monkey. *Science,* 130: 421–432.

Hutt, S. J., et al. 1965. A behavioral and electroencephalographic study of autistic children. *Journal of Psychiatric Research,* 3: 181–197.

Joliffe, T., et al. 1992. Op. cit.

Konner, M. 1982. *The tangled wing.* Holt, Rinehart, Winston, New York.

Mason, W. A. 1960. The effects of social restriction on the behavior of rhesus monkeys. *Journal of Comparative Physiology and Psychiatry,* 6: 582–588.

Melzack, R., and Burns, S. K. 1965. Neurophysiological effects of early sensory restriction. *Experimental Neurology,* 13: 163–175.

Miller, G. 2005. Reflecting on another's mind. *Science,* 308: 945–947.

Rapoport, J. L. 1989. *The boy who couldn't stop washing.* E. P. Dutton, New York.

Sagan, C. 1977. *The dragons of Eden: speculations on the evolution of human intelligence.* Random House, New York.

Simons, D., and Land, P. 1987. Early tactile stimulation influences organization of somatic sensory cortex. *Nature,* 326: 694–697.

Williams, D. 1994. Op. cit.

Chapter 5   The Ways of the World: Developing Autistic Talent

REFERENCES

Grandin, T. 1990. Needs of high-functioning teenagers and adults with autism. *Focus on Autistic Behavior,* April 1990, pp. 1–8.

Grandin, T. 1992. Making the transition from the world of school into the world of work. *The Advocate,* Autism Society of America, Spring 1992, pp. 8–9.

Grandin, T., and Duffy, K. 2004. *Developing Talents, Careers for Individuals with Asperger Syndrome and High Functioning Autism.* Autism Asperger Publishing Co., Shawnee Mission, Kansas.

Louv, R. 2005. *Last Child in the Woods, Saving our Children from Nature Deficit Disorder.* Algonquin Press, Chapel Hill, North Carolina.

McAfee, J. 2002. *Navigating the Social World.* Future Horizons, Arlington, Texas.

McKean, T. 1994. Op. cit.

Paradiz, V. 2005. *Elijah's Cup: A Family's Journey into the Community and Culture of High Functioning Autism and Asperger's Syndrome.* Jessica Kingsley, London.

Shore, S. 2001. *Beyond the Wall—Personal Experiences with Autism and Asperger Syndrome.* Autism Asperger Publishing, Shawnee Mission, Kansas.

Trivedi, B. 2005. Autistic and Pour, *New Scientist,* June 18, pp. 36–40.

OTHER READINGS

Kanner, L. 1971. Follow-up study of eleven autistic children originally reported in 1943. *Journal of Autism and Childhood Schizophrenia,* 1: 112–145.

Kanner, L., Rodriguez, A., and Ashender, B. 1972. How far can autistic children go in matters of social adaptation? *Journal of Autism and Childhood Schizophrenia,* 2: 9–33.

Szatmari, P., Bartolucci, G., Bond, S., and Rich, S. 1989. A follow-up study of high-functioning autistic children. *Journal of Autism and Developmental Disorders,* 19: 213–225.

Chapter 6 Believer in Biochemistry: Medications and New Treatments

REFERENCES

Barrett, R. P., Feinstein, C., and Hole, W. T. 1989. Effects of naloxone and naltrexone on self-injury: A double-blind placebo-controlled analysis. *American Journal of Mental Retardation,* 93: 644–651.

Bowden, C. L., Brugger, A. M., Swann, A. C., Calabrese, J. R., Janicak, P. G., Petty, F., Dilsaver, S. C., Davis, J. M., Rush, A. J., Small, J. G., et al. 1994. Efficacy of divalproex vs. lithium and placebo in the treatment of mania. *Journal of the American Medical Association,* 271: 908–924.

Cohen, S. A., Fitzgerald, R. J., Khan, S. R., and Khan, A. 2004. The effect of a switch to ziprasidone (Geodon) in an adult population with autistic disorders: Chart review of naturalistic open label treatment. *Journal of Clinical Psychiatry,* 65: 110–113.

Comings, D. E. 1990: *Tourette Syndrome and human behavior.* Hope, Duarte, California.

Cook, E. H. Jr., Rowlett, R., Jaseiskis, C., and Leventhal, B. 1992. Fluoxetine treatment of children and adults with autistic disorder and mental retardation. *Journal of the American Academy of Child and Adolescent Psychiatry,* 31, 4: 739–745.

Couzin, J. 2004. Volatile chemistry: Children and antidepressants. *Science,* 305: 468–470.

Delong, G. R., Teague, L. A., and Kaufman, M. M. 1998. Effect of fluoxetine (Prozac) treatment in young children with idiopathic autism. *Developmental Medicine and Child Neurology,* 40: 551–562.

Dodman, N. H., et al. 1987. Investigation into the use of narcotic antagonists in the treatment of stereotypic behavior pattern (crib biting) in the horse. *American Journal of Veterinary Research,* 48: 311–319.

Donovan, S. J., Stewart, J. W., and Nunes, E. W. 2000. Divalproex treatment of youth with explosive temper and mood liability. A double-blind placebo-controlled crossover design. *American Journal of Psychiatry,* 157: 818–820.

Edwards, J. G. and Anderson, L. 1999. Systematic review and guide to selective serotonin reuptake inhibitors. *Drugs,* 57: 507–533.

Fankhauser, M., Karumanchi, V., German, M., Yates, A., and Karumanchi, S. D.

1992. A double-blind, placebo-controlled study of the efficacy of transdermal clonidine in autism. *Journal of Clinical Psychiatry,* 53, 3: 77–82.

Fieve, R. R. 1994. *Prozac: Questions and answers for patients, family and physicians.* Avon, New York.

Gedye, A. 1989. Episodic rage and aggression attributed to frontal lobe seizures. *Journal of Mental Deficiency Research,* 33: 369–379.

Gedye, A. 1992. Anatomy of self-injurious, stereotypic, and aggressive movements: Evidence for involuntary explanation. *Journal of Clinical Psychology,* 48, 6: 766–778.

Gillberg, C. 1991. The treatment of epilepsy in autism. *Journal of Autism and Developmental Disorders,* 21: 61–77.

Gordon, C. T., State, R. C., Nelson, J. E., Hamburger, S. D., and Rapoport, J. L. 1993. A double-blind comparison of clomipramine, desipramine, and placebo in the treatment of autistic disorder. *Archives of General Psychiatry,* 50: 441–447.

Grandin, T. 1984. Op. cit.

Grandin, T. 1992. An inside view of autism. In E. Schopler and G. B. Mesibov (eds.), *High-functioning individuals with autism.* Plenum, New York, pp. 105–126.

Grandin, T., and Scariano, M. 1986. Op. cit.

Hardy, P. M. 1989. National Conference of the Autism Society of America. Seattle, Washington, July 19–22, 1989 (personal communication). Lecture with no published paper.

Horvath, K., and Perman, J. A. 2002. Autism and gastrointestinal symptoms. *Current Gastroentorology Reports,* 4: 251–258.

Jamison, K. R. 1993. *Touched with fire.* Free Press, New York.

Knivesberg, A. M., Reichelt, K. L., Hoien, T. and Nodland, M. 2002. A randomized controlled study of dietary intervention in autistic syndromes. *Nutritional Neurosciences,* 4: 251–261.

Kwon, H. 2004. Tardive dykinesia in an autistic patient treatment with risperidone. *American Journal of Psychiatry,* 161: 757–758.

Lerman, P., Lerman-Sagie, T., and Kivity, S. 1991. Effect of early corticosteroid therapy for Landau-Kleffner syndrome. *Developmental Medicine and Child Neurology,* 33: 257–266.

Lewis, L. 1998. *Special Diets for Special Kids.* Future Horizons, Arlington, Texas.

Lewis, L. S. 2005. Gf and Cf plain and simple. *Autism Asperger Digest Magazine,* Jan/Feb., pp. 10–11.

Lindsay, R. L., and Aman, M. G. 2003. Pharmocologic therapies and treatment for autism. *Pediatric Annals,* 32: 671–676.

Martin, A., Scahill, L., Anderson, G. M., and Aman, M., et al. 2004. Weight and leptin changes among risperidone treatment youths with autism: 6-month prospective data. *American Journal of Psychiatry,* 161: 1125–1127.

Martineau, J., Barthelemy, C., Garreau, B., and Lelord, G. 1985. Vitamin B_6, magnesium and combined B_6-Mg. Therapeutic effects in childhood autism. *Biological Psychiatry,* 20: 467–478.

Martineau, J., Barthelemy, C., and Lelord, G. 1986. Long-term effects of combined vitamin B_6-magnesium administration in an autistic child. *Biological Psychiatry,* 21: 511–518.

Mathews, A. W. and Abboud, A. L. 2005. FDA raises concerns about ADHD drugs. *Wall Street Journal,* June 29, pp. D1 and D5.

McClellan, J. M. and Werry, J. S. 2003. Evidence based treatments in child and adolescent psychiatry. *Journal of American Academy of Child and Adolescent Psychiatry.* pp.

McDougle, C. J., Kem, D. L., and Posey, D. J. 2003. Core Series: Use of ziprasidone for maladaptive symptoms in youths with autism. *Journal of American Academy of Child and Adolescent Psychiatry,* 41: 921–927.

McCracken, J. T., McGough, J., Shah, B., Cronin, P., and Hong, D., et al. 2002. Risperdone in children with autism and serious behavioral problems. *New England Journal of Medicine,* 347: 314–321.

Millward, C., Ferrita, M., Calver, S., and Connell-Jones, G. 2004. Gluten and casein free diets. *Cochrane Database Systems Review,* 2: CD003498.

Panksepp, J., and Lensing, P. 1991. Brief report: a synopsis of an open-trial of naltrexone treatment of autism with four children. *Journal of Autism and Developmental Disorders,* 21, 2: 135–140.

Plioplys, A. V. 1994. Autism: electroencephalogram abnormalities and clinical improvement with valproic acid. *Archives of Pediatrics and Adolescent Medicine,* 148: 220–222.

Rapp, D. 1991. *Is this your child? Discovering and treating unrecognized allergies.* William Morrow, New York.

Ratey, J. J., et al. 1987: Autism: The treatment of aggressive behaviors. *Journal of Clinical Psychopharmacology* 7, 1: 35–41.

Richardson, A. J., and Montgomery, P. 2005. The Oxford-Durham study—a randomized controlled trial of dietary supplementation with fatty acids in children with developmental coordination disorder. *Pediatrics,* 115: 1360–1366.

Ricketts, R., et al. 1993. Fluoxetine treatment of severe self-injury in young adults with mental retardation. *Journal of the American Academy of Child and Adolescent Psychiatry,* 32, 4: 865–869.

Rimland, B. 1994. *Parent ratings of behavioral effects of drugs and nutrients.* Autism Research Institute, San Diego, California.

Rimland, B. 1995. Children's shots: no longer a simple decision. *Autism Research Review* 9(1), p. 1–7.

Rosack, J. 2004. FDA issues controversial black box warning. *Psychiatric News,* 29(21): 1 and 48.

Sandman, C. A., Barron, J. L., and Colman, H. 1990. An orally administered opiate blocker, naltrexone, attenuates self-injurious behavior. *American Journal on Mental Retardation,* 95, 1: 93–102.

Sheehan, D. V., Beh, M. B., Ballenger, J., and Jacobsen, G. 1980. Treatment of endogenous anxiety with phobic, hysterical and hypochondriacal symptoms. *Archives of General Psychiatry,* 37: 51–59.

Swann, A. C., Shoaib, A. M., and Bowers, T. C. 1993. The manic syndrome: factors which may predict a patient's response to lithium, carbamazepine and valproate. *Journal of Psychiatry and Neuroscience,* 18(2): 61–66.

Trivedi, H. K., Wang, B., and Gonzalez-Heydrich, J. 2005. Anti-epileptic drugs (AEDs) in the treatment of aggression in children and adolescents, *Child and Adolescent Psychopharmacology News,* vol. 10, no. 1, pp. 6–10.

Tsai, L. 2001. *Taking the Mystery Out of Medications.* Future Horizons, Arlington, Texas.

Waldman, P. 2005. Mercury and Tuna: U.S. Advice Leaves Lots of Question, *The Wall Street Journal,* August 1, pp. 1 and 5.

Walters, A., Barrett, R., Feinstein, C., Mercurio, A., and Hole, W. 1990. A case report of naltrexone treatment of self-injury and social withdrawal in autism. *Journal of Autism and Developmental Disorders,* 20, 2: 169–176.

Whittington, C. J., Kendall, T., Fonagy, P., Cotrell, D., Cotgrove, A., and Boddington, E. 2004. Selective serotonin reuptake inhibitors in childhood depression: Systematic review of published versus unpublished data. *Lancet,* 363: 1341–1345.

Wild, J. 2005. Adult Suicide Linked to Popular Antidepressant (Paxil). *Nature,* 436: 1073.

Chapter 7   Dating Data: Autism and Relationships

REFERENCES

Asperger, H. 1944. Op. cit.

Barron, J., and Barron, S. 1992. Op. cit.

Baron-Cohen, S., Ring, H. A., Bullmore, E. T., Wheelwright, S., Ashwin, C., and Williams, S. C. 2000. The amygdale theory of autism. *Neuroscience Biobehavior Review,* 24: 355–364.

Baron-Cohen, Ring, H. A., Wheelwright, S., Bullmore, E. T., and Brammer, M. J., et al. 1999. Social intelligence in the normal and autistic brain: An FMRI study. *European Journal of Neuroscience,* 11: 1891–1898.

Baron-Cohen, S. 2004. The cognitive neuroscience of autism. *Journal of Neurology, Neurosurgery Psychiatry,* 75: 945–948.

Cesaroni, L., and Garber, M. 1991. Op. cit.

Cutler, E. 2004. *A Thorn in My Pocket.* Future Horizons, Arlington, Texas.

Frith, U. 1989. Op. cit.

Haznedar, M. M., Buchsbaum, M. S., Wei, T. C., Hof, P. R., Cartwright, C., Bienstock, C. A., and Hollander, E. 2000. Limbic circuitry in patients with positron tomography and magnetic resonance imaging. *American Journal of Psychiatry,* 157: 1994–2001.

McDonnell, J. T. 1993. Op. cit.

Sinclair, J. 1992. Op. cit.

Chapter 8 A Cow's Eye View: Connecting with Animals

REFERENCES

Bemporad, M. L. 1979. Op. cit.

Giger, W., Prince, R. P., Westervelt, R. G., and Kinsman, D. M. 1977. Equipment for low stress animal slaughter. *Transactions of the American Society of Agricultural Engineers,* 20: 571–578.

Grandin, T. 1980. Observations of cattle behavior applied to the design of cattle handling facilities. *Applied Animal Ethology,* 6: 19–31.

Grandin, T. 1987. Animal handling. *Veterinary Clinics of North America, Food Animal Practice,* 3: 323–338.

Grandin, T. 1991. Double-rail restrainer for handling beef cattle. Paper No. 91-5004, American Society of Agricultural Engineers, St. Joseph, Michigan.

Grandin, T. (ed.) 1993. *Livestock handling and transport.* CAB International, Oxon, England.

Grandin, T. 1994. Euthanasia and slaughter of livestock. *Journal of the American Veterinary Medical Association,* 204: 1354–1360.

Grandin, T., and Johnson, C. 2005. *Animals in Translation.* Scribner, New York.

Grandin, T. 1997. Assessment of stress during handling and transport. *Journal of Animal Science,* 75: 249–257.

Hedigar, H. 1968. *The psychology and behavior of animals in zoos and circuses.* Dover, New York.

Joliffe, T., et al. 1992. Op. cit.

LeDoux, J. 1998. *The Emotional Brain.* Simon and Schuster, New York.

McConnel, P. B., and Baylis, 1985. Interspecific communication in cooperative herding: acoustic and visual signals from human shepherds and herding dogs. *Zeitschrift für Tierpsychologie,* 67: 302–328.

Souse, B., and Wheeler, M. 1997. *A Treasure Chest of Behavioral Strategies for Individuals with Autism,* Future Horizons, Arlington, Texas.

Westervelt, R. G., Kinsman, D. M., Prince, R. P., and Giger, W. 1976. Physiological stress measurement during slaughter of calves and lambs. *Journal of Animal Science,* 42: 831–837.

Chapter 9   Artists and Accountants: An Understanding of Animal
Thought

REFERENCES

Beck, B. B. 1980. *Animal tool behavior.* Garland STPM Press, New York.

Brown, P. 1994. Understanding inner voices. *New Scientist,* 143(1933): 26–31.

Brown, S. A., et al. 1987. Naloxone compulsive tail chasing in a dog. *Journal of the American Veterinary Medical Association,* 190: 884–886.

Dawkins, M. S. 1993. Through our eyes only. In *The search for animal consciousness.* W. H. Feeman, New York.

Dodman, N. H., et al. 1987. Use of narcotic antagonist (Nalmefene) to suppress self-mutilative behavior in a stallion. *Journal of the American Veterinary Medical Association,* 192: 1585–1586.

Dodman, N. H. 1996. *The Dog Who Loved Too Much.* Bantam, New York.

Duncan, I. J. H. 1994. Practices of concern. *Journal of the American Veterinary Medical Association,* 204: 372–377.

Grandin, T. 1996. Factors that impede animal movement at slaughter plants, *Journal of American Veterinary Medical Association,* 209: 757–759.

Grandin, T., and Johnson, C. 2004. *Animals in Translation.* Scribner, New York.

Gray, P. M., et al. 2001. The music of nature and the nature of music. *Science,* 291: 52–54.

Hemsworth, P. H. 1987. Human-animal interactions. *Veterinary Clinics of North America, Food Animal Practice,* 3: 339–356.

Kagan, J., Reznick, J. S., and Snidman, N. 1988. Biological bases of childhood shyness. *Science,* 240: 167–171.

LeDoux, J. E. 1994. Emotion, memory and the brain. *Scientific American,* June, pp. 50–57.

Overall, K. L. 1992. Behavioral drugs, behavioral clinic, veterinary hospital, University of Pennsylvania. Proceedings, Iowa Veterinary Medical Association Annual Meeting, Des Moines, Iowa, pp. 79–86.

Papi, F. 1992. *Animal homing.* Chapman and Hall, New York.

Park, C. 1992. Op. cit.

Pascoe, P. J. 1986. Humaneness of electroimmobilization unit for cattle. *Journal of Veterinary Research,* 10: 2252–2256.

Pepperberg, I. 1987. Evidence for conceptual qualitative abilities in the African grey parrot: Labeling of cardinal sets. *Ethology,* 75: 37–61.

Rapoport, J. L. 1989. Op. cit.

Rapoport, J. L., Ryland, D. L., and Kriete, M. 1992. Drug treatment of canine acral lick. An animal model of obsessive-compulsive disorder. *Archives of General Psychiatry,* 49: 517–521.

Rimland, B. 1978. Inside the mind of the autistic savant. *Psychology Today,* August.

Smalley, S. L., McCracken, J., and Tanguay, P. 1995. Autism, affective disorder and social phobia. *American Journal of Medical Genetics,* 60: 19–26.

Smolker, R. 2002. *To Touch a Wild Dolphin.* Anchor, New York.

Stookey, J. M., Nickel, T., Hanson, J., and Vandenbosch, S. 1994. A movement-measuring device for objectively measuring temperament in beef cattle. *Journal of Animal Science,* Supl. 1, 72: 207.

Terrace, H. S. 1986. Positive transfer from sequence production to sequence discrimination in a nonverbal organism. *Journal of Experimental Psychology: Animal Behavior Processes,* 12: 215–234.

Thomas, E. M. 1993. *The hidden life of dogs.* Houghton Mifflin, Boston.

Treffert, D. A. 1989. *Extraordinary people: Understanding savant syndrome.* Harper and Row, New York.

Voith, V. L. 1984. Possible pharmacological approaches to treating behavioral problems in animals. In R. S. Anderson (ed.), *Nutrition and behavior in dogs and cats.* Pergamon, Oxford, England.

Welling, H. 1994. Prime number identification in idiot savants. *Journal of Autism and Developmental Disorders,* 24: 199–207.

Chapter 10   Einstein's Second Cousin: The Link Between Autism and Genius

REFERENCES

Andreason, N. C. 1987. Creativity and mental illness prevalence rates in writers and first-degree relatives. *American Journal of Psychiatry,* 144: 1288–1292.

Asperger, H. 1944. Op. cit.

Baron-Cohen, S. 2000. Is Asperger syndrome/high functioning autism necessarily a disability? *Developmental Psychopathology,* 12: 480–500.

Callow, P. 1990. *Vincent van Gogh: a life.* Ivan R. Dee, Chicago.

Clark, R. P. M. 1993. A theory of general impairment of gene expression manifesting as autism. *Personal Individual Differences,* 14: 465–482.

Clark, R. W. 1971. *Einstein: the life and times.* Thomas Y. Crowell, New York.

Delong, G. R., and Dwyer, J. T. 1988. Correlation of family history and specific autistic subgroups: Asperger's syndrome and bipolar affective disease. *Journal of Autism and Developmental Disorders,* 18: 593–600.

Dowling, C. G. 2005. MIT Nerds. *Discover,* June, pp. 36–43.

Folstein, S., and Rutter, M. 1977. Op. cit.

Gardner, H. 1993. *Creating minds.* Basic Books, New York.

Gillberg, G., and Schaumann, H. 1981. Infantile autism and puberty. *Journal of Autism and Developmental Disorders,* 11: 365–371.

Gleick, J. 1993. *Genius: Richard Feynman and modern physics.* Little, Brown, New York.

Grant, A. 1885. *Charles Darwin.* Appleton, New York.

Grant, V. W. 1968. *Great abnormals.* Hawthorn, New York.

Hermelin, B. 2001. *Bright Splinters of the Mind.* Jessica Kingsley, London.

Highfield, R., and Garter, P. 1993. *The private lives of Albert Einstein.* St. Martin's, New York.

Jamison, K. R. 1993. Op. cit.

Kevin, G. 1967. *Inspired amateurs.* Books for Libraries Press, Freeport, New York.

Kincheloe, J. L., Steinberg, S. R., and Tippins, D. J. 1992. *The stigma of genius.* Hollowbrook, Durango, Colorado.

Landa, R., Piven, J., Wzorek, M. M., Gayle, J. O., Chase, G. A., and Folstein, S. E. 1992. Social language use in parents of autistic individuals. *Psychological Medicine,* 22: 245–254.

Ledgin, N. 2002. *Asperger's and Self Esteem.* Future Horizons, Arlington, Texas. This book profiles famous scientists and musicians who were Asperger's.

Malcolm, N. 1984. *Ludwig Wittgenstein: a memoir.* Oxford University Press, New York.

Miller, B. L., Boone, K., Cummings, J. L., Read, S. L., and Mishkin, F. 2000. Functional correlates of musical and visual ability in fronto-temporal dementia. *British Journal of Psychiatry,* 176: 458–463.

Miller, B. L., Cummings, J., Mishkin, F., Boone, K., Prince, F., Ponton, M., and Cotman, C. 1998. Emergence of art talent in fronto-temporal dementia. *Neurology,* 51: 978–981.

Munk, R. 1990. *Ludwig Wittgenstein: the duty of genius.* Free Press, New York.

Myerson and Boyle. 1941. The incidence of manic-depressive psychosis in certain socially prominent families, p. 20. In K. R. Jamison, 1993. *Touched with Fire.* The Free Press, New York.

Narayan, S., Moyer, B., and Wolff, S. 1990. Family characteristics of autistic children: a further report. *Journal of Autism and Developmental Disorders,* 20: 523–535.

Pais, A. 1994. *Einstein lived here.* Oxford University Press, New York.

Patten, B. M. 1973. Visually mediated thinking: a report of the case of Albert Einstein. *Journal of Learning Disabilities,* 6, 7: 15–20.

Persson, C. B. 1987. Possible biological correlations of precocious mathematical reasoning ability. *Trends in Neuroscience,* 10: 17–20.

Plomin, R., Owen, M. J., and McGuffin, G. 1994. Op. cit.

Rapoport, J. L. 1989. Op. cit.

Ring, H. A., Baron-Cohen, S., Wheelwright, S., Williams, S. C., Brammer, M., Andrew, C., and Bullmore, E. T. 1999. Cerebral correlates of preserved cognitive skills in autism: A functional MRI study of embedded figures task performance. *Brain,* 122: 1305–1315.

Ritvoe, E. R., Freeman, B. J., Pingree, C., et al. 1989. The UCLA-University of Utah epidemiological survey of autism: prevalence. *Journal of Psychiatry,* 146: 194–199.

Robertson, J. W. 1923. *Edgar A. Poe: a psychopathic study.* Putnam, New York.

Sacks, O. 1994. Op. cit.

Sacks, O. 1995. Prodigies. *The New Yorker,* January 9, pp. 44–65.

Time. 1994. Anon. Diagnosing Bill Gates. January 24, p. 25.

Snyder, A. W., and Mitchell, J. D. 2000. Is integer arithmetic fundamental to arithmetic? The mind's secret arithmetic. *Proceedings of the Royal Society,* 266: 587–592.

Snyder, A. W., Mulcathy, E., Taylor, J. L., Mitchell, D. J., Sachdew, P., and Gandevia, S. 2003. Savant like skills exposed in normal people by suppressing the left fronto-temporal lobe. *Journal of Integrative Neurosciences,* 2: 149–158.

Treffert, D. A. 1989. *Extraordinary people: understanding the savant syndrome.* Harper and Row, New York.

Witelson, S. F., Kigar, D. L., and Harvey, T. 1999. The exceptional brain of Albert Einstein. *Lancet,* 353: 2149–2153.

Wheelwright, S., and Baron-Cohen, S. 2001. The link between autism and skills such as engineering, math, physics, and computing: A reply to Jarrold and Routh. *Autism,* 5: 223–227.

Chapter 11 Stairway to Heaven: Religion and Belief

REFERENCES

Appenzeller, T. 1994. Recreating the universe's fateful flaws. *Science,* 263: 921.

Brinkley, D. 1994. *Saved by the light.* Villard, New York.

Budiasky, S. 1989. The ancient contract. *U.S. News & World Report,* March 20, pp. 75–79.

Dixon, R. 1981. The mathematical daisy. *New Scientist,* December 17, pp. 791–795.

Eadie, B. J. 1992. *Embraced by the light.* Old Leaf Press, Placerville, California.

Einstein, A. 1940. Science and religion. *Nature,* 146: 605.

Einstein, A. 1949. *Albert Einstein, philosopher-scientist.* P. S. Tudor, New York.

Einstein, A. 1973. *Ideas and opinions.* Based on *Mein Weltbild,* C. Seelig, 1954. Dell, New York.

Fraser, J. G. 1963. *The Golden Bough,* Vol. 1 (Abridged ed.), Macmillan, New York.

Freedman, D. H. 1994. Quantum consciousness. *Discover,* June, pp. 89–98.

Gleick, J. 1987. *Chaos: making a new science.* Penguin, New York.

Gleick, J. 1992. Op. cit.

Grandin, T. 1988a. Behavior of slaughter plant and auction employees towards the animals. *Anthrozoos,* 1: 205–213.

Grandin, T. 1988b. Double-rail restrainer for livestock handling. *Journal of Agricultural Engineering Research,* 41: 327–338.

Grandin, T. 1990. Humanitarian aspects of shehitah in the United States. *Judaism,* 39: 436–446.

Hegstrom, R. A., and Kondepudi, D. K. 1990. The handedness of the universe. *Scientific American,* January, pp. 108–115.

Horgan, J. 1992. Quantum philosophy. *Scientific American,* July, pp. 92–104.

Maurer, R. 1991. Autism Society of America Conference, July 10–13. Indianapolis, Indiana.

McCrone, J. 1994. Quantum states of mind. *New Scientist,* August 20, pp. 35–38.

Moody, R. 1973. *Life after life.* Bantam, New York.

Moody, R. 1977. *Reflections on life after life.* Bantam, New York.

Ohno, S. 1987. Play the right bases and you'll hear Bach. *Discover,* March, p. 10.

Penrose, R. 1989. *The emperor's new mind.* Oxford, New York.

Penrose, R. 1994. *Shadows of the mind.* Oxford, New York.

Peterson, I. 1994. Islands of growth: working out a building code for atomic structures. *Science News,* 145: 218–219.

Rollin, B. 1981. *Animal rights and human morality.* Prometheus Books, Buffalo, New York.

Serpell, J. 1986. *In the company of animals.* Basil Blackwell, New York.

Siegal, R. K. 1977. Hallucinations. *Scientific American,* October, pp. 132–152.

While surfing the Internet to find information on the Golden Rule, I stumbled across the name of the author of the quote in the cattle chute catalogue. He is Charles Caleb Cotton, an English clergyman who lived in the 1800s.

RESOURCE LIST

Associations and Sources of Information

Autism Society of America
7910 Woodmont Avenue, Suite 300
Bethesda, Maryland 20814-3067
301-667-0881
800-3-AUTISM
www.autism-society.org
Largest parent support group in the U.S. Has many local chapters.

Autism Research Institute
4182 Adam Avenue
San Diego, California 92116
www.autismwebsite.com
www.autism.org
www.autism.com
Information on biomedical treatments, auditory training, sensory
   problems, and many other treatments. They publish a very infor-
   mative newsletter on new treatments and scientific research.

Gluten Free Casein Free Support Group
www.gfcfdict.com

MAAP Services, Susan Moreno
P.O. Box 529
Crown Point Indiana 46307
219-662-1311
www.maapservices.org
chart@netnitco.net
Information for older high-functioning individuals and Asperger's
syndrome.

Judevine Center for Autism
1101 Olivette Executive Parkway
St. Louis, Missouri 63132
314-482-6200
www.judevine.org or *www.judevine.org/autism/resources.html*
Contains excellent links in their resources section to many autism
and Asperger sites.

National Institute of Mental Health
Office of Communications
6001 Executive Blvd. Room 8184, MSC 9663
Bethesda, Maryland 20892
301-443-4513
866-615-6464
www.nimh.nih.gov/publicat/autism.cfm
Contains basic information about autism.

National Autistic Society in England
393 City Road
London, England ECIV ING
44-(0)20-7833-2299
www.nas.org.uk
Good general information site. Has good objective information on
auditory training and other treatments. Use the search box located
on this site. Searches for many different kinds of information can
be done.

Tonyattwood.com.au
A good source of information on Asperger's Syndrome.

www.thegraycenter.org
Contains information on teaching social skills to children with autism.

Emily Post's The Etiquette Advantage in Business: Personal Skills for Professional Success by Peggy Post and Peter Post. This practical book provides many tips on how people should behave at work. It will be useful for learning work-related social skills.

Physician's Desk Reference
Order from www.Amazon.com
The Doctor's Bible for information on medications. They also have books on herbal and nutritional supplements. They are available in many libraries and at your doctor's office. All FDA Black Box warnings are in these books.

Pubmed—provides free access to summaries of studies published in scientific journals. This database is run by the National Institute of Health. To access, type *Pubmed* into either the Google or Yahoo! search engine. There are several different Pubmed search pages that search different databases. The best one is labeled NCBI PUBMED NATIONAL LIBRARY OF MEDICINE and it has an easy-to-use search box near the top of the page.

Google Scholar searches scientific papers. Go to www.google.com and click on "scholar" on the tool bar.

Therafin
19747 Wolf Road
Mokena, Illinois 60448
800-843-7231
708-479-7300
www.therafin.com
The squeeze machine manufacturer.

Irlen Institute
5380 Village Road
Long Beach, California 90808
www.irlen institute.com

IrlenInstitute@irlen.com
Has information on colored glasses and colored overlays to help with
  visual processing problems.

Sensory Integration International
P.O. Box 5339
Torrance, California 90510-5339
www.sensoryint.com
Information on sensory problems.

College of Optometrists in Vision Development (COVD)
243 N. Lindberg Blvd., Suite 310
St. Louis, Missouri 63141
314-991-4007
888-268-3770
www.covd.org
info@covd.org
Information on finding doctors who can treat visual processing
  problems.

Publishers of Books on Autism and Asperger Syndrome

Autism Asperger Publishing Company
P.O. Box 23173
Shawnee Mission, Kansas 66283-0173
877-277-8254
913-897-1004
www.asperger.net

Future Horizons
721 West Abram Street
Arlington, Texas 76013
800-489-0727
www.futurehorizons-autism.com

Jessica Kingsley Publishers
116 Pentonville Road
London NI 9JB United Kingdom
44-(0)20-7833-2307
www.jkp.com

Pro-Ed Inc.
8700 Shoal Creek Blvd.
Austin, Texas 78757-6897
www.proedinc.com
Has books on Lovaas, ABA, and discreet trial methods.

Sites Run by People with High-Functioning Autism or Asperger's Syndome
www.autismtoday.com
Karen Simmons
info@autismtoday.com
A good site for parents to get information and to communicate with
   other parents.

Grasp—the Global and Regional Asperger Syndrome Partnership
125 East 15th Street
New York, NY 10003
645-242-4003
info@grasp.org
www.grasp.org
Contains lots of links to other sites, run by people with autism or
   Asperger's.

www.neurodiversity.com
Web site with lots of information run by Kathleen Seidel.
In her profile she writes, "We've recognized the characteristics of
   autism in both sides of our family and no longer regard autism as an
   aberration, but regard ourselves and our loved ones as a remarkable
   tribe."

www.WrongPlanet.net
A great Web site with lots of links made by Alexander Plank, a
   student who has created an online community.

www.aspennj.org contains an extensive list of state support groups
   and has information on bullying and teasing.

I would like to conclude this list of sources with a warning. There
is no magic cure for autism and parents must be cautious to avoid
being misled by extravagant claims by people who are promoting
their brand of therapy. Treatments that are effective should work

with reasonable amounts of effort. A treatment program that works for one child may be useless for another. Treatments and educational programs that are effective can be implemented without spending huge sums of money. Dedicated parents and good teachers have made their own effective programs after reading different books. They did not have to have expensive training. A parent should follow his or her own good instincts. Try different programs or methods and keep the things that work and eliminate the things that do not work. Combining several different approaches is often effective.

With a perspective like that of no other expert in the field, Temple Grandin translates how animals think, feel, and act. *Animals in Translation* is an insightful guide to the world of animal pain, fear, aggression, and love, and will forever change the way we think about our fellow creatures.

ISBN 0-15-603144-2 • $15.00 / Higher in Canada

 Harcourt